The Presence of the Past
T.S. Eliot's
Victorian Inheritance

Studies in Modern Literature, No. 8

A. Walton Litz, General Series Editor

Professor of English
Princeton University

Ronald Bush

Consulting Editor for Titles on T.S. Eliot
Associate Professor of Literature
California Institute of Technology

Other Titles in This Series

The Presence of the Past
T.S. Eliot's
Victorian Inheritance

by
David Ned Tobin

UMI RESEARCH PRESS
Ann Arbor, Michigan

Produced and distributed by
UMI Research Press
an imprint of
University Microfilms International
Ann Arbor, Michigan 48106

Library of Congress Cataloging in Publication Data

Tobin, David N.
   The presence of the past.

   (Studies in modern literature ; no. 8)
   Revision of thesis (Ph.D.)—Princeton University, 1977.
   Bibliography: p.
   Includes index.
   1. Eliot, T. S. (Thomas Stearns), 1888-1965—Criticism and interpretation. 2. Eliot, T. S. (Thomas Stearns), 1888-1965—Knowledge—Literature. 3. English poetry—19th century—History and criticism. 4. Tennyson, Alfred Tennyson, Baron, 1809-1892—Influence—Eliot. I. Title. II. Series.

PS3509.L43Z879 1983   821'.912   83-5733
ISBN 0-8357-1413-6

Contents

Preface

When we assume that a literature exists we assume a great deal. . . . We suppose not merely a corpus of writings in one language, but writings and writers between whom there is a tradition; and writers who are not merely connected by tradition in time, but who are related so as to be in the light of eternity contemporaneous, from a certain point of view cells in one body, Chaucer and Hardy.

But in the long run we can see that the continuity of the language has been the strongest thing; so that however much we need French or Italian literature to explain English literature of any period, we need, to explain it, the English inheritance still more.

Both of these quotations are taken from a review written by T. S. Eliot in 1919 ("Was There a Scottish Literature?" *Athenaeum,* 1 August). The first one sounds familiar to anyone acquainted with the precepts of "Tradition and the Individual Talent," written later that same year. The second reminds us of what too many critics of Eliot's poetry have long overlooked: the influence of the Victorians. Taken together, the two quotations justify the task of this book: studying Eliot's work in relation to his Victorian predecessors.

"Comparison and analysis," Eliot wrote in "The Function of Criticism" (1923), "are the chief tools of the critic" (*SE* 32-33). These tools are used to refine one's understanding of an artist's work, which is, according to Eliot's point of view, the understanding of its unique place in the whole body of works forming a vital tradition. His concept of tradition and the talent which cannot afford to be isolated from it lies behind a basic technique of his own criticism: the consideration of poets in terms of their predecessors. "No poet, no artist of any art," he wrote in "Tradition and the Individual Talent" (1919), "has his complete meaning alone":

His significance, his appreciation is the appreciation of his relation to the dead poets and artists. You cannot value him alone; you must set him, for contrast and comparison, among the dead. (*SE* 15)

"I mean this," Eliot adds significantly, "as a principle of aesthetic, not merely historical, criticism." His "aesthetic" revaluations of the English poetic tradition grew from comprehending the complex interrelationship of works of art both past and present.

Eliot's own poetry has of course been studied in terms of this comparative critical mode. Dante, Elizabethan and Jacobean drama, seventeenth-century metaphysical verse, and nineteenth-century French poetry have all been seen as parts of the tradition in which Eliot consciously placed his own poems. But what of his more immediate "English inheritance," which, because of "the continuity of the language," ought to be quite relevant to an appreciation of his work? With all this talk of the poet's relation to the past, there appears a considerable hiatus in Eliot studies. Although it would seem reasonable, considering nothing more than the chronological factor, to suggest that Eliot has as much to do with the Victorians as, for instance, metaphysical poetry with the Elizabethans, little attention has been directed towards Eliot's relationship to Victorian poetry, which still overshadowed the literary landscape when he began taking his poetic aspirations seriously. "Outside of several brief studies that identify 'echoes,' " Ronald Schuchard wrote in 1974, "there is in print no full exploration of Eliot and the Victorians."[1] This statement remains true today. More than a few distinguished critics have suggested aspects of Eliot's Victorian ancestry, but only as curiosities or minor literary sources, with not at all the same importance as his relation to authors of another language or another time.

There are several reasons for this long-standing bias in the extensive study of Eliot's achievement. Perhaps most influential of all has been Eliot's own testimony. Although critics have long been aware that an artist's pronouncements about the nature of his own work are far from infallible, the eminent position of T. S. Eliot—elder statesman, aged eagle, chief mandarin of modern poetry—gave to his assertions the nimbus of sanctified truth. His early criticism, represented by *The Sacred Wood* and *Homage to John Dryden,* sought to justify the "new" poetry of the English avant-garde in large part by dismissing the great Victorians. This was a necessary act in the complex struggle of what Harold Bloom calls "the anxiety of influence."

Moreover, we have for a long time naively accepted Eliot's own account of his artistic development, neglecting some essential qualifications which are explained throughout this book. He has told us that, finding most of nineteenth-century English verse totally unsuited to his needs as a poet and quite foreign to his sensibility, he turned instead to other literatures and other ages in order to find those models that would enable him to arrive at a new poetic voice distinctly his own. Scholars went scurrying back, obviously with good reason, to Eliot's announced sources—Laforgue, Baudelaire, Webster and others—and English writers of the nineteenth century were ignored in the catalogue of forces shaping his poetry.

Another reason for the disappearance of the Victorian tradition in Eliot studies has to do with the whole transition from "Victorian" to "modern," which is explored in chapters 5 and 6. The Modernists were quite anxious to announce their liberation from all things Victorian. Their strident proclamations (typified by Wyndham Lewis's declaration in a 1914 *Blast* manifesto: "years 1837 to 1900/CURSE Abysmal inexcusable middle-class"[2]), which were apparently confirmed by much of the undeniably new work they were producing, seemed quite convincing. W. J. Bate, in *The Burden of the Past and the English Poet,* writes of this "immense effort of the arts, including music, of the early and middle twentieth century to get the nineteenth century off their backs." It is important to remember, however, that "what we are trying desperately to be unlike can tell a great deal about not only what we are doing but why, and a movement may often be better understood by what it concretely opposes than by its theoretical slogans."[3] This concept can certainly be applied to Eliot and the Victorians.

Finally, there is the matter of historical perspective. Only in the past ten years or so have we begun to view Modernism objectively, and to see it as a distinct phase rather than the final say of English literature. As time enables us to distance ourselves from the Modernist movement, we perceive more and more of its connections with the nineteenth century. This is not unlike the change in Romantic studies initiated in the late 1920s and '30s, when scholars began to discover so many of the roots of Romanticism in, of all places, the eighteenth century.

As I have already noted, much of Eliot's criticism is based upon the perception of the poet's inevitable involvement in the work of his predecessors. Again and again, Eliot begins his discussion of a writer with the question of his literary influences: the influence of Pater on Wilde, the influence of Ibsen on Joyce, the influence of Poe on Baudelaire. Yet Eliot was aware of an important distinction to be made concerning the subject of literary influence. He made it in a 1927 review dealing with Edgar Allen Poe:

> After the death of Byron it may be said that romanticism became diffused. Two men, and perhaps two men only, inherited the spirit of English romanticism: Poe and Heine. I should add Baudelaire, but Baudelaire is already influenced by Poe—although it is impossible to decide . . . how much is influence and how much simple kinship.[4]

Comparing Eliot's poems to those of Arnold, Newman, Kipling and Tennyson, one sometimes finds it difficult to decide "how much is influence and how much simple kinship." But this by no means invalidates this book's objective, which is to place Eliot more clearly in the English poetic tradition and to see how his poetry grew from what Victorian poets had done. Both "influence" and a more general affinity are equally revealing signs of Eliot's Victorian inheritance.

The phrase "literary influence" encompasses a great deal, from unconscious echoings and the passing-on of words, images, situations and attitudes, all the way to the effects of struggling to be free from the burdensome weight of past monuments. Eliot's Victorian influences are manifold indeed. For this book to limit itself to any one type or theory of literary influence would be to narrow its scope without good reason.

In much of his early poetry, Eliot was remembering Arnold's major poems (chapter 2); "Gerontion" would not have been the same poem without Newman's "The Dream of Gerontius" looming in the background (chapter 3); in writing "Prufrock," Eliot was recollecting and strangely transforming a story of Kipling's (chapter 6); the presence of Tennyson was felt throughout Eliot's poetic career, from the early days when one could not avoid him (chapter 5) to the writing of the *Quartets,* when Eliot made a final pact with his dead master (chapter 7). All these topics represent varieties of literary influence; they are all parts of Eliot's profound relation to the Victorians. In order to reach a more balanced perspective on T. S. Eliot's achievement, this relationship must be acknowledged and understood.

I am most grateful to A. Walton Litz of Princeton University for his generous help in the writing of this book, which began as a dissertation written under his direction. In addition to countless specific suggestions, Professor Litz's knowledge and patience were truly invaluable. I am also indebted to Professor E. D. H. Johnson of Princeton, whose command of Victorian literature prevented me from getting by with too many conveniently oversimplified generalizations. Lyndall Gordon's enthusiasm and willingness to discuss with me her excellent work on Eliot were of great benefit, as was Herbert Levine's informed energy. Cynthia Blanton Thomiszer helped me in more ways than I can recount. The book is dedicated to my mother and father, Joseph and Hilda Tobin, without whose support it could not have been written.

Abbreviations

AW	*Ash-Wednesday*
Berg material	Unpublished poems by Eliot, dating from the Harvard and Paris years, now in the Berg Collection of the New York Public Library
CPP	T. S. Eliot, *The Complete Poems and Plays, 1909-1950*. New York: Harcourt, Brace & World, 1952
BN	"Burnt Norton"
DS	"The Dry Salvages"
EC	"East Coker"
FLA	*For Lancelot Andrewes: Essays on Style and Order*. London: Faber, 1928
FQ	*Four Quartets*
FT or *Facsimile and Transcript*	*The Waste Land: A Facsimile and Transcript of the Original Drafts Including the Annotations of Ezra Pound*, ed. Valerie Eliot. New York: Harcourt Brace Jovanovich, 1971

Gallup

Donald Gallup, *T. S. Eliot: A Bibliography*, Revised and Expanded Edition. New York: Harcourt, Brace & World, 1969

IM

In Memoriam

LG

"Little Gidding"

Notebook

Eliot's bound notebook, containing over fifty pages of holograph drafts of mostly unpublished poems, now in the Berg Collection of the New York Public Library

OPP

On Poetry and Poets. New York: Farrar Straus, 1957, rpt. Noonday-Farrar, 1974

PT

Poems of Tennyson, ed. Christopher Ricks. New York: Norton, 1972

SE

Selected Essays, Third Enlarged Edition. London: Faber and Faber, 1951, rpt. 1972

SW

The Sacred Wood: Essays on Poetry and Criticism. London: Methuen, 1920, rpt. University Paperbacks, Methuen, 1972

TCC

To Criticize the Critic. New York: Farrar Straus, 1965, rpt. Noonday-Farrar, 1970

UPUC

The Use of Poetry and the Use of Criticism. Cambridge, Mass.: Harvard University Press, 1933, rpt. London: Faber Paperback, 1970

WL

The Waste Land

Part 1

Eliot's Victorian Quest

1

Charlotte Eliot

The Victorian poet most closely related to Eliot was his mother. Charlotte Champe Stearns was writing and transcribing poetry years before her marriage, at age twenty-five, to Henry Eliot.[1] Raising four daughters and two sons, devoting herself to St. Louis community affairs, she still managed to turn out a great amount of verse, much of which found its way into print in religious journals like the *Christian Register* or *The Unitarian*. "All her life," Herbert Howarth has noted, "she wrote poems."[2] Yet she was objective and perceptive enough to recognize early on that her youngest child, Tom, was by far the better poet; one day she quietly took the boy aside and told him so. He already knew enough about his mother's own literary aspirations to realize that this admission must have been for her a painful one.

"[There] is a convenient distinction between 'religious' and 'devotional' [poems,]" Eliot wrote in 1930: "I call 'religious' what is inspired by religious feeling of some kind; and 'devotional' that which is directly about some subject connected with revealed religion."[3] Charlotte Eliot's poetry is mostly devotional. One of her notebooks, now in the library of the Missouri Historical Society, contains numerous drafts of verse narratives describing episodes from the life of Jesus.[4] In a voluminous scrapbook in the Houghton Library's Eliot Collection, there are dozens of clippings of her printed poems, with titles like "Christ's Entry into Jerusalem," "The Vision of St. Francis," "All Saints' Day," "The Apostles," "Giordano Bruno in Prison," "Theodosius and St. Ambrose."[5] Both Herbert Howarth and Lyndall Gordon have commented in some detail on her poetry, noting its ingenuous moral fervor, its didactic nature, and its use of images and themes that recur in Eliot's poetry.[6]

By 1930, Eliot considered doubt, spiritual ennui, and even blasphemy to be kinds of "religious feeling" that were steps in the quest towards full belief. Thus his own poems are "religious" in the larger sense defined above, far from the optimistic certainties expressed by his mother. Still, Charlotte Eliot's poetry, solidly rooted in the liberal nineteenth-century point of view, provides the appropriate starting point for an examination of Eliot's Victorian inheritance.

Poetry was for Charlotte Eliot a means of exploring and celebrating her religious faith. Her poems deal most often with salvationist themes, rejoicing in Christ's power to heal and to redeem. She returns again and again to the death-and-resurrection aspect of the Christian myth, in Easter hymns and songs and carols, in "Christ Risen" and "The Raising of Lazarus," playing upon the strange mingling of life and death that her son would carry further in the opening lines of *The Waste Land*. For him, the overwhelming questions are answered in *Ash-Wednesday,* a poem enacting the agonies of purgation and scourging our perpetually inadequate natures. Mrs. Eliot chose rather to dwell on the glory of God, to which man tends:

> Towards righteousness the world is moving still,
> Since onward swept by the Eternal Will.[7]

Her poems read like a catalogue of standard nineteenth-century notions and hopes, many of which Eliot would reject in the development of his own convictions. This is made clear in her echoings of Tennyson, whose work she obviously knew. "Ring, Easter Bells!" for instance, imitates the climactic 106th lyric of *In Memoriam:* "Ring out, wild bells, to the wild sky. . . ." Tennyson's bells signal the death of the old year (the old, mournful life), and the beginning of the new; Mrs. Eliot's cleanse the world and man's soul with the message of eternal life:

> Ring out the doubts that like a cloud enfold us,
> Ring in the faith that clearer vision brings!
> . . . .
>
> Ring out the world's temptation and illusion!
> Ring in immortal hopes that shall endure!
> . . . .
>
> Ring, Easter Bells, the story hath no ending,
> Soul shall not be imprisoned in the tomb,
> Near to God its upward path is tending!
> Ring, Easter bells, dispel all doubt and gloom.

Throughout her poetry, one finds themes traced in *In Memoriam*. In "Giordano Bruno in Prison," the hero proclaims one of that poem's essential ideas:

> I do believe the human and divine
> Forever meet and mingle and combine;
> The human is the ladder that we climb
> In struggling upward nearer the divine.

Of course, this concept was anathema to Eliot, who, along with Paul Elmer More and T. E. Hulme, believed in the discontinuity of natural and supernatural. Like Tennyson, Charlotte Eliot needed the assurance of immortality to make life meaningful:

> Is life worth living? Not if death have power
> To chill the soul within that self-same hour
> That limbs grow stiff and light forsakes the eyes. . . .[8]

Also like Tennyson, she shows an anti-ecclesiastic bias, trusting in the individual's capacity to reach toward God, independent of the Church, which was the rock of T. S. Eliot's faith:

> Not in the records of the Church
>   Nor in historic creeds,
> We find Him, but in noble thoughts
>   That blossom into deeds.[9]

In the introduction to his mother's closet drama *Savonarola,* published in 1926, Eliot made note of this "opposition to ecclesiasticism; the author of *Savonarola* opposes it directly by exhibiting the beauty of a character which was certainly above fanaticism, and which was not without moral grandeur, in conflict with the hierarchy of its place and time."[10] In the same essay, he described how a work of historical fiction, whether in prose or verse, "is much more a document on its own time than on the time portrayed. . . . This Savonarola is a disciple of Schleiermacher, Emerson, Channing and Herbert Spencer . . ." (pp. vii, x). The same could be said of Bruno, and the other martyrs and saints Mrs. Eliot was drawn to. "Its own time" was the time of Eliot's youth. His list of names represents those forces that shaped, in a negative way, his own spiritual development: Protestantism, Unitarianism, optimistic faith in human progress, evolutionary theory applied to all branches of experience. These ways of seeing life did not at all correspond to his own deepest feelings, expressed in the early, unpublished poems now in the Berg Collection of the New York Public Library: the sense of life's utter meaninglessness, the intimations of a higher, untouchable reality, and the humiliation over the demands and weaknesses of his physical nature. A young Eliot exploring the towns of pre-World War I Europe, bewildered by their decadence as well as his own desires, had no place for the Unitarian vision of benign social progress and the abiding goodness of human nature.[11]

One review of *Savonarola,* which Eliot clipped and mailed to his mother, made the same point about the historical perspective:

> There is no indication of the date at which this poem was composed, but spiritually it is a product of the Victorian era. . . . She sees life as life was seen from the more

enlightened parsonages and manses of fifty years ago. This Savonarola, "a great moral reformer," [Mrs. Eliot's words] is one of the Victorian prophets, a Carlyle, a Matthew Arnold, or a Ruskin, who in the habit of a Dominican has slipped back into 15th-century Florence, exactly as some of the Victorians were apt to wish they could do.[12]

Charlotte Eliot's work presents a peculiar combination of elements. She was a Unitarian preoccupied with Christ's life and the lives of His saints, who changed Renaissance priests into nineteenth-century "moral reformers," and who demonstrated a sympathy for the mystical state in such poems as "The Vision of St. Francis" or the "Hymn to Divine Madness" in *Savonarola*. This tension continues, elements inverted so to speak, into Eliot's work: the Anglo-Catholic, twentieth-century Matthew Arnold, who dissociates himself from the age preceding his own but assumes its principal task of finding a faith that will endure.

Savonarola, dedicated "To My Children," describes a life of public achievement—of suffering and denial and painfully achieved religious devotion. Eliot, ignoring his family motto ("Tacuit et fecit"), not "acting" and not being silent in those early years, actually went on to try to live that life. He followed Arnold and Carlyle and the other Victorian prophets in trying to save civilization—in his case, by trying to save the language.

Charlotte Eliot, then, was a woman of strong literary interests, expressing in her poetry devotion to the life of the spirit. A woman of her character would no doubt have been aware of Mr. Matthew Arnold's lecture tour in America in the winter of 1883-84, and it is not unreasonable to assume that, when Arnold was in St. Louis, Mrs. Eliot was either in the audience or at least paying close attention to the newspaper reports. On January 30, 1884, Arnold spoke on "Numbers; or The Majority and the Remnant," exploring the dangers of unlimited American democracy; on February 1, he delivered the lecture, "Emerson," which R. H. Super has called "one of Arnold's best and most engaging essays in criticism."[13]

Eliot knew this essay, as he knew so much of Arnold's work: he refers to it in "Lancelot Andrewes" (1926):

When Andrewes begins his sermon, from beginning to end you are sure that he is wholly in his subject, unaware of anything else, that his emotion grows as he penetrates more deeply into his subject, that he is finally 'alone with the Alone', with the mystery which he is seeking to grasp more and more firmly. One is reminded of the words of Arnold about the preaching of Newman. (*SE* 351)

These "words of Arnold" appear at the beginning of "Emerson," as he reviews the inspirational figures of his youth: Carlyle, Goethe, Emerson, and finally Newman:

Who could resist the charm of that spiritual apparition, gliding in the dim afternoon light through the aisles of St. Mary's, rising into the pulpit, and then, in the most entrancing of voices, breaking the silence with words and thoughts which were a religious music,—subtle, sweet, mournful? I seem to hear him still, saying: "After the fever of life, after weariness and sickness, fightings and despondings, languor and fretfulness, struggling and failing, struggling and succeeding; after all the changes and chances of this troubled, unhealthy state,—at length comes death, at length the white throne of God, at length the beatific vision."[14]

Arnold's quotation shows that Newman's emotion, like Andrewes', does indeed grow "as he penetrates more deeply into his subject" through the use of rhythmic repetitions. Arnold continues, still showing that keen nostalgia for religious discipline found in "Stanzas from the Grande Chartreuse," written over thirty years before:

Or, if we followed him back to his seclusion at Littlemore, that dreary village by the London road, and to the house of retreat and the church which he built there,—a mean house such as Paul might have lived in when he was tent-making at Ephesus, a church plain and thinly sown with worshippers,—who could resist him there either, welcoming back to the severe joys of church-fellowship, and of daily worship and prayer, the firstlings of a generation which had well-nigh forgotten them? Again I seem to hear him: "The season is chill and dark, and the breath of the morning is damp, and worshippers are few; but all this befits those who are by profession penitents and mourners, watchers and pilgrims. More dear to them that loneliness, more cheerful that severity, and more bright that gloom, than all those aids and appliances of luxury by which men nowadays attempt to make prayer less disagreeable to them. True faith does not cover comforts; they who realize that awful day when they shall see Him face to face, whose eyes are as a flame of fire, will as little bargain to pray pleasantly now, as they will think of doing so then."[15]

These words—both Arnold's retreat through time to a timeless moment, and Newman's stern cadences—must have struck to the heart of a poet who wrote of such moments; who was to think of Little Gidding as the model of spiritual devotion; who found "daily worship and prayer" so important; who became by profession a penitent and mourner, watcher and pilgrim; and who described the terrors of that final confrontation:

> The eyes are not here
> There are no eyes here . . .
>
> Not that final meeting
> In the twilight kingdom[16]

But why this apparent digression into a St. Louis lecture hall? "History has many cunning passages," muses the speaker of "Gerontion." Consider the one we have noticed; conjure up the scene. Charlotte Eliot (she *should* have been there if she wasn't), rapt listener, sits before the critic with whom her youngest child will engage in the kind of struggle described by Harold Bloom in *The Anxiety of Influence*. The subject of his talk is Emerson, the son of a Unitarian minister (she was the daughter-in-law of a most prominent one) and another of Eliot's literary forebears,[17] who argued that "the highest revelation is that God is in every man"—a doctrine with which Eliot would do battle. "Matthew and Waldo, guardians of the faith," are both there—the line from Eliot's "Cousin Nancy" (1915) perfectly illustrates his defensive need to get the nineteenth century off his back. He would certainly reject the nineteenth century's version of "the faith," but he was still a product of that era and its literature.

In the lecture hall, "Matthew" begins, his words taking on a distinct rhythm. It is a tone of yearning that characterizes Eliot's own poetry. "Forty years ago, when I was an undergraduate at Oxford, voices were in the air there which haunt my memory still"—the phrase itself strangely transports us to the garden of "Burnt Norton." One of those voices, Newman's, sounds through the lecture hall via Arnold: " 'The season is chill and dark, and the breath of the morning is damp, and worshippers are few. . . .' " According to Arnold, that was the voice of one who, in the very prime of life, "seemed about to transform and to renew what was for us the most national and natural institution in the world, the Church of England" (165). Times, however, have changed:

> But he [Newman] is over eighty years old; he is in the Oratory at Birmingham; he has adopted, for the doubts and difficulties which beset men's minds today, a solution which, to speak frankly, is impossible. (165)

This is a conclusion with which the socially conscious, Unitarian Mrs. Eliot would agree. But her son, struggling with similar "doubts and difficulties," was to embrace the same "solution" as Cardinal Newman, an old man waiting for death.

At this moment in history—February 1, 1884—the whole of Eliot's quest is symbolically presented. Charlotte Eliot and Ralph Waldo Emerson represent variations of the faith no longer acceptable, no longer living. They are the beginning. Newman represents the end. He has learned how to "sit still" as he approaches death in the Oratory of St. Philip Neri, a community of prayer and observance less than a hundred miles from the "secluded chapel" of Little Gidding, symbol of a similar community, a like discipline. And in the middle is the figure of Arnold, wandering between the worlds of faith and disbelief. The steps along the way, one sees, are marked by Victorians; it is through them that Eliot's quest unfolds.

2

Eliot and Arnold: "Between Two Worlds"

A basic effort in Victorian poetry is the struggle towards belief. Faith—whether in the Incarnation, a divine Presence, the Truth of one's own deepest feelings, or the ultimate Good of human sympathy and selflessness—was the goal, difficult to achieve but necessary to strive for. A major pattern in Eliot's poetry, discernible not only in individual poems but in his work as a whole, is this archetypal Victorian quest through the fires of despair and doubt towards a state of religious affirmation. Although Eliot moved towards a creed which many Victorians had abandoned, the movement, the struggle *itself*—the need to achieve belief in something that gave meaning and purpose to life in a materialist world—places him with the Victorians in their quest.

One could spend a good deal of time qualifying this assertion, listing all the inevitable differences of circumstance and habit of mind between the generations. The possibility of a Godless universe became less and less threatening and incomprehensible—more and more *reasonable*—as the years passed. The Victorian poets confronted a world thrown into confusion, a world acutely, at times obsessively aware of and dissatisfied with that confusion. Eliot, however, faced a society that had settled rather comfortably into the resignation of unbelief. It was a skeptical, secular world which was busy accommodating itself to the "new" sciences. The Victorians, moreover, did not have to come to terms with a war which shattered once and for all the assumptions behind the near-sacred notion of Progress; they were not witness to what had come perilously close to the collapse of a civilization. The spiritual pilgrimages of Eliot and his predecessors were marked by different signs and different forces. Still, the pilgrimages are analogous and point to the essential continuity of the English poetic tradition, placing Eliot with the great Victorian poets who treated the problems of doubt and faith as a basic part of their experience.

One must be careful here not to confuse Eliot the poet with Eliot the

Anglo-Catholic literary and social critic. The prose of the latter often reveals an apparently serene, unquestioning conviction in matters of faith, especially when concerned with the need to accept as Truth the central dogmas of the Church. Thus, concluding a discussion of Matthew Arnold in 1933, Eliot pronounces that "Perhaps he cared too much for civilization, forgetting that Heaven and Earth shall pass away, and Mr. Arnold with them, and there is only one stay" (*UPUC* 119). It would be obtuse to ignore the strategic irony that gives this statement its bite; nevertheless, it is the voice of a believer.

His poetry, though, is a different matter. The strict pronouncements of the later criticism; the droning, hortatory choruses from *The Rock*; the massive finality of the *Quartets*; and perhaps more than anything else the image of the pious, devout public figure—all of these things have tended to obscure the fact that much of Eliot's poetry concerns itself with the awful, doubt-ridden struggle *towards* a faith that cannot be grasped. In this respect he is returning to the dilemma which preoccupied the major Victorian poets.

Eliot insisted in his criticism that doubt was a *part* of the religious experience, and it must be returned to again and again. Belief was by no means a final rest on the plateau of serene conviction, but rather a series of bouts with the demons which are always assaulting it. "To believe *anything* (I do *not* mean merely to believe in some 'religion') will probably become more and more difficult as time goes on," Eliot wrote in 1927. "For those of us who are higher than the mob, and lower than the man of inspiration, there is always *doubt*; . . . [and] doubt and uncertainty are merely a variety of belief."[1]

Several years later (1931), soon after completing *Ash-Wednesday* (his most intense exploration of religious "doubt and uncertainty"), Eliot was able to be more specific, in "The Pensées of Pascal":

> For every man who thinks and lives by thought must have his own scepticism, that which stops at the question, that which ends in denial, or that which leads to faith and which is somehow integrated into the faith which transcends it. And Pascal, as the type of one kind of religious believer, which is highly passionate and ardent, but passionate only through a powerful and regulated intellect, is in the first sections of his unfinished Apology for Christianity facing unflinchingly the demon of doubt which is inseparable from the spirit of belief. (*SE* 411)

The invisible poet, so reticent about biographical matters, put much of his own experience into his criticism, discussing the works of others in terms of thinly disguised personal history. One could almost construct a concentrated autobiography from the criticism: again and again the reader cannot help but apply to Eliot's own poetry and life what he writes about the poetry and lives of other figures. In the above quotation, Eliot surely had his own development in mind, a development which, in its various alternatives (the kinds of scepticism), recalls the similar struggles of poets like Alfred Tennyson and Matthew Arnold.

The examples of Tennyson and Arnold are relevant to an understanding of what may be called Eliot's Victorian quest, defined as the struggle to achieve and maintain faith, whether this be in the context of a doubt-ridden or more thoroughly secular world. Eliot considered *In Memoriam* to be a profoundly religious poem, "not religious because of the quality of its faith, but because of the quality of its doubt":

> Its faith is a very poor thing, but its doubt is a very intense experience. *In Memoriam* is a poem of despair, but of despair of a religious kind. And to qualify its despair with the adjective 'religious' is to elevate it above most of its derivatives. (*SE* 336)

The place of Tennyson and *In Memoriam* in Eliot's poetry is the subject of Part 2 of this book. The rest of this chapter turns principally to Matthew Arnold, whose struggle with the problem of faith ended quite differently than did Eliot's and yet still belonged to the same tradition Eliot was to follow.

In his 1933 Harvard lecture on "Matthew Arnold," Eliot says at one point:

> A French friend said of the late York Powell of Oxford: 'Il était aussi tranquille dans son manque de foi que le mystique dans sa croyance.' You could not say that of Arnold; his charm and his interest are largely due to the painful position that he occupied between faith and disbelief. (*UPUC* 144)

A much earlier lecture, one he gave for a course on Victorian literature in 1917-18, was called "Three Poets of Doubt—Matthew Arnold, Edward Fitzgerald, James Thomson."[2] Although Eliot had no sympathy for Arnold's unorthodox attempts in prose to reinterpret traditional religious beliefs, and although he frowned upon Arnold's occasional lapses in poetic craftsmanship (*UPUC* 107n, 111n), he still found himself coming back to the poetry:

> But Arnold is a poet to whom one readily returns. . . . With all his fastidiousness and superciliousness and officiality, Arnold is more intimate with us than Browning, more intimate than Tennyson ever is except at moments, as in the passionate flights of *In Memoriam*. He is the poet and critic of a period of false stability. All his writing in the kind of *Literature and Dogma* seems to me a valiant attempt to dodge the issue, to mediate between Newman and Huxley; but his poetry, the best of it, is too honest to employ any but his genuine feelings of unrest, loneliness and dissatisfaction. (*UPUC* 105-6)

"Unrest, loneliness and dissatisfaction" also characterize Eliot's early verse:

> I remain self-possessed
> Except when a street piano, mechanical and tired
> Reiterates some worn-out common song
> With the smell of hyacinths across the garden
> Recalling things that other people have desired.
> Are these ideas right or wrong?[3]
>
> Sometimes these cogitations still amaze
> The troubled midnight and the noon's respose.[4]

The "essential advantage for a poet," the 1933 lecture continues, "is to be able to see beneath both beauty and ugliness; to see the boredom, and the horror, and the glory. The vision of the horror and the glory was denied to Arnold, but he knew something of the boredom. . . . His tone is always of regret, of loss of faith, instability, nostalgia" (*UPUC* 106-7)—another list of qualities that also describe the tone of many of Eliot's poems.

The world of Arnold's poetry represents a stage in the development of Eliot's own point of view. "The boredom" is part of what dominates his earlier poems (including much of the *vers de société* in the Berg material):

> Time for you and time for me,
> And time yet for a hundred indecisions,
> And for a hundred visions and revisions,
> Before the taking of a toast and tea.[5]

But Eliot's early work, culminating in *The Waste Land,* also reaches past boredom into other domains of experience, into the horror and the glory, which are both further on in the struggle towards religious faith. In Eliot's view, Arnold never got very far—never got beyond the ennui of "the neutral territory between two worlds"—but he was on the same quest. The principal concerns of Arnold's best poetry are also those of the young Eliot; they define a state of mind which Eliot expressed, but beyond which he endeavored to move. By comparing themes, images and language in selected poems of the two writers, it is possible to demonstrate that the spiritual dilemma conveyed in Eliot's earlier poetry goes back to and is defined by Arnold's major poems.

"The neutral territory between two worlds"—this important phrase comes from Part II, Scene iii of *The Family Reunion.* Agatha is responding to Mary's fear over Harry's strange commitment to exile:

> We must all go, each in his own direction,
> You, and I, and Harry. You and I,
> My dear, may very likely meet again
> In our wanderings in the neutral territory
> Between two worlds.   (*CPP* 285)

The play is about these "two worlds" and the crucial differences between them. One is the world of death-in-life:

> . . . a crowded desert
> In a thick smoke, many creatures moving
> Without direction, for no direction
> Leads anywhere but round and round in that vapour—
> Without purpose, and without principle of conduct
> In flickering intervals of light and darkness. . . .   (*CPP* 235)

The other is the world of spiritual enlightenment, of "agony, renunciation,/But birth and life" (*CPP* 284). Agatha's words echo Matthew Arnold's oft-quoted description of his sorrowful dilemma in "Stanzas from the Grande Chartreuse":

> Wandering between two worlds, one dead,
> The other powerless to be born. . . .[6]

This image, along with its many implications, struck Eliot deeply; it reached into the depths of his own experience and became part of his poetic world. One finds quiet echoes and direct references to these lines in both his criticism and his poetry, from an early *Waste Land* fragment to the Dante imitation in "Little Gidding." Why should Eliot have seized upon this particular image? The answer to this places Eliot's poetry in the Victorian tradition.

"Wandering between two worlds . . ." describes not only the feelings of the speaker in "Grande Chartreuse," but also the attitude of many Victorian writers towards what they took to be the peculiarly transitional nature of their age. Walter E. Houghton has asserted that "this is the basic and almost universal conception of the period."[7] Thus John Stuart Mill wrote in 1831 that "mankind have outgrown old institutions and old doctrines, and have not yet acquired new ones."[8] In the same year, in an essay which Arnold knew and drew upon, Carlyle wrote of the same phenomenon in terms that strikingly foreshadow Eliot's poetic landscape of a world without faith:

> The Godlike has vanished from the world. . . . how many a poor Hazlitt must wander
> on God's verdant earth, like the Unblest on burning deserts; passionately dig wells,

and draw up only the dry quicksand. . . . The doom of the Old has long been pronounced, and irrevocable; the Old has passed away: but, alas, the New appears not
in its stead; the Time is still in pangs of travail with the New. Man has walked by the
light of conflagrations, and amid the sound of falling cities; and now there is darkness,
and long watching till it be morning. The voices even of the faithful can but exclaim:
"As yet struggles the twelfth hour of the Night: birds of darkness are on the wing,
spectres uproar, the dead walk, the living dream. . . ."⁹

"Stanzas from the Grande Chartreuse" precisely illustrates Arnold's
"painful position . . . between faith and disbelief," to use Eliot's words
describing Arnold's place in the neutral territory.

The poet, participating in the Victorian quest even in his apparent
denial, journeys up a mountain, through a desolate landscape of "dark
forges long disused" (3), "wet smoke" (11), the "strangled sound" (9) of
a river called *Guiers Mort,* "spectral vapours" (13), "limestone scars"
(14), to arrive at the place of the cross, the "Carthusians' world-famed
home" (30). Eliot of course makes use of the same archetypal pattern:
the pilgrimage through a sinister, surreal world to the Chapel Perilous.
But instead of finding graves and dry bones, "only the wind's home" (*WL*
389), Arnold stands silent before

> The chapel, where no organ's peal
> Invests the stern and naked prayer—
> With penitential cries they kneel
> And wrestle; rising then, with bare
> And white uplifted faces stand,
> Passing the Host from hand to hand. . . .   (37-42)

Although the poet cannot participate in the rituals of the most orthodox form of the creed he no longer believes in, he is drawn instinc-
tively, almost against his will, to the "ghostlike . . . Cowl'd forms" (35-36).
For five stanzas Arnold dwells on the purposeful discipline of the mon-
astery life, in which each gesture, however painful, is at least graced with
meaning—for the participants, if not for the enervated observer. Here,
then, is one form of the "agony, renunciation" that both Harry in *The
Family Reunion* and Eliot himself will finally embrace as part of their
faith. Arnold, however, speaks of the Carthusians' "death in life" (54),
and hears with guilt the imagined remonstrance of his liberal teachers:
"*What dost thou in this living tomb?*" (72). He is indeed torn between
two worlds.

Like Eliot in *The Waste Land,* Arnold scans his version of the literary
tradition in "Grande Chartreuse," making the attempt to shore fragments
against his ruin: Goethe, Byron, Shelley, and Senancour are all alluded
to (133-50). But their voices and their visions fade before the materialistic

dominance of the present. There is no doubt that the poet is in awe of the powers of the steadfast unbelievers, whose technology has enabled them to triumph over time and space (165-66). He is irresistibly attracted to the "action and pleasure" of the secular city (175-92). But at the same time, he has no hope at all—only grief over the loss of something precious, only the instinctive clinging to "our desert" (210) of failed belief.

Near the end of the poem, Arnold likens himself and others of his age to

> . . . children rear'd in shade
> Beneath some old-world abbey wall,
> Forgotten in a forest glade,
> And secret from the eyes of all.
> Deep, deep the greenwood round them waves,
> Their abbey, and its close of graves!   (169-74)

The image of the Carthusian chapel has been replaced by that of a secluded cloister and its graveyard. Instead of the thunder of spiritual demands, however, one hears only the seductive bugle-music of the secular city: "*Ye shy recluses, follow too!*" (192). The poet-recluse does not heed the call, but he has nothing to fall back upon.

The material world, which claims a bleak triumph in "The Grande Chartreuse," bursts into pieces and falls away by the end of *The Waste Land,* as Eliot leaves behind the disillusioned, exhausted persona of Arnold's poem. Fleeing the flowing, groping corpses of the secular city, the *Waste Land* protagonist confronts solitude and the possibility of new life. The crowing cock (392-93) and the flash of lightning illuminating, perhaps transforming "this decayed hole among the mountains" (386) are emblems of a possible transcendence of the tortuous wandering amongst the scenes and voices of a dead world.

In "Stanzas from the Grande Chartreuse," the poet succumbs to the spiritual enervation of the neutral territory. Still yearning for the faith his reason has condemned to death, he remains paralyzed in "the painful position . . . between faith and disbelief." The protagonist of *The Waste Land* knows that same paralysis, yet manages the journey to a point where the towers and bridges of all unreal cities burst in the violet air. The sounds of the thunder provide intimations of another reality.

It is clear, then, that the two poems end quite differently, and these contrasting conclusions emphasize the diverging paths of Eliot's and Arnold's quest. But Eliot still recognized in Arnold's predicament the roots of his own, and he transformed the image of "Wandering between two worlds, one dead,/The other powerless to be born" into a private symbol for the alternatives with which he was faced.

As Lyndall Gordon has shown, Eliot was struggling through an intense religious crisis years before the publication of *The Waste Land*. Indeed, she maintains that the early fragments of the poem are "the purely personal record of a man who saw himself as a potential candidate for religious life":

> Although the ground of Eliot's ordeal shifts—sometimes the domestic scene, sometimes the divine visitation, sometimes the imaginary trial by fire or water—he is always present, blighted and sceptical, hovering between the remote role of a religious candidate and a more immediate despair.[10]

To affirm that he was seriously contemplating religious candidacy is, I think, pushing things a bit far. Eliot's poems in the Berg Collection, upon which Ms. Gordon bases her conclusions, are just that: a collection of poems and not a journal. Still, she has uncovered an important aspect of Eliot's development. Although he eventually achieved, in his own life, a thoroughgoing Anglo-Catholic faith, the experience of "wandering between two worlds" remains a crucial one in his poetry, through *Ash-Wednesday* and *The Family Reunion* (which describes Harry's frightful journey across the frontier, leaving behind those who will always wander in the neutral territory or "live in this world, this world only" [*CPP* 285]) and into *Four Quartets*. Echoes of Arnold's essential phrase emphasize Eliot's relationship to the Victorian crisis of faith.[11]

In his poetry, Arnold hovers between the dead world of traditional Christian belief and the unknowable possibilities of a godless future. For him, this future is "powerless to be born," to be realized in his own soul, because he is still too much attached to the forms and emotions of what has passed away. Eliot's poetry unfolds in the territory between the godless world which Arnold foresaw (and which Eliot despised as utterly without life) and the possibilities of traditional Christian belief.

Eliot's position between two worlds is depicted in one of the *Waste Land* fragments, "Song" (originally "Song for the Opherion"), one of his poems echoing the crucial lines in "Stanzas from the Grande Chartreuse."[12] "Song" remained a part of *The Waste Land* for quite a while in the prolonged genesis of the long poem until, in January 1922, Pound finally persuaded Eliot to drop it.[13] Eliot had thought enough of the poem to publish it (with a slightly different title) in Wyndham Lewis's *Tyro*, April 1921:

SONG TO THE OPHERIAN

The golden foot I may not kiss or clutch
Glowed in the shadow of the bed

Perhaps it does not come to very much
This thought this ghost this pendulum in the head
Swinging from life to death
Bleeding between two lives
    Waiting that touch

The wind sprang up and broke the bells,
Is it a dream or something else
When the surface of the blackened river
Is a face that sweats with tears?
I saw across the alien river
The campfire shake the spears.

It is important to dwell for a moment on the background of this poem, since it provides an entrance into Eliot's poetry in terms of his religious predicament: the approach towards faith, and its obstacles. An understanding of this dilemma brings him closer to Arnold's (and Tennyson's) poems.

Much of the unpublished early poetry in the Berg Collection,[14] confessional and tormented in nature, employs again and again a basic image or scene: the speaker isolated in a nondescript room or garret, often late at night or in the unearthly pre-dawn hours, struggling with terror or confusion, finally becoming dimly aware of what are for him the nightmarish commonplaces of the everyday world. Some of this comes across in "Preludes" and "Rhapsody on a Windy Night," although in those pieces the poet has managed to distance himself through minor strategies of objectification, such as addressing his consciousness as if it were someone else (a technique finding its culmination in the first line of "Prufrock"):

    The lamp said,
'Four o'clock,
Here is the number on the door,
Memory!
You have the key,
The little lamp spreads a ring on the stair.
Mount.
The bed is open; the tooth-brush hangs on the wall,
Put your shoes at the door, sleep, prepare for life.'

The last twist of the knife.[15]

You tossed a blanket from the bed,
You lay upon your back, and waited;
You dozed, and watched the night revealing

> The thousand sordid images
> Of which your soul was constituted;
> They flickered against the ceiling.
> And when all the world came back
> And the light crept up between the shutters
> And you heard the sparrows in the gutters
> You had such a vision of the street
> As the street hardly understands. . . .[16]

In many of the Berg poems, the speaker is haunted by broken, incomplete visions of the "Absolute" that seem to cancel out the world in their intensity. The poet likens these overpowering intuitions to locomotives rushing over desert plains: gone in an instant, they leave the observer baffled, questioning the reality of the experience. Repelled by his sexual needs and by the emptiness of the polite intellectual society around him, the poet yearns for a total surrender to belief in the Absolute, which he senses but cannot grasp. He wanders in the limbo between two worlds, the limbo to which Tennyson and Arnold were also condemned.

By the time Eliot wrote "Song for the Opherion," he was adopting the same kind of poetic shorthand that Pound developed in revising the early Cantos.[17] Situations and states of mind were alluded to by signs and images which usually had a quite specific meaning in the poet's own mind, but which could point in many different, often confusing directions in the impersonal, "rich and strange" world of the poem itself—rich and strange because of its ambiguous suggestivity. This should be kept in mind as one unravels the imagery and language of the "Song," tracing this minor poem to some of its roots in order to better understand it and the impulses behind it, *not* necessarily to arrive at a definitive reading.

References in "Song to the Opherian" to "the shadow of the bed," the stirring of the wind at dawn (in several of the unpublished poems, early morning hours are associated with renewed movement of the wind), and the hallucinatory vision all point to the "agony in the garret" state of mind. The poet in his waking dream sees but cannot embrace or in any way worship the supernatural visitant: "The golden foot I may not kiss or clutch . . ." (foot of the Buddha?). Elsewhere Eliot wrote of "The golden vision [that] reappears" but remains beyond the afflicted observer.[18] It prompts not joy, but terror and pain and doubt:

> Perhaps it does not come to very much
> This thought this ghost this pendulum in the head
> Swinging from life to death
> Bleeding between two lives

Those last two lines ironically recall Arnold's "wandering between two worlds," conjuring a more fatal neutral territory.

In the typescript of the "Song," the next line originally read "Waiting that touch." Eliot revised this to:

> Waiting a touch   a breath[19]

The speaker awaits the inspiration—the breath of grace, of spiritual life—without which he must remain on the verge of the Hell of unbelievers, where "the surface of the blackened river/Is a face that sweats with tears." This is the river of death: on one side are the lost souls, of which the poet is one so long as he cannot achieve faith; on the other are those damned for all eternity. In the typescript, the final lines of the poem are:

> Waiting that touch
> After thirty years.

But Eliot crossed these lines out, heavily and repeatedly. He was thirty-two when the poem was published, and presumably had written it several years before. In those excised lines, the personal, indeed confessional nature of the poem rises briefly to the surface. One can see into the feelings, the spiritual dilemma out of which the poem grew. This dilemma—swinging like a pendulum from life to death, from faith to disbelief—lies at the heart of the poem to which "Song to the Opherian" once belonged, *The Waste Land*.

Eliot stressed this important aspect of *The Waste Land* in "A Note on Poetry and Belief" (1927), which was a response to I. A. Richards's assertion that the poem effected "a complete severance between his poetry and *all* beliefs, and this without any weakening of the poetry. . . ."[20] Eliot argued that Richards seemed to have a simple-minded conception of "belief" as a totally static phenomenon that never changed with the times—a mere process of dreamy assent. But this is simply not the case, for "belief has been in constant mutation . . . from the beginning of civilization." Limiting oneself for the moment to the Christian tradition, Eliot explains, there are the faiths of Dante, of Crashaw, of Christina Rossetti: faiths equally strong, and in agreement on certain basic dogmas, but still quite different from one another.

As for the poem of my own in question [*The Waste Land*], I cannot for the life of me see the "complete separation" from all belief—or it is something no more complete than the separation of Christina Rossetti from Dante. A "sense of desolation," etc. [Eliot is quoting Richards's account of *The Waste Land,* which continues: ". . . of uncertainty, of futility, of the baselessness of aspirations, of the vanity of endeavour, and a thirst for a life-giving water which seems suddenly to have failed . . ."] (if it is that) is not a separation from belief; it is nothing so pleasant. In fact, doubt, uncertainty, futility, etc., would seem to me to prove anything except this agreeable partition; for doubt and uncertainty are merely a variety of belief.[21]

Eliot is suggesting that the conditions of the modern world have made doubt and the emotions associated with it an inseparable component of religious faith. This "complication of belief is merely another complication to be put up with." It is easy to conclude from Eliot's remarks that *The Waste Land* is in the same poetic tradition as Arnold's "Stanzas" or Tennyson's *In Memoriam,* both of which struggle with "doubt, uncertainty, [and] futility."

Richards's conception of belief, Eliot says, "seems to me to be slightly under the sentimental influence of Matthew Arnold, whom he pertinently quotes at the head of his article; wandering between two worlds, one dead, etc." That "etc." is typical of Eliot's defensive attempts to trivialize or otherwise dismiss the work of his Victorian predecessors, a strategy I examine more closely in chapter 6. It of course implies that the image and implications of "wandering between two worlds" were of little interest to a writer who could not even bring himself to finish the phrase.

But in fact Richards did not even take his epigraph from "Grande Chartreuse"; rather, he went to "Stanzas in Memory of the Author of 'Obermann' ": "—Yet we/Have a worse course to steer" (63-64). In that poem, Arnold has been describing Goethe, the principal member of his Tradition, as one of the few spirits "In this our troubled day" (46) who have been able "to see their way":

> Strong was he, with a spirit free
> From mists, and sane, and clear;
> Clearer, how much! than ours—yet we
> Have a worse course to steer.
>
> For though his manhood bore the blast
> Of a tremendous time,
> Yet in a tranquil world was pass'd
> His tenderer youthful prime.
>
> But we, brought forth and rear'd in hours
> Of change, alarm, surprise—
> What shelter to grow ripe is ours?
> What leisure to grow wise?
>
> Like children bathing on the shore,
> Buried a wave beneath,
> The second wave succeeds, before
> We have had time to breathe.   (61-76)

Eliot's misreading of Richards's epigraph indicates that "wandering between two worlds" was for Eliot a memorable image that the name of Arnold immediately evoked. Although the horizons were different for the two poets, both were concerned with what Kenneth Allott has called the "spiritual No Man's Land" (see note 9), a realm characterized by the debilitating lack of faith.

Another echo of Arnold's phrase is found in line 218 of *The Waste Land*: "I Tiresias, though blind, throbbing between two lives." Tiresias, who sees but cannot act upon his insight, wanders in the No Man's (or Woman's) Land. He witnesses the parade of the dead and recognizes its sterility, but he is condemned to remain among the shades. This is the world that Arnold's poems decry. It is the world that his scholar-gipsy has managed to escape in order to seek out moments of poetic inspiration, far from those "Who fluctuate idly without term or scope" (167):

> Of whom each strives, nor knows for what he strives,
> And each half lives a hundred different lives;
> Who wait like thee, but not, like thee, in hope.
>
> . . . Light half-believers of our casual creeds,
> Who never deeply felt, nor clearly willed,
> Whose insight never has borne fruit in deeds,
> Whose vague resolves never have been fulfill'd;
> . . . Who hesitate and falter life away. . . .

These lines from "The Scholar Gipsy" (168-78) place us directly in the twittering world Eliot's poetry has made familiar. Here are the aimless movement, the effort without purpose, the distractions and lack of control, the desire without proper end—all symptoms of spiritual enervation. Tiresias sees and knows them all. Gerontion and the hollow men will join those who wait without hope; Prufrock will come to represent those "Whose insight never has borne fruit in deeds, . . . Who hesitate and falter life away." This is the dead land, perceived by two poets wandering in the neutral territory, aware of a faith that, for different reasons, they cannot embrace. Their plight is that of Tiresias, who sees as the seer but cannot act upon his vision, and who is burdened with a knowledge which those around him do not share.

"The misery of the present age," Arnold wrote, "is not in the intensity of men's suffering—but in their incapacity to suffer, enjoy, feel at all, wholly and profoundly; in their having their susceptibility eternally *agacée* by a continual dance of ever-changing objects . . . the eternal tumult of the world mingling, breaking in upon, hurrying all away."[22] But for a few quirks of nineteenth-century syntax, this could be Eliot speaking.

As we have seen, both poets express the plight of wandering between two worlds. They describe in similar terms one of these worlds: the secular city, which is the figurative desert of lifeless souls. As far back as the early sonnet "Written in Emerson's Essays" (1844), Arnold rejects the response of the "monstrous, dead, unprofitable world" to the oracular voice (in this case, Emerson's):

> Man after man, the world smiled and pass'd by;
> A smile of wistful incredulity
> As though one spake of life unto the dead. . . .

He distinguishes in "Rugby Chapel" between those bound to pursue the quest "On, to the City of God" (208) and those bound

> . . . without aim to go round
> In an eddy of purposeless dust,
> Effort unmeaning and vain.   (76-78)

The quest in "Rugby Chapel" moves through a waste land which, as Curtis Dahl has pointed out,[23] prefigures Eliot's landscape:

> Years they have been in the wild!
> Sore thirst plagues them, the rocks,
> Rising all round, overawe;
> . . . .
> Sole they shall stray; in the rocks
> Stagger for ever in vain,
> Die one by one in the waste.   (177-87)

Gerontion, ruminating in the waste of "Rocks, moss, stonecrop, iron, merds" also sees that "eddy of purposeless dust":

> De Bailhache, Fresca, Mrs. Cammel, whirled
> Beyond the circuit of the shuddering Bear
> In fractured atoms.

Indeed, Arnold's vision of "the fretful foam/Of vehement actions without scope or term,/Called history"[24] is like Gerontion's, that old man who, like many an elderly Victorian, was robbed by time not only of sense but also of faith, leaving dry thoughts and nothing more.[25]

The nightmare of history leads to World War I. The darkling plain of what Arnold called, in "Memorial Verses" (1850), "Europe's dying hour" (23) remains a feature of Eliot's waste world. The vision in "Dover Beach" of ignorant armies on that plain, and of "confused alarms of struggle and flight," becomes the horrifying reality of trench warfare:

> Who are those hooded hordes swarming
> Over endless plains, stumbling in cracked earth
> Ringed by the flat horizon only   (*WL* 369-71)

For Arnold and Eliot, these visions of contemporary society are inseparable from the loss of faith. Man no longer *believes*; consequently his feelings and will are no longer ordered or nourished as they once were; they wither away; society becomes a hot, fretful race of isolated souls, dead and dying. Returning to Arnold's words, "The misery of the present age is . . . in [men's] incapacity to suffer, enjoy, feel at all, wholly and profoundly." This judgment is reflected in Eliot's array of those who know nothing of Kurtz's horror, or the saint's glory, or even genuine doubt. "The majority of people live below the level of belief or doubt," he wrote.[26]

In the *Waste Land* manuscripts, Eliot occasionally faltered from his stance of dramatic objectivity, spelling out his judgment of contemporary society in a way that Arnold would immediately have recognized:

> London, the swarming life you kill and breed,
> Huddled between the concrete and the sky;
> Responsive to the momentary need,
> Vibrates unconscious to its formal destiny,
>
> Knowing neither how to think, nor how to feel . . .
> London, your people is bound upon the wheel![27]

There is indeed little to distinguish this from the stern voice of the Victorian poet condemning the failings of his time. Pound pounced on this lapse into outmoded directness, slashed the passage through, and wrote "B⸺S." Regardless of the quality of the verse, Eliot was far too close here to the Victorian poetic attitude. He was not making it new.

One way of depicting the temper of a faithless age is to evoke images of other ages, which suggest great contrasts or illuminating parallels or both. "Both Arnold and Eliot have seen a mechanized and commercialized world of spurious or sordid values, a world of parched or greasy souls," Douglas Bush has written; ". . . both poets resort to classic myth from a partly identical impulse, the hunger for a glimpse of the ideal felt in the midst of arid and ugly actuality."[28] "A glimpse of the ideal" might be simplifying matters too much (especially in Eliot's case), but Bush is certainly right in recognizing the dynamic interplay of past and present which both poets employ. For instance, Arnold's bold "end-symbol" in "The Scholar-Gipsy"—the extended simile involving the Tyrian and Greek traders—has the same kind of suggestiveness coloring the whole poem, the same jarring shift of vision, as Eliot's closing lines in "Sweeney among the Nightingales," which transport us from a sinister gathering of whores to the scene of Clytemnestra's revenge.

The comparison of past and present, however, whatever the specific technique, is obviously a fundamental impulse for many poets. The one aspect of this past-present exchange that *does* suggest a real affinity between Arnold and Eliot is the system of allusions, whether explicit or indirect, to what each poet conceives to be the Great Literary Tradition. Dante, Shakespeare, and the Jacobeans all lie behind much of Eliot's poetry, providing *points of view* with which to observe and describe the modern malady. Similarly, Arnold refers to Wordsworth, Goethe and others when describing the diminished present, thus establishing a greater perspective. In "Heine's Grave" (which Eliot considered "good poetry" and "very fine criticism" [*UPUC* 112, 111]) Arnold invokes the tradition:

> Ah, I knew that I saw
> Here no sepulchre built
> In the laurell'd rock, o'er the blue
> Naples bay, for a sweet
> Tender Virgil! no tomb
> On Ravenna sands, in the shade
> Of Ravenna pines, for a high
> Austere Dante! no grave
> By the Avon side, in the bright
> Stratford meadows, for thee,
> Shakespeare! loveliest of souls,
> Peerless in radiance, in joy.   (55-66)

Their specific techniques of allusion are utterly unlike (compare "Austere Dante!" with Eliot's reference to the *Inferno*, "I had not thought death had undone so many"), but this should not obscure the poets' parallel use of their relation to a literary past in order to define the present.

Of course, Arnold does more than just define the conditions of modern life. In trying to find a sure foundation for it, he moves beyond describing the collapsed structure of revealed religion to explore the possibilities of the romantic love-ideal, which might perhaps fill in the vacuum left by the disappearance of God. The series of Marguerite poems, as well as others, define love's ultimate failure; they trace the process by which the poet's heart learns "How vain a thing is mortal love."[29] Arnold's treatment of the poet and his beloved looks forward to the situations of Eliot's early verse, and the relationship of some central poems suggests a considerable influence.

Arnold creates a particular scene in several of the love poems: the poet confronts his beloved (or remembers a confrontation), and yearns for the kind of communion which, he has discovered, even love can rarely provide. His expectations have been broken by the overwhelming fact of man's isolation, a fact only confirmed by intimate relations with another. Here lies the paradox: it is the experience of love itself, *with* its consolations, *with* its moments of joy and apparent enlightenment, which leads the poet to his vision of estrangement. The most memorable example of this, "Dover Beach," is hardly a celebration of love's success. The poet's cry, "Ah, love, let us be true/To one another!" comes across as a hopeless, last-ditch plea drowned out by that "long, withdrawing roar" and its implications. This nocturnal union has resulted not in fulfillment but in a feeling very close to despair.

Similarly, the voices of Eliot's early verse are trapped in the spheres of self, and this predicament is only confirmed by the attempts to break through to another. Love (or the emotion approaching it, or at least the *attempt* at love) *fails* in Arnold's and Eliot's poetry because it does not bridge the gulf; rather, it seems only to emphasize its width. Repeatedly, Eliot creates a scene analogous to Arnold's: confrontation (with the gestures of conventional union), and subsequent disillusion. Prufrock (his is after all a *love* song), the speaker in "Portrait of a Lady," the fastidious arranger of "La Figlia Che Piange," the protagonist of *The Waste Land*— all participate in (or at least painfully approach) some form or echo of romantic union, and all emerge from it with an intensified sense of their own isolation. Their experience echoes Arnold's, who also "heard the key/Turn in the door once and turn once only":

> For most men in a brazen prison live,
> Where, in the sun's hot eye,
> With heads bent o'er their toil, they languidly
> Their lives to some unmeaning taskwork give,
> Dreaming of nought beyond their prison-wall.[30]

By focusing on a specific poem of Arnold's, "The Buried Life"—by using it as a central reference point—one can range throughout Eliot's early work in order to demonstrate how he echoes and adapts Arnold's vision of human relationships. The poem made enough of an impression on Eliot for him to refer to it explicitly in "Portrait of a Lady."[31] The woman speaks:

> 'Yet with these April sunsets, that somehow recall
> My buried life, and Paris in the Spring,
> I feel immeasurably at peace, and find the world
> To be wonderful and youthful, after all.'

It is difficult to limit the impressions evoked by "My buried life," which might mean simply "my past," or suggest passionate feelings unstirred for so long, or be a carefully placed literary allusion designed by the lady to impress her young man. One cannot be sure in this, the most Jamesian and one of the most elusive of Eliot's poems. She continues, Arnold's poem remaining in the background:

> 'I am always sure that you understand
> My feelings, always sure that you feel,
> Sure that across the gulf you reach your hand.'

But the narrator does nothing of the sort: he only observes obsessively the actions and reactions of himself and another. The contrast emerges between Arnold's yearning to express and share our deepest feelings, those usually buried by "the thousand nothings of the hour" (69), and the narrator's fastidious maneuvers to *evade* the confrontation that would involve those feelings, and to deliberately lose himself in "the thousand nothings":

> —Let us take the air, in a tobacco trance,
> Admire the monuments,
> Discuss the late events,
> Correct our watches by the public clocks,
> Then sit for half an hour and drink our bocks.

The whole of *Prufrock and Other Observations* (1917), with its *conversations galantes,* its crowded streets and protagonists who are, in Arnold's words, "alien to the rest/Of men, and alien to themselves" (21-22), presents the same view of the lost, subterranean soul expressed in "The Buried Life."[32] The more one examines Eliot's earlier poetry, the more does it reveal certain connections, conscious or unconscious reminiscences, and parallel images arising from shared experience and a knowledge of Arnold's poems.

The direct contact of eyes, eyes clouded with tears, is a central image in "The Buried Life" (2, 10-11, 81), signifying the earnest attempt to plumb the soul's depths and thus achieve real communion. It is a standard romantic image (cf. for instance Tennyson's use of it in "Love and Duty"), which Eliot inherited and employed to his own ends. In the waste world of hollow men, that kind of communion becomes threatening and must be avoided at all cost: "Eyes I dare not meet in dreams. . . ."

The very notion of "buried life" runs throughout Eliot's early verse, reflected through various shades of irony. "These April sunsets" of which the Lady speaks color the opening of *The Waste Land,* stirring unpleasant emotions, recalling the buried life of memory and desire. The displaced people in "The Burial of the Dead," like Arnold's hurried souls "Eddying at large in blind uncertainty" ("The Buried Life," 42), are only *threatened* by what lies beneath, and want to keep it buried.

> But often, in the world's most crowded streets,
> But often, in the din of strife,
> There rises an unspeakable desire
> After the knowledge of our buried life. . . .   (45-48)

This "unspeakable desire" thrusts itself, sardonic and twisted, into the nightmare of Eliot's Unreal City, in the midst of a bridge crowded with dead souls:

> A crowd flowed over London Bridge, so many . . .
> There I saw one I knew, and stopped him, crying: "Stetson!"
> "You who were with me in the ships at Mylae!
> "That corpse you planted last year in your garden,
> "Has it begun to sprout? Will it bloom this year?
> "Or has the sudden frost disturbed its bed?"

Here, the image of the buried life has turned into a fertile corpse.

It is in this first section of *The Waste Land,* Eliot's version of "The Buried Life," that we find the romantic confrontation (or at least the memory of it). Arnold describes it as the redeeming moment of intensity, when "A bolt is shot back somewhere in our breast,/And a lost pulse of feeling stirs again" (84-85):

> "You gave me hyacinths first a year ago;
> "They called me the hyacinth girl."

But something is wrong. The romantic setting could not be better—garden, hyacinths, rain, thrilling background music from Wagner's *Tristan und Isolde*[33]—but instead of Arnold's transient yet climactic moment of communication, when "Our eyes can in another's eyes read clear,/ . . . The eye sinks inward, and the heart lies plain,/And what we mean, we say, and what we would, we know" (81-87), something quite different is depicted:

> . . . I could not
> Speak, and my eyes failed, I was neither
> Living nor dead, and I knew nothing. . . .

Desolate and empty the sea. In this strange moment of ecstasy and despair, the protagonist still cannot connect with another. The romantic
confrontation has brought on a desolating enlightenment. He remains
trapped within himself, like the "mass of men" in Arnold's poem with
locked hearts and chained lips (13, 28). The Arnoldian cage of everyday
distractions or "thousand nothings," confirmed by the failure of love,
merges with the Bradleyan cage of one's own perceptions, the Jamesian
cage of paralyzed observation, and the Cumaean Sibyl's cage of endless
time.

Arnold goes on in his poem to describe how reminiscences of the
buried life intrude into the everyday waste:

> Yet still, fron time to time, vague and forlorn,
> From the soul's subterranean depth upborne
> As from an infinitely distant land,
> Come airs, and floating echoes, and convey
> A melancholy into all our day.   (72-76)

So goes the experience of the protagonist in *The Waste Land,* haunted by
airs and echoes from the depths of his own consciousness. One illustration
of this comes from the section originally called "In the Cage":

> "Do you know nothing? Do you see nothing? Do you remember
> "Nothing?"
>   I remember
> The hyacinth garden. Those are pearls that were his eyes, yes!
> "Are you alive, or not? Is there nothing in your head?"
>   But
> 0 0 0 0 that Shakespeherian Rag . . .[34]

Echoes of Arnold's poem are by no means limited to *The Waste
Land.* We have already taken into account "Portrait of a Lady," and
noted how the encounters in "Prufrock" and "La Figlia Che Piange"
result only in intensified alienation. In one of the unpublished poems in
the Berg Collection, the poet describes a disillusioning scene in which he
realizes how far he is from real communion with the woman of his atten-
tions. They walk together under the April trees; he seizes her hand; but
his deepest feelings remain buried beneath the debris of fears and hesi-
tations. Words are inadequate, and the scene ends in silent frustration.
The speaker has succumbed to the endless process of Laforguian self-
inspection, which confirms the prison.

Arnold reaches the same point of failure in the relationship traced by the Marguerite poems. It is a failure described in "The Buried Life":

> Are even lovers powerless to reveal
> To one another what indeed they feel?
> I knew the mass of men conceal'd
> Their thoughts, for fear that if reveal'd
> They would by other men be met
> With blank indifference, or with blame reproved . . .
> But we, my love!—doth a like spell benumb
> Our hearts, our voices?—must we too be dumb?   (14-25)

Regardless of his answer (which is quite unsure of itself), these words approach Prufrock's world and Prufrock's fears:

> If one, settling a pillow or throwing off a shawl,
> And turning towards the window, should say:
>   "That is not it at all,
>   That is not what I meant, at all."

This involves more than the inadequacy of words to express properly what one means. The would-be lovers who speak in Eliot's early poetry are unable or at least unwilling to translate their feelings into any kind of significant commitment or action. They recall one of Arnold's typical figures, described by A. Dwight Culler as the "Divided Soul":

> Such a person, common among the second-generation Romantics, is a would-be Byron without the Byronic force, a kind of Hamlet who has the "motive and the cue to passion" but in whom passion itself has petered out. Self-knowledge and the sense that it has all been done before undercut his rebellion and reduce his agony to the mere unrest of a mid-Victorian Prufrock.[35]

After *Prufrock and Other Observations,* however, the lovers (or couplers, to be more precise) in Eliot's poetry quite simply have nothing to feel, and are all too eager to act. The mechanics of lust become their sole reality in a corporeal world without life. By this point we are quite a ways from Arnold's lover, striving to mine his way to a consoling view of humankind's potential.

Eliot found a better way to objectify the state of wandering between the worlds of death and faith in "Journey of the Magi" (1927) and "A Song for Simeon" (1928). In these poems he speaks through the masks of old men who are, historically, precisely at the midpoint of the neutral territory. Through these masks, he could explore the tensions of private experience.

The old men are from the old world, but they have been exposed by the grace of God to signs which denote the advent of the new. "We would see a sign!" the unbelievers cry; the Magus has asked for nothing but has been given signs aplenty, which he cannot understand. All he knows is that he has been made aware of a new kind of death, and a new kind of birth. He has suffered through a barely comprehended experience which, as Hugh Kenner has observed, "has rendered quotidian pleasures meaningless, and protracted life a preliminary death."[36] This is the experience of the young Eliot, struggling through nights of visitation and despair, obsessed with the possibilities of a faith he cannot yet hold, plagued by the "voices singing in our ears, saying/That this was all folly" ("Magi," 19-20). The Magus' quest has ended only in a question: "were we led all that way for/Birth or Death?" Those two grand words are repeated eight times in four lines (36-39), until they blur and become part of the same thing; thus the poetry *itself* explains the Incarnation. But the old man remains in doubt, "no longer at ease here, in the old dispensation," anxious to end the uncertainty with "another death," his own. "Journey of the Magi" describes one of the steps through doubt towards what can never be absolutely realized. It describes that "Painful position. . . between faith and disbelief."

The Magi's quest is one of many undertaken in Eliot's poetry. It is a motif he shared with Arnold and other Victorian writers. Douglas Bush has observed that "a quest was one of Arnold's archetypal images."[37] We have already discussed the quest of the speaker in "Stanzas from the Grande Chartreuse," who journeys up to austere heights only to be confronted with what he has lost. In "Rugby Chapel," the quest becomes a metaphor for life itself, or rather for the life of those mortals "whom a thirst/Ardent, unquenchable, fires,/Not with the crowd to be spent . . ." (73-75). Empedocles suffers from a similar kind of thirst; we follow his doomed pilgrimage, representative of a life-long quest, past the watered valley, past "the highest skirts of the woody region," on to the "charr'd, blacken'd, melancholy" summit of Etna, where he quenches his thirst with the fire of self-destruction. And of course in the Oxford diptych, the whole notion of the quest dominates both structure and theme, whether it be the quest of the scholar-gipsy, or the quest of Arnold himself in "Thyrsis," groping towards the vision of "That single elm-tree bright," or moving back through successive layers of time.[38] Eliot's use of the quest motif, to be explored in the next chapter, provides another means of establishing how his poetry grew from the poetic world of his Victorian predecessors.

3

The Quest: 1905–1925

The quest embodies a state of mind which is unfulfilled. The restless movement forward, whether across a waste plain or ocean, or up a barren peak, or through city streets, suggests what Newman called "spiritual dryness."[1] This impels the dissatisfied soul to *seek* the healing Fountain which will bring relief. In the Victorian context the pilgrimage becomes a complex, by no means wholly consistent image for the religious struggle: the search for faith and the exploration of its alternatives. Thus, "Grande Chartreuse" examines the emotions which can no longer find release in a vital dogma; *Empedocles* describes the cul-de-sac of a certain kind of radical scepticism; "Rugby Chapel" tries to define a secular faith based on the social commitment typified by Arnold's father; and the Oxford poems, against a natural landscape revealing the presence not of Divinity but only of Time and its changes, endeavor to shift the source of man's inspiration from God to the imagination.

The Victorians took the traditional idea of the quest, a basic literary motif from *The Aeneid* to *Alastor,* and transformed it into a unique property of their own age. One thinks not only of the examples in Arnold's poetry, but of Tëufelsdrockh's "world-pilgrimage"[2]; of Childe Roland's "whole world-wide wandering" (19); and of Tennyson's voyagers ("The Lotos-Eaters," "Ulysses," "The Voyage") and knights. Almost every one of the *Idylls of the King* centers around the quest of a central character. Not every one of these quests refers specifically to the problem of religious faith, but they do suggest different facets of the radical impulse underlying so much of Victorian literature, including the very concept of Progress: the need to push on through an unsatisfactory world towards what must certainly be a better realm, whether of the individual spirit or society as a whole. Ulysses' call to his men may be in part a veiled yearning for oblivion, but his action also implies the desire to seek better worlds:

It may be we shall touch the Happy Isles,
And see the great Achilles, whom we knew.

Many of Eliot's poems center on quests of one sort or another. I use this term in a general sense that includes any kind of pilgrimage towards a supreme trial, with antagonists and temptations as well as the presiding goal.[3] Of course, Dante's journey from the Inferno to Paradise in *The Divine Comedy* was for Eliot the supreme quest of the spirit, which became the pattern not only for his poetry but for his life. But Eliot's quests can still be seen as versions of the Victorian struggle towards resolution through faith, whatever form that faith assumes.

The Waste Land is the most obvious example. With the publication of the *Waste Land* manuscripts and the subsequent appreciation of the poem's long development, many readers no longer regard the poem's anthropological scheme—derived from Frazer and Weston, and imposed by Eliot at a late stage of composition—as the most important prerequisite for an understanding of the poem. Still, it would be wrongheaded to dismiss the presence and implications of the Quest for the Holy Grail. We have not only Eliot's own reference, in the *Waste Land* notes, to the elucidative significance of "Miss Jessie L. Weston's book on the Grail legend," but also the record of his soon-forgotten project to complete a sequel to *The Waste Land,* about the actual "coming of the Grail."[4]

The landscape and action of "What the Thunder said" define all that has preceded in terms of a quest pattern. The faces, voices, scenes and memories become parts of a whole. They all contribute to the "continuous phantasmagoria" (Eliot's phrase for Dante's journey in the *Inferno* [*SE* 256]) through which the consciousnesses of poet and reader move towards the Chapel Perilous.

As we follow "The road winding above among the mountains" (333), the protagonist senses the presence of Him whose terrible absence seems confirmed by contemporary actuality: "He who was living is now dead. . . . When I count, there are only you and I together." The quest for the Grail (the platter which held Christ's last earthly sustenance and his blood) culminates in a dizzying look backwards at the whole journey, in lines which are a nightmarish echo-chamber recalling as well as distorting what has gone before (*The Waste Land,* ll. 367-85).

The faint moonlight (387) reveals no sign of Christ—only fossils of faith. "Dry bones can harm no one": no danger, no life. But suddenly, four lines (392-95) bring an abrupt turnabout: there appear a cock on the rooftree crowing (a sign of resurrection, of putting wandering spirits to rest, of approaching light), a flash of lightning instead of dawn's glimmer, and a "damp gust/Bringing rain." The Grail turns out to be not a vision, but the sounds of fabled thunder; one culture is dropped for another in the poet's gesture towards synthesis. The movement of the quest ceases:

> I sat upon the shore
> Fishing, with the arid plain behind me

What remains is the exhausted realization that these are indeed "fragments" that have been shored. The chanting of a "Peace which passeth understanding" floats over images of destruction ("London Bridge is falling down") and madness ("Why then Ile fit you"). Closure is attained in words pointing to a nondiscursive mode of enlightenment: an end as mysterious and untranslatable as Childe Roland's or Galahad's in Tennyson's "The Holy Grail." What Houghton and Stange have said of Browning's quester can be applied here to Eliot's:

> His hero is not fired by the possibility of romantic action; weary and disillusioned, he continues his search through a doomed and wasted world. The meaning of the search, of the goal itself, is not made clear to us. What is clear is the agony of the journey, and the necessity which compels it.[5]

The pattern and implications of the quest motif are by no means limited to *The Waste Land.* Throughout Eliot's poetry, from the urban peregrinations of the early poems, through the perilous ocean voyage of the original "Death by Water," to the painful ascent up mountain or Sacred Stair, the movement and energy of questing play an important part. We cannot define precisely the ultimate goal of the journey—Prufrock's "overwhelming question" remains as vague and unanswerable as the broken prayers of *Ash-Wednesday*—but we can see whence it moves: from the emptiness of a world without God, where man becomes the measure of all things, and all things become small and meaningless. "Not fare well," Eliot wrote in *Four Quartets,* a poem that looks back upon his own quest towards the precarious mastery of language and belief, "But fare forward, voyagers."

The Smith Academy graduation piece (1905) presents the first version of the quest in Eliot's poetry: the dangerous ocean voyage becomes an image for life itself. The poem is all clichés about the past and the present and the future, but it is given form and purpose by the memory of Tennyson's voyagers. Here the presence of Tennyson is in the theme and manner of the poem as a whole, as well as in echoes of poems like "Ulysses," "Crossing the Bar," and "Merlin and the Gleam":

I

Standing upon the shore of all we know
We linger for a moment doubtfully,
Then with a song upon our lips, sail we
Across the harbor bar—no chart to show,
No light to warn of rocks which lie below,
But let us yet put forth courageously.[6]

The metaphor shifts from sea to land, in lines which foreshadow poems
and images to come:

Although the path be tortuous and slow,
Although it bristle with a thousand fears,
To hopeful eye of youth it still appears
A lane by which the rose and hawthorn grow.

As Eliot grew older, he found and shaped a poetic world more suited to
his own vision. It was a shabby urban world, presented by means of what
might be called the unconscious quest: the apparently aimless wanderings
of a restless soul, compelled to drift through city streets towards vaguely
sinister rooms or questions, or terrible silences, all of them tests through
which he may or may not have the courage to pass.

Many of the unpublished poems in Eliot's holograph Notebook, now
in the Berg Collection of the New York Public Library, clearly depict this
world. These poems were written in Cambridge and Paris, mostly between 1909 and 1912.[7] They all rehearse the ominous wandering that will
find perfect expression in "Rhapsody on a Windy Night" and "The Love
Song of J. Alfred Prufrock." The wandering hints at an unspoken and
inexpressible yearning. The unnatural landscape and unavoidable temptations characteristic of the quest are found in these rough early pieces:
rubbish, mud, sand, black trees, and buildings standing like mindless
beggars; evil houses laughing at the speaker and pointing a finger at him.
Only in one poem do we hear anything about an ultimate goal: lines of
city lights lead to a cross on which the bleeding soul is spread. The poems
oscillate between intense spiritual crisis and the agony of humiliation.
The self-conscious quester of these poems both pursues and awaits a sign:
of what, he is not sure, but it surely has to do with a moment of transcendence that effaces Arnold's "thousand nothings of the hour."

"In the context of the development of Eliot's poetry," Stephen
Spender has written, "Prufrock is a searcher, and his quest, like that of
other individuals in Eliot's poetry, is for a grail."[8] "Rhapsody on a Windy
Night" presents the consciousness of another of these searchers. It is no
doubt reasonable to discuss this poem in terms of Bergsonian influence[9]

or musical organization.[10] These approaches, however, ignore an aspect of the poem that gives it greater coherence, making it more than a "loosely flowing experiment"[11] with only a "precarious and arbitrary imposition of order."[12] This is the quest pattern, specifically the failed quest typified by Arnold's "Stanzas from the Grande Chartreuse," or Tennyson's "The Holy Grail," or Browning's "Childe Roland to the Dark Tower Came." I am not trying to push Eliot's poem back into the nineteenth century, but simply pointing to a motif Eliot drew upon again and again in ways recalling its use in Victorian poetry.

Compare, for instance, "Rhapsody" to "Childe Roland." In both poems the quest is indeterminate, both goal and motivation remaining problematic. This results in "an imagistic concentration on objects that dwells, as a painter might, on their quiddity while hinting at their larger implications"—the words are Bernard Bergonzi's, describing "Rhapsody," but they apply quite aptly to Browning's poem. What Eliot calls, in "Rhapsody," "the floors of memory" (5) are dissolved in both poems. Past and present fuse, again in Bergonzi's words, "with many dream-like juxtapositions."[13] The landscape *becomes* the poem, thrusting itself upon us in a linear progression of surreal clarity. Finally, with no warning, the speakers suddenly find themselves at their destination, which turns out to be nothing more than an awful trap. Both feel "The last twist of the knife."

"Childe Roland" opens with a sinister cripple, his "malicious eye/Askance. . . ." In "Rhapsody," the first figure to whom the street-lamp directs the poet's attention is a tattered whore, equally threatening. " 'And you see the corner of her eye/Twists like a crooked pin.' " Browning's knight passes an abandoned instrument with "rusty teeth of steel" (144); Eliot's searcher passes a rusty spring "Hard and curled and ready to snap." In "Rhapsody," the disfigured moon ("A washed-out smallpox cracks her face") "smooths the hair of the grass," another reflection of Childe Roland's world:

> As for the grass, it grew as scant as hair
> In leprosy. . . .   (73-74)

Childe Roland finds resolution in an instant of supreme knowledge coincident with his own death. The restless, frustrated spirit in Eliot's poem, imprisoned rather than liberated by memory (cf. the last two stanzas of "Childe Roland"), reaches only a travesty of the final ascent or ultimate phase of the quest: the staircase of his boarding-house, which leads only to bed and tooth-brush. "The little lamp spreads a ring on the stair"—a mocking, meaningless aureole bringing to mind the grail he has not found.

The background of "Rhapsody" includes more than one Victorian. The movement of a cat's tongue reminds the speaker of something else he once saw:

> So the hand of a child, automatic,
> Slipped out and pocketed a toy that was running along the quay.
> I could see nothing behind that child's eye.   (38-40)

These lines are an ironic echo of Arnold's "To a Gipsy Child by the Sea-Shore," in which, by a "cluster'd pier," Arnold catches a glimpse of a child's expression and finds in it a world of sorrow and resignation:

> Who taught this pleading to unpractised eyes?
> Who hid such import in an infant's gloom?
> . . . .
> With eyes which sought thine eyes thou didst converse,
> And that soul-searching vision fell on me.   (1-2, 15-16)

Although genuine communication is rare in Arnold's poetry, he can still speak of eyes as windows to the soul. In "The Buried Life," there comes a moment when "Our eyes can in another's eyes read clear" (81). But for Eliot, eyes are only barriers, the implications of which haunt the speaker in poems like "Eyes that last I saw in tears," *The Hollow Men,* and, of course, "Rhapsody on a Windy Night."

The quest becomes more explicit in one of the earliest *Waste Land* fragments, "So through the evening," written just a few years after "Rhapsody on a Windy Night."[14] The poem has been published in *The Facsimile and Transcript of the Original Drafts,* pp. 112-15.

The urban peregrination becomes a visionary pilgrimage into the wilderness: "out from town" comes to represent the direction of Eliot's questers, from St. Narcissus to the Magi:

> If he walked in city streets
> He seemed to tread on faces, convulsive thighs and knees.
> So he came out under the rock.[15]

> And the cities hostile and the towns unfriendly
> And the villages dirty and charging high prices:
> A hard time we had of it.
> At the end we preferred to travel all night. . . .[16]

"So through the evening" contains eight lines (13-16, 19-22) that eventually became part of *The Waste Land*. It is very close to an embryo—a kind of primitive *Waste Land* in miniature. We have a journey through desert land and away from the city (6, 9, 33); a questing consciousness exposed to "strange images" and hallucinatory visions, searching for the Grail of religious enlightenment ("The This-do-ye-for-my-sake . . . The one essential word that frees/The inspiration that delivers and expresses"); a "Death by Water" section that performs the similar function of suddenly changing the movement and tone of the poem, and posing an image of the supposedly life-giving water as agent of suffocation; and even a corpse that will not stay dead. The obvious difference is that instead of achieving the perilous ascent in order to hear and *perhaps* understand what the thunder says, there is only a return to endless unfulfillment: "So in our fixed confusion we persisted, out from town."

The nature of the quest depends upon its goal. The speaker of this poem seeks (or waits for) something having to do with the phrase "This-do-ye-for-my-sake": "Concatenated words from which the sense seemed gone," but words still vivid enough to haunt the restless consciousness of the poem. When does it come?—that question is the "One tortured meditation" of all questers for the Grail. The phrase refers to the service of Holy Communion, specifically to the point when the priest, taking the bread, repeats the words of Jesus: "Take, eat, this is my Body which is given for you: Do this in remembrance of me." Like the speaker in "Song to the Opherian," the wanderer in "So through the evening" is "waiting that touch," the sense of communion with God Himself, which liberates him from the labyrinth of secular days and ways ("This wrinkled road which twists and winds and guesses"). "This-do-ye-for-my-sake" will cease to be only a string of empty, run-together words when the inspiration of belief in a living God has been granted.

The poet compares his "fixed confusion" to that of a deaf mute underwater, with no sense of direction, swimming deeper and deeper into the sea. This image brings us to the original "Death by Water," where the landscape of the quest becomes a haunted seascape.

"Fear death by water," warns Madame Sosostris, foreshadowing the protagonist's transfiguring fate as well as the actual configuration of the poem. The original "Death by Water" (*FT* 54-69) consisted of three distinct sections. First came three introductory quatrains, the form of which Eliot had already used in the typist episode of "The Fire Sermon." Next came seventy lines of blank verse, a first-person narrative describing the doomed voyage of some New England fishermen. Finally, there was the "Phlebas, the Phoenician" lyric—all that was to remain of Part IV after Pound's strenuous revising.

Most critics have accepted Pound's cuts here with unqualified approval, dismissing the first eighty-two lines as inadequate verse, marred by "trouble with idiom, trouble with rhythm, trouble with tone,"[17] verse "slackly written,"[18] mere "seamanship and literature."[19] Behind these convenient dismissals, however, lie at least two problematic assumptions. One is that the verse is in fact bad poetry, a conclusion with which Stephen Spender, who ought to know about such things, disagrees:

> In contrast to this [the Fresca scene] there is a passage which has the holidaying sense of pastoral release of certain allegrettos of Beethoven:
>
> > Kingfisher weather, with a light fair breeze,
> > Full canvas and the eight sails drawing well . . .
>
> linked (perhaps with some straining of intellectual purpose), with Dante's account in the *Inferno* of the last voyage of Ulysses. The omission of this is, poetically speaking, the only long passage to be regretted.[20]

Another questionable assumption is that these lines could not have been worked into something better—a transformation we know to be at least possible from the several versions of the typist episode. Instead of treating the early version of "Death by Water" as only an abortive indulgence giving Eliot the opportunity to play sailor, one might do well to take it more seriously as material that was once a significant part of *The Waste Land,* at least in Eliot's mind, contributing to the complex effect of the whole. In this light, certain images and themes—for one, the pattern of the quest for faith—stand out more clearly, unobscured by Pound's insistence upon radical ellipsis.

In the original "Death by Water," Eliot made sure to establish in the reader's mind the presence of Ulysses, archetypal voyager and hero of one of the oldest quests in Western literature. He did this by means of a few carefully placed and, for him, relatively explicit allusions to the Ulysses of Homer, Dante, and Tennyson. Homer's hero appears with a paraphrase (signalled by quotation marks) of the description of Ulysses that opens the *Odyssey*:

> From his trade with wind and sea and snow, as they
> Are, he is, with "much seen and much endured" . . .   (9-10)

"So the crew moaned," the sailor-narrator recounts in the second section, and "the sea with many voices/Moaned all about us . . ."   (42-43). These lines recall a passage from Tennyson's "Ulysses":

> The lights begin to twinkle from the rocks;
> The long day wanes; the slow moon climbs; the deep
> Moans round with many voices.   (54-56)

In 1929, Eliot wrote that the last of these three lines, "a true specimen of Tennyson-Virgilianism, is too *poetical* in comparison with Dante, to be the highest poetry" (*SE* 248). But it was one of those lines that stuck in his mind. He used it again in Part VI of *Ash-Wednesday,* describing "the lost sea voices," and in "The Dry Salvages": "The sea has many voices,/Many gods and many voices" (*CPP* 130-31).

The sailor continues his account. The women "who sang above the wind/A song that charmed my senses" (55-56) recall the sirens of the *Odyssey,* Book XII. Unlike Ulysses, however, Eliot's sailor does not escape the wrack to which their music leads. His ship runs against an iceberg, leading to the horror and utter confusion of death at sea:

> My God man there's bears on it.
> Not a chance. Home and mother.
> Where's a cocktail shaker, Ben, here's plenty of cracked ice.
> Remember me.   (78-81)

The narrative concludes:

> And if *Another* knows, I know I know not,
> Who only know that there is no more noise now.   (82-83)

The word that Eliot capitalized and underscored refers us to another first-person account of a shipwreck: Ulysses' relation of his fate to Dante in Canto XXVI of the *Inferno.* The canto ends with these words:

> ". . . a storm came up from the new land, and caught the stem of our ship. Three times it whirled her round with all the waters; the fourth time it heaved up the stern and drove her down at the head, as pleased Another [*com' altrui piacque*]; until the sea closed over us."[21]

That single phrase—"*com' altrui piacque*"—struck Eliot deeply. As far back as his first "Dante" essay (pub. April 1920), he singled it out for comment:

> . . . if Mr. Sidgwick had pondered the strange words of Ulysses,
>
> com' altrui piacque,

he would not have said that the preacher and prophet are lost in the poet. "Preacher" and "prophet" are odious terms; but what Mr. Sidgwick designates by them is something which is certainly not "lost in the poet," but is part of the poet. (*SW* 166)

In the "Dante" essay of 1929, comparing Dante's handling of Ulysses to Tennyson's, he writes:

We do not need, at first, to know what mountain the mountain was [which Ulysses and his men spot shortly before their death], or what the words mean *as pleased Another*, to feel that Dante's sense has further depths. (*SE* 250)

Eliot wrote that Dante's Ulysses episode has "the quality of *surprise* which Poe declared to be essential to poetry" (*SE* 247). One can see that *"com' altrui piacque"* embodies that "quality of surprise." In those three words, Dante has the pagan—in Eliot's words, "a legendary figure of ancient epic" (*SE* 247)—casually and unexpectedly acknowledge the presence of a divinely sanctioned Order; all that he has said takes on a new intensity of meaning. Ulysses' damnation has brought Knowledge.

Eliot praised the Ulysses episode in Canto XXVI more than once, always insisting that it was "better"—simpler, more moving, more exciting—than Tennyson's "Ulysses." It "reads like a straightforward piece of romance, a well-told seaman's yarn" (*SE* 250); it sets before you "real men talking . . . real events moving" (*SE* 331). He was no doubt trying to capture this realism in his own version of the final voyage.

We have spent several pages seeing how Eliot evokes Ulysses in his account of some hard-bitten American fishermen on a cursed voyage. They pick bugs from their grub, dream about Marm Brown's joint, sail, and die. This juxtaposition represents the technique Eliot described in *"Ulysses*, Order, and Myth" (1923) as "manipulating a continuous parallel between contemporaneity and antiquity."[22] Perhaps the Ulysses allusions are not as successful as Eliot's balancing the vision of Sweeney fallen amongst bumbling crooks with that of Agamemnon's fall, or not as sustained as the image of maidens old and new drifting down the Thames. Still, they are certainly more than mere "mechanical efforts to link it [the original "Death by Water"] with the rest of the poem," which is how Hugh Kenner dismisses them.[23]

The interplay of past and present, of the everyday and the heroic, is no simpler here than elsewhere in Eliot's poetry. A drunken sailor, "Staggering, or limping with a comic gonorrhea" (8), is suddenly associated with the great voyager burdened with the knowledge of " 'much seen and much endured.' " The dying sailor, passing the stages of his age and youth ("Where's a cocktail shaker, Ben" is probably the remembered voice of one of Marm Brown's girls) utters words reminiscent of Arnaut

Daniel's parting cry in Canto XXVI of the *Purgatorio*: "Remember me" (81), "*sovegna vos*." But Daniel dives into "that fire which refines," which brings new life; the sailor is on the other hand swallowed by waters of oblivion, where "there is no more noise" (83). This technique is no mere glorification of the splendid past in relation to a diminished present. Rather, it is a placing of the present in time so as to achieve the effect of experiencing several periods of time and several planes of reality at once.

The original "Death by Water" presents different reflections of an archetypal voyage in which man and his spirit are opposed to the sea, with its demons and its dread blank force. The desire "To follow knowledge like a sinking star" ("Ulysses," l.31), or the concentration of will "against the tempest and the tide" (2), which Ben and his crew display to the full, are both manifestations of that spirit. The voyage of "Death by Water" exalts man but at the same time reduces him to nothing, for it ends in death. The waters will overwhelm both him and his aspirations; the sea closes over both the aged king Ulysses and the anonymous fisherman plagued with gleet. It is an end, Eliot implies, redeemed only by that knowledge of Another, which is difficult to attain. Ben dies "know[ing] not" (82); Dante's Ulysses attains it in Hell.

The concluding lyric about Phlebas effects an abrupt shift of time and place. From the turbulence of storm and destruction, Eliot cuts to the curiously restful image of a corpse rotting undersea, a dead man of Phoenicia—a civilization as ancient as Ulysses' Ithaca.

Eliot had read about Phoenicians in Frazer's *Adonis, Attis, Osiris,* which he cites in the *Waste Land* notes. Chapter 5 of the first volume describes the Phoenicians' custom of burning the chief god of the city in effigy, or in the person of a human representative. Chapter 7 of the same volume discusses the ancients' view of this kind of death by fire as an apotheosis, purging away the mortal parts of man and leaving only the immortal.[24]

But with Phlebas, Eliot was probably recalling the merchant-seaman who appears in Book XIV of *The Odyssey,* who is an archetypal Bleistein-Mr. Eugenides figure. Ulysses recounts:

> ". . . But when the eighth circling year was come, then there came a man of Phoenicia, well versed in guile, a greedy knave, who had already wrought much evil among men. He prevailed upon me by his cunning, and took me with him, until we reached Phoenicia, where lay his house and his possessions. There I remained with him for a full year."[25]

This Phoenician, governed by thoughts of "the profit and the loss" (*WL* 314), suffers the same fate as Phlebas:

". . . he sent me on a seafaring ship bound for Libya, having given lying counsel to
the end that I should convey a cargo with him, but in truth that, when there, he might
sell me and get a vast price. So I went with him on board the ship. . . . But when we
had left Crete, and no other land appeared, but only sky and sea, then verily the son
of Cronos set a black cloud above the hollow ship, and the sea grew dark beneath it.
. . ." (294-304)

Zeus strikes the ship with lightning, and all save Ulysses are lost.

For Eliot, the Phoenician is another whose death is only the terminus
that renders life meaningless.

> Gentile or Jew,
> O you who turn the wheel and look to windward,
> Consider Phlebas, who was once handsome and tall as you.

These lines are addressed to all: pagans, Jews, and Christians; Ulysses
and Ben; Eliot himself, who loved sailing and was a strikingly handsome,
tall young man; those "who turn the wheel" and the dead and dying souls
"bound upon the wheel" (*FT* 31) in all unreal cities. Consider death—a
proper meditation at this point, serving as prelude to "What the Thunder
said," which gropes towards new life.

I have been considering how the original "Death by Water" worked
as a distinct, tripartite poetic unit. It is also necessary to observe how it
would have affected one's reading of the rest of the poem—especially the
final section, which Eliot thought the strongest, and upon which any
argument about the unity of *The Waste Land* has finally to rest.

The original "Death by Water" and "What the Thunder said" were
written in November and December 1921, at Lausanne.[26] They contrast
two kinds of journey: one on the sea, leading only to death; and one in
the desert, leading to the possibility of renewed life. We turn from the
horror of death as *end,* to a crucifixion that, in Christian terms, makes
death a *beginning*:

> After the torchlight red on sweaty faces
> After the frosty silence in the gardens
> After the agony in stony places . . . (322-24)

Each journey has its own demons—"voices singing" from the top of the
mast (66-68) or out of empty cisterns. And each journey has its own
apocalyptic terrors: "the illimitable scream/Of a whole world about us"
(64-65), or, over the mountains, explosions "in the violet air." In the storm
of the original "Death by Water," there are sirens on the cross-trees,
singing of ruin; in the storm bringing lightning and rain to "this decayed
hole among the mountains," a cock on the rooftree sings of resurrection.

The thunder speaks, bringing us towards the moment of illumination which stills the tempest and quickens the dead:

> The boat responded
> Gaily, to the hand expert with sail and oar
> The sea was calm. . . .

The early version of "Death by Water," then, was joined with Part V to act as a unit, with deliberate contrasts and unifying points of contact. The fire-water dichotomy of "The Fire Sermon" was expanded more fully with the extended account of a doomed sea-journey followed by a quest through the desert. "The roar of waves upon the sea" (58) and the "sharper note of breakers on a reef" (59) are replaced by sounds of water's absence:

> If there were the sound of water only
> Not the cicada
> And the dry grass singing
> But sound of water over a rock

Part IV, in its original form, brought about a balance in the poem as a whole. The dreary couplings and empty souls of the waste land were set in a more comprehensive perspective by the image of seamen not unusually heroic or noble, but, despite their watery end, *alive*. This notion is presented but hardly developed in "The Fire Sermon":

> . . . I can sometimes hear
> Beside a public bar in Lower Thames Street,
> The pleasant whining of a mandoline
> And a clatter and chatter from within
> Where fishmen lounge at noon. . . .   (260-63)

Like Ulysses, even like the saint or pilgrim in the desert, they are devoted with "concentrated will" (2) to a meaningful purpose, and their struggle is not against boredom or having a sixth child (*WL* 160), but with the elements of wind and earth and sea. The inherent worthiness of their trade goes all the way back to the metaphor of Christ as the fisher of men's souls.

The sea-storm of the original "Death by Water" also played its part in *The Waste Land* as a whole. Not only did it provide a focal point for Eliot's scattered echoes of Ariel's elegy for the father apparently lost in the shipwreck opening *The Tempest,* but it also recalled the Psalm that is, according to the Anglican *Book of Common Prayer,* one of the "Forms of Prayer to be used at Sea" for thanksgiving after a storm:

Some went down to the sea in ships, doing business on the great waters;
These see the works of the LORD, and his wonders in the deep.
For he commandeth, and raiseth the stormy wind, which lifteth up the waves thereof.
They mount up to the heaven, they go down again to the depths: their soul is melted
  because of trouble.
They reel to and fro, and stagger like a drunken man, and are at their wits' end.
Then they cry unto the LORD in their trouble, and he bringeth them out of their
  distresses.
He maketh the storm a calm, so that the waves thereof are still.
Then are they glad because they be quiet; so he bringeth them unto their desired
  haven.   (Psalm 107: 23-30)

Psalm 107 offers praise for "God's providence in divers varieties of life,"[27] addressing itself to "wayfarers who have received divine guidance, liberated prisoners, the sick who have been healed, and seafarers rescued from the storm."[28] It is an anti-poem to *The Waste Land,* which concerns the *absence* of God "in divers varieties of life," addressing itself to wayfarers still lost in the desert, prisoners confirming the prison, the sick one awaiting the healing vision, and seafarers overwhelmed by the storm. "They wandered in the wilderness in a desert way;"

They found no city of habitation.
Hungry and thirsty,
Their soul fainted in them.
Then they cried unto Jehovah in their trouble,
And he delivered them out of their distresses. . . . (Psalm. 107: 4-6)

It is that cry in the wilderness, an essential part of the quest for faith, towards which *The Waste Land* points. We finally hear it, "even among these rocks" (*AW* VI), in the last line of *Ash-Wednesday,* the last step of the quest: "And let my cry come unto Thee."

I am not trying to sneak Psalm 107 into the already overcrowded roll call of *Waste Land* sources, although one could certainly argue that Eliot had it in the back of his mind when he began tying the pieces of his unwieldy poem together. But it does help to remind us that the central image of *The Waste Land* by no means has to be glossed by referring to books on fertility rites or mystical schemata:

He turns rivers into a desert,
   springs of water into thirsty ground,
a fruitful land into a salty waste. . . .
He turns a desert into pools of water,
   a parched land into springs of water.
. . . .
Whoever is wise, let him give heed to these things;
   let men consider the steadfast love of the LORD.   (Psalm. 107: 33-43)

The quest for faith in *The Waste Land*—for that which makes life more than the passing of time, and death more than the disintegration of tissue—becomes clearer with the presence and implications of the original "Death by Water." It forms a part of the pattern.

Of course, not all of Eliot's personae in the poems written in or before 1922 move through the streets of cities, or past the rocks of the desert, or over the breakers of storms at sea. Some are quite stationary, too old or too empty to move at all. But the nature of their paralysis further illuminates the nature of the quest.

Gerontion is one who has stopped moving. He waits—for rain, and for death, which both attracts and terrifies him. Memory provides neither solace nor escape, but only images of withered souls and a decayed history. Even the prospect of death cannot purge him of "a thousand small deliberations" which intrude and occupy the brain.

Northrop Frye has called "Gerontion" "a parody of Newman's *The Dream of Gerontius.*"[29] But neither Frye nor other scholars have bothered to carry the comparison any further than that. Indeed, B. C. Southam, in his standard *Guide to the Selected Poems of T. S. Eliot,* mentions Newman's poem not at all. Yet *The Dream of Gerontius* is as significant a source for Eliot's poem as the plays of the Jacobeans. Viewing the two poems together places "Gerontion" more clearly in relation to the quest for faith.

Martin J. Svaglic has described "how seriously it [*The Dream of Gerontius*] was taken in England, where almost 30,000 copies were sold in the two decades after Newman's death [1890-1910]. . . ."[30] In the same year that Eliot travelled to Oxford (1914), H. Milford came out with the "Oxford Edition" of *The Dream of Gerontius and other Poems*. Sir Edward Elgar's oratorio *The Dream of Gerontius,* first performed in 1900, quickly became a standard piece. Both works made the name "Gerontius" a widely recognized symbol of the saved Christian soul. In the mind of early twentieth-century England, Gerontius's ordeal represented the ordeal of every true Christian: struggling with death's terror, momentarily succumbing to fear of the abyss, but finally emerging triumphant, credo intact, overwhelmed by the love and presence of God. The descent into purgatory which ends both Newman's and Elgar's works is the joyfully accepted pathway to that state of purity enabling the soul, "possest/Of its Sole Peace," to "rise, and go above,/And see him in the truth of everlasting day."[31] Elgar's composition ends with the souls in Purgatory, Gerontius's "Guardian Spirit," and the "Choir of Angelicals" all singing a magnificent contrapuntal paean to the glory of God.

The popularity of Elgar's work did not diminish during the war years. In May 1916, for example, when Eliot was teaching at the Highgate School near London, a series of Red Cross concerts was performed at Queen's Hall, which included a daily performance of *The Dream of Gerontius*. This was, according to Basil Maine, Elgar's biographer, "a remarkable achievement at a time when music-making on a large scale had almost completely ceased. . . . The music of 'Gerontius,' during that week in the spring of 1916, shone with a new significance and became a symbol of intercession."[32] Eliot seized upon the symbol of Gerontius to write a poem that would embody, not civilization's salvation, but its death throes. The memory of Newman's archetypal figure provided the perfect foil for Eliot's despairing vision.

Both poems describe an old man's preparation for death. Like Gerontion, Gerontius's exhaustion is both physical and spiritual:

> . . . I am near to death. . . .
> 'Tis this strange innermost abandonment . . .
> This emptying out of each constituent
>   And natural force, by which I come to be.
> . . . .
> I can no more; for now it comes again,
> That sense of ruin, which is worse than pain,
> That masterful negation and collapse
> Of all that makes me man. . . .   (1-12, 108-11)

And Gerontius has his own tormenting "Tenants of the house," his own nightmare:

> A fierce and restless fright begins to fill
> The mansion of my soul. . . .
> Some bodily form of ill
> Floats on the wind, with many a loathsome curse
> Tainting the hallow'd air, and laughs, and flaps
> Its hideous wings,
> And makes me wild with horror and dismay.   (119-25)

But Eliot has diminished the old man, using the diminutive form, Ger-*on*i*on*, "little old man." Like his name, his world has been trivialized. His companions are not the friends who pray for Gerontius, not the priest who encourages with words like "Go forth upon thy journey, Christian soul!" (150), but "the jew" squatting on the window sill, a boy, and a kitchen-woman, sneezing and poking. "Here I am, an old man," staring at death and waiting for rain, which will not forestall it. Verbs involve action or identity; Gerontion can no longer rise to either:

> I an old man,
> A dull head among windy spaces.

In contrast to Newman's poem, which begins with the cries of a dying old man but becomes by the end a stately exposition of the workings of salvation and eternal judgment, "Gerontion" remains throughout the thoughts of one dry brain, or rather, the *dream* of one, a notion supported by Eliot's epigraph (". . . an after dinner sleep/Dreaming of both") as well as the illogically connected pieces of the old man's life floating into consciousness:

> . . . by Mr. Silvero
> With caressing hands, at Limoges
> Who walked all night in the next room;
> By Hakagawa, bowing among the Titians;
> By Madame de Tornquist, in the dark room
> Shifting the candles. . . .

Eliot's epigraph, like his title, recalls Newman's poem concerning "The Dream" of the departed Christian soul. The Angel tells the Soul of Gerontius:

> And thou art wrapp'd and swathed around in dreams,
> Dreams that are true, yet enigmatical;
> For the belongings of thy present state,
> Save through such symbols, come not home to thee.   (536-39)

"In other words," Alec Robertson has written, "the experiences of Gerontius are real, but they are like a dream, because he does not perceive them through his bodily senses."[33] "Nor touch, nor taste, nor hearing hast thou now," the Angel explains (525). Gerontion's state is similar: "I have lost my sight, smell, hearing, taste and touch."

Gerontion's senses are dead. But he is still trapped in life, like Tithonus—trapped in a death-in-life made fearful by the suspicion that "We have not reached conclusion, when I/Stiffen in a rented house." In Eliot's poem, death has extended its dominion so that even Christ, symbol of the new life which Gerontion and the Hofgarten crowd cannot possibly tolerate, becomes an agent of destruction:

> . . . In the juvescence of the year
> Came Christ the tiger
> . . . .
> The tiger springs in the new year. Us he devours.

Eternal life, the poet suggests, becomes a parody of itself without the possibility of salvation; it becomes Gerontion's eternal death. Eliot has turned the dream of Gerontius into a nightmare.

Eliot took his epigraph from *Measure for Measure,* III.i:

> . . . Reason thus with life:
> If I do lose thee, I do lose a thing
> That none but fools would keep;
> . . . .
> Thou hast nor youth nor age,
> But as it were an after-dinner's sleep,
> Dreaming on both. . . .

Although the Duke is addressing Claudio, "Thou" refers to life itself. Gerontion is reasoning with life from the perspective of "palsied eld," with "neither heat, affection, limb, nor beauty" (*Measure for Measure,* III.i.36-37). He has settled into a kind of ultimate post-prandial stupor, in which self-justification mingles wearily with self-contempt. With just the slightest shake of these elements held in suspension, Gerontion's state becomes that of Europe, dazed and helpless after the awful indulgences of the Great War.

The Dream of Gerontius is about salvation, while "Gerontion" is about the loss of salvation: "After such knowledge, what forgiveness?" The way to salvation is found, finally, in *Ash-Wednesday,* which like Newman's poem describes "the time of tension between dying and birth" (*AW* VI). As the Soul of Gerontius ascends the "Sacred Stair" (746), the Angelicals sing of man's fallen nature and the Incarnation, which redeems both time and man. "The shame of self at thought of seeing him," Gerontius's Soul learns, "Will be thy veriest, sharpest purgatory" (737), as the speaker in *Ash-Wednesday* also discovers:

> . . . strength beyond hope and despair
> Climbing the third stair.
>
> Lord, I am not worthy
> Lord, I am not worthy
>
> but speak the word only.

In *Ash-Wednesday,* the revivifying waters, awaited since Gerontion's futile vigil, finally appear: "But the fountain sprang up"; "The white sails still fly seaward, seaward flying"; "spirit of the river, spirit of the sea." The Soul of Gerontius, "scorch'd and shrivell'd" in the presence of Christ, ends his journey (or rather that part of it which can be conveyed through

words) in the same element, the same peace. His Angel speaks the concluding lines:

> And carefully I dip thee in the lake,
>   And thou, without a sob or a resistance,
> Dost through the flood thy rapid passage take,
>   Sinking deep, deeper, into the dim distance. . . .   (889-92)

Before *Ash-Wednesday* began taking shape, however, Eliot pieced together another major poem in which the quest towards faith is stalled. In
The Hollow Men, published in 1925, Eliot again explored the point of
view of those who are not a part of the quest or the questing consciousness. The title-page epigraph, ''Mistah Kurtz—he dead,'' refers to one
of the most unforgettable quests in modern literature: Marlow's journey
into the heart of darkness. But here in ''the dead land'' there is no half-
apprehended goal, no impulse to seek the intensity of full realization and
commitment—whether that commitment be towards God or, with Kurtz,
towards Evil. In fact, there is no forward movement of any kind. Here
they lean together (3) and grope together (58). Their actions are without
direction; they behave ''as the wind behaves,'' recalling Arnold's ''eddy
of purposeless dust'' (77) in ''Rugby Chapel'':

> Here we go round the prickly pear
> Prickly pear prickly pear
> Here we go round the prickly pear
> At five o'clock in the morning.

Even if one ''equates the eyes, the rose, and the star with the Grail
of the earlier poem as different modes of imagining the (as yet unattained)
redeeming value'' or symbol, as G. W. Foster has done in her Jungian
reading of Eliot's poems,[34] there remains the fact that this transfigured
grail image is for the hollow men something to be avoided. It cannot be
forgotten but certainly cannot be pursued, let alone faced:

> Eyes I dare not meet in dreams
> In death's dream kingdom . . .
>
> Let me be no nearer
> In death's dream kingdom . . .
>
> Not that final meeting
> In the twilight kingdom.

Up till now the forbidding level of enlightenment has been sought or
yearned after; it has provided Eliot's wanderers with their most basic

impulse, however much they have understood it. Not so in *The Hollow Men*. The stuffed, empty voices represent those who do *not* cross to another realm (13-14). They keep stars and "direct eyes" at an illimitable distance, so far away that the heavens, suggesting that other realm, are reduced to one twinkling, fading star.

What precisely is the nature of that barely comprehended realm (the guiding vision of the now-paralyzed quest) reached by "Those . . . With direct eyes"? What lies beyond the cactus land of broken stone and broken men? To answer this question we must surrender ourselves to the experience of reading the poem, which involves putting aside much of the elaborate Dantesque apparatus constructed in most readings of the poem. Critics have referred to Dante not so much to direct the reader's attention to a point of view taken from *The Divine Comedy* and no doubt a part of *The Hollow Men,* but rather to engage us in the fruitless task of trying to categorize the realms that follow one another in the poem like successive dreams on a troubled night. In equating this "kingdom" with one state and that "kingdom" with another, they have turned the poem into a literary jigsaw puzzle designed to test and improve our knowledge of Dante. This results in conflicting accounts of how many kingdoms there are and what they all mean, so that the reader is left figuring out the distinctions between "death's dream kingdom" and "the twilight kingdom," instead of paying attention to the poem's articulation through rhythm and sound. One should remember F. R. Leavis's cautionary remark, which certainly applies here:

> Well-equipped commentators would do well, for a simple illustration of the kind of dangers and temptations awaiting them, to consider how Eliot uses Dante in *Ash-Wednesday,* and how easy it would be with the aid of a Dante primer to work out an illuminating commentary that would save grateful readers the trouble of understanding the poem.[35]

The word "kingdom" sounds again and again in *The Hollow Men,* becoming a center of gravity around which are organized our impressions of the dried voices and their situation. We hear of "death's other Kingdom," "death's dream kingdom," "the twilight kingdom," "death's other kingdom," "our lost kingdoms," and "death's twilight kingdom." In this poem, the verbal austerity of which gives each word a preternaturally heightened presence, it is not enough to roughly equate "dream" with "twilight" or even "Kingdom" with "kingdom." The result is a kind of uneasy confusion over boundaries, a dreamscape in which we are sure only of a hollow valley filled with hollow men, *and* of a frightening Beyond, where evasions and empty gestures are impossible.

The climactic fifth section presents a dramatic change in both tone and method. Instead of enervated first-person monotones there are the disconcertingly jaunty nightmare-lyrics, built around an impersonal quasi-litany which juxtaposes death and life, the Shadow and God. First a voice proclaims, in a hammering rhythm without pause, the presence of that which paralyzes in this valley of death:

> Between the idea
> And the reality
> Between the motion
> And the act
> Falls the Shadow

Then another voice, set off by italics and placement on the page, recites a fragment of the Lord's Prayer ("For Thine is the Kingdom"). This is of course the first part of the concluding doxology, which runs in full: "For Thine is the kingdom, The power, and the glory, For ever and ever. Amen." Once again the term "kingdom" appears, but this time there is no doubt as to what it represents. The phrase, taken from the prayer given to the Church by Christ, points to the reality of God's Kingdom. It is towards *that* kingdom, or at least an awareness of it, that Eliot's questers strive. But the echo of the potentially redeeming fragment of prayer grows fainter, broken into still smaller pieces in the hollow valley:

> For Thine is
> Life is
> For Thine is the

The Shadow has fallen. We return to the unholy dance:

> This is the way the world ends
> This is the way the world ends
> This is the way the world ends
> Not with a bang but a whimper.

Eliot's own reading of *The Hollow Men* (in *The Waste Land and Other Poems read by T. S. Eliot,* Caedmon TC 1326) supports what I have been suggesting. He begins the fifth section with a totally new rhythm: the parody-lyric quite literally runs, nervous and hurried, with the tones of individual words varying not at all. This is in marked contrast to the rich, measured chanting of the previous sections, which returns with "Between the idea/And the reality. . . ." Then comes the Lord's Prayer fragment, detached from the rest of the verse just as much by Eliot's voice as it is by its appearance on the page. His tone is low, soft, and distant, sounding very much like murmured words of prayer. Behind this tone lies a whole world: it is a glimpse of the Grail and the coming of "The This-do-ye-for-my-sake" (see above, p. 38). The pattern repeats itself over the next fourteen lines, as the stentorian proclamation of the Shadow is interrupted by unworldly words. Finally, in the same tone as "For Thine is the Kingdom," we hear the broken, frustrated prayer—and then an abrupt return to the opening cadence, the opening dance, obliterating what has gone before in a rushed death-jingle.

It is important to comprehend the nature of the prayer which unexpectedly intrudes itself into *The Hollow Men*. The Lord's Prayer is the archetypal prayer in Christian devotion. St. Augustine called it the source of all other prayers, and it occupies a climactic place in Christian liturgies, including the celebration of the Eucharist. According to Luke—and this is essential for an understanding of its place in Eliot's poem—Jesus gave it to his disciples in answer to their request, "Lord, teach us to pray" (Luke 11: 1-4).

Eliot recognized that the need for prayer was part of the movement towards faith. In the essay "Poet and Saint . . . ," published less than two years after *The Hollow Men* (and included in *For Lancelot Andrewes* as "Baudelaire in Our Time"), he quotes from an essay by Charles Du Bos, which he calls "the finest study of Baudelaire that has been made":

> La notion de péché, *et plus profondement le besoin de prière,* telles sont les deux réalités souterraines qui paraissent appartenir à des gisements enfouis bien plus avant que ne l'est la foi elle-même. (*FLA* 95; emphasis mine)

In the world of hollow men, prayer is false, misdirected, and meaningless:

> Lips that would kiss
> Form prayers to broken stone.

The possibility of genuine prayer, which the Lord's Prayer represents, appears and then disintegrates. "Kingdom," necessary for completion of the essential phrase, disappears. For Thine is the. . . . Gone too are the power and the glory, in this dead land, leaving only the boredom and the horror.[36]

The failure of the quest in *The Hollow Men* is confirmed, then, by the poem's conclusion. But the sense of those "deux réalités souterraines qui paraissent appartenir à des gisements enfouis" is certainly present at the end: the Shadow of man's corruption, and the appeal to God, both of which are part of the quest. In the Baudelaire essay just referred to, Eliot wrote:

And being the kind of Christian that he was, born when he was, he had to discover Christianity for himself. In this pursuit he was alone in the solitude which is only known to saints. To him the notion of Original Sin came spontaneously, and the need for prayer.

The "notion of Original Sin . . . and the need for prayer" govern Eliot's final version, and completion, of the quest: *Ash-Wednesday.*

4

"End of the Endless Journey": Poetry, Belief, and *Ash-Wednesday*

That hold on human values, that firm grasp of human experience, . . . is a formidable achievement of the Elizabethan and Jacobean poets. This wisdom, cynical perhaps but untired . . . , leads toward, and is only completed by, the religious comprehension. . . .

Eliot, "Andrew Marvell" (1921)

'Tis not the prompting of mine own desire
That thus consumes me like an inward fire.
Ah no! I only ask to know God's will,
That thus the eternal tumult be forever still.
Sin only can divide my soul from Thine,
Lord, make me wholly pure. Thy will be mine.

Charlotte Eliot, *Savonarola*

. . . the religion of Carlyle or that of Ruskin or that of Arnold or that of Tennyson or that of Browning, is not enough.

Eliot, "Arnold and Pater" (1930)

The 1920s were for Eliot a time of great trial and resolution, when his quest for faith culminated in conversion to Anglo-Catholicism. Struggling through severe personal problems having to do in large part with his wife and their crumbling relationship, he was also discovering that baptism, confirmation, and all the discipline of the Church did not signal an end to the quest. With Tennyson, he learned to accept the life of faith in "honest doubt" (*IM* 96). With Pascal, he would always return to face "the demon of doubt which is inseparable from the spirit of belief" (*SE* 411), the demon which appears in *Ash-Wednesday*:

Struggling with the devil of the stairs who wears
The deceitful face of hope and of despair.[1]

Ash-Wednesday is the culmination of years of religious hope and despair, when Eliot was grappling with the concept of belief both in his own criticism and in the contents of the journal he edited, *The Criterion.* What is "belief"? What are its varieties? How is it achieved? How is it related to poetry? These were the questions that preoccupied Eliot during the middle and late 1920s; these were the concerns that led to *Ash-Wednesday.* In order to better understand the poem and its place in the quest for faith, one should turn first to the debate of these years over belief in the modern world. In doing so, one discovers that it was rooted in the opposed viewpoints of two Victorians, John Henry Newman and Matthew Arnold. In a sense, the composition of *Ash-Wednesday* was overseen by these two figures.

We have already noted Newman's presence in the background of "Gerontion." But Eliot knew his work well before the publication of that poem: "John Henry Newman" was one of the subjects included in his 1916 syllabus for a tutorial class in Modern English Literature. His coverage was rather conventional:

> His temperament, with regard to his change in religious attachment. Relation to the Oxford Movement. Reasons for joining the Church of Rome. His thought. Style. Read: *Apologia, Idea of a University.*[2]

Eliot's interest in Newman's writings increased as he approached the Anglican faith and the experience of conversion. Writing in 1926 about the sermons of Lancelot Andrewes, he likens their intensity to "the preaching of Newman" (see chapter 1):

> Andrewes' emotion is purely contemplative; it is not personal, it is wholly evoked by the object of contemplation, to which it is adequate; his emotions wholly contained in and explained by its object. (*SE* 351)

Andrewes' prose, moreover, "is not inferior to that of any sermons in the language, unless it be some of Newman's" (*SE* 353).

Indeed, one of Newman's sermons, as V. J. E. Cowley has pointed out, may be the source for the term "objective correlative," a term that Eliot certainly had in mind when he wrote the above words about the right relation of Andrewes' emotion to the object of contemplation.[3] "Love, the Safeguard of Faith against Superstition," published in *Sermons Chiefly on the Theory of Religious Belief,* has for text John 10: 4-5: "The sheep follow Him, for they know His voice. And a stranger will they not follow, but will flee from him, for they know not the voice of strangers." Newman wrote:

> It is the doctrine, then, of the text, that those who believe in Christ, believe because they know Him to be the Good Shepherd. . . . The divinely-enlightened mind sees in

Christ the very Object whom it desires to love and worship,—the Object correlative of its own affections; and it trusts Him, or believes, from loving Him.[4]

Emotion or "affections," mind, and object—all the components of Eliot's "formula" are here. "The artistic 'inevitability,' " Eliot wrote to clarify his definition, "lies in this complete adequacy of the external to the emotion" (*SW* 101); Newman reasoned that the inevitability of *belief* lay in the "complete adequacy" of Christ to the emotion of love.

More references to Newman appear, scattered through essays written around the composition of *Ash-Wednesday*. "One feels," Eliot wrote in his essay on F. H. Bradley (1927), "that the emotional intensity of Ruskin is partly a deflection of something that was baffled in life, whereas Bradley, like Newman, is directly and wholly that which he is" (*SE* 445). In "Arnold and Pater" (1930), he made clear just how he saw Newman in relation to his contemporaries:

The purpose of the present paper is to indicate a direction from Arnold, through Pater, to the 'nineties, with, of course, the solitary figure of Newman in the background. (*SE* 431)

In "The 'Pensées' of Pascal" (1931), Eliot set forth "the process of the mind of the intelligent believer":

The Christian thinker—and I mean the man who is trying consciously and conscientiously to explain to himself the sequence which culminates in faith . . .—proceeds by rejection and elimination. He finds the world to be so and so; he finds its character inexplicable by any nonreligious theory: among religions he finds Christianity, and Catholic Christianity, to account most satisfactorily for the moral world within; and thus, by what Newman calls 'powerful and concurrent' reasons, he finds himself inexorably committed to the dogma of the Incarnation. (*SE* 408)

Eliot was of course speaking from his personal experience, which always lay beneath the impersonal pronouncements of his criticism. This is made clear by comparing the above quotation to part of a talk he gave on "Christianity and Communism" in 1932:

Towards any profound conviction one is borne . . . by what Newman called "powerful and concurrent reasons." . . . In my own case, I believe that one of the reasons was that the Christian scheme seemed to me the only one which would work. . . . The Christian scheme seemed the only possible scheme which found a place for values which I must maintain or perish . . . , the belief, for instance, in holy living and holy dying, in sanctity, chastity, humility, austerity.[5]

Eliot attached importance to the phrase, "powerful and concurrent reasons." It comes from the conclusion of Newman's *A Grammar of Assent*:

> Christianity is addressed, both as regards its evidences and its contents, to minds which are in the normal condition of human nature, as believing in God and in a future judgment. Such minds it addresses both through the intellect and through the imagination; creating a certitude of its truth by arguments too various for enumeration, too personal and deep for words, too powerful and concurrent for reversal.[6]

He probably knew this passage firsthand, but it appears also in an essay he included in the January 1926 *Criterion,* Frederic Manning's "A French Criticism of Newman."[7]

Manning's was one of a series of three essays appearing in *The Criterion* in the mid-twenties, which focused on Newman's conception of religious belief. Ramon Fernandez's "The Experience of Newman" (October 1924), translated by Richard Aldington, presents Newman as "the philosopher of religious experience" and the "most inexhaustible among the thinkers capable of furnishing solutions to modern problems."[8] Manning's response (January 1926) criticizes Fernandez for distorting Newman's ideas by ignoring their intellectual and historical contexts. Finally, in October 1926, Eliot published Fernandez's "The Experience of Newman: Reply to Frederic Manning" (this time translated by F. S. Flint), which restates and clarifies his position.

In his reply, Fernandez objects to Manning's confusion of religious belief with poetry and the arts in general. This confusion was repeatedly denounced by Eliot himself during these years. He never tired of attacking the substitution of literature for religion. In this, he was aligning himself with Newman. Alvan S. Ryan explains:

> Arnold would find in literature "a criticism of life," a dealing with man's total humanity, with his moral nature, that supersedes religion and philosophy by virtue of its imaginative quality. . . .
> Eliot and Newman, on the other hand, are affirming the role of the teaching Church against this approach. It is the whole theological, apologetic and philosophical tradition of Catholicism—Anglo-Catholicism for Eliot, Roman Catholicism for Newman—that offers ultimate truth concerning man's nature and his destiny. . . . Their concern with what the Christian Faith is leads them to insist on what literature is not; and yet, paradoxically, both writers consider that through such distinctions they are serving the interest not only of religious truth, but of literature as well.[9]

In the 1920s, Newman's forces were Eliot, Fernandez, and the French critics Maritain and Rivière; on the side of Arnold were Manning, Middleton Murry, and I. A. Richards.

Richards's statement in 1925 that *The Waste Land* "effected a complete severance between his [Eliot's] poetry and *all* beliefs,"[10] and the corresponding argument that modern man, no longer able to believe in traditional religious creeds, must turn to poetry to find the values and psychological satisfactions necessary for a meaningful existence, set off a debate with Eliot that would last almost a decade. The whole controversy forms an important part of the background of *Ash-Wednesday.*

Eliot's first response to Richards came in January 1927. "A Note on Poetry and Belief" pronounces for the first time what Eliot would say again in the years to come: "doubt and uncertainty are merely a variety of belief," and Richards's misconceptions about belief and the role of poetry identify him with Matthew Arnold.[11] Later that year, he called Richards's *Science and Poetry* (1926) "a revised version of Literature and Dogma":

> "Poetry is capable of saving us," he says; it is like saying that the wall-paper will save us when the walls have crumbled.[12]

Richards did not hesitate to acknowledge his debt to Arnold. The epigraph for *Science and Poetry,* a popularized version of *Principles of Literary Criticism,* comes from Arnold's "The Study of Poetry" (1880):

> The future of poetry is immense, because in poetry, where it is worthy of its high destinies, our race, as time goes on, will find an ever surer and surer stay. There is not a creed which is not shaken, not an accredited dogma which is not shown to be questionable, not a received tradition which does not threaten to dissolve. Our religion has materialized itself in the fact, in the supposed fact; it has attached its emotion to the fact, and now the fact is failing it. But for poetry the idea is everything.[13]

Arnold was also the mentor of Middleton Murry, who contributed to the debate. Eliot's "Mr. Middleton Murry's Synthesis" appeared in the October 1927 *Criterion.* It confirms how the whole controversy grew from the assumptions and implications not only of Matthew Arnold but of nineteenth-century English poetry in general:

> But when Mr. Murry makes poetry a substitute for philosophy and religion—a higher philosophy and a purer religion, he seems to me to falsify not only philosophy and religion, but poetry too. And here is a passage from an essay by Jacques Rivière which sums up the Murry attitude better than Mr. Murry has summed it up himself:
>
> "In the seventeenth century . . . if it had occurred to anyone to ask Molière or Racine why they wrote, they would surely have been able to reply in no other way than by saying: 'to amuse the better sort' (*pour distraire les honnêtes gens*). It is only with Romanticism that the literary act began to be conceived as a sort of approach towards the absolute, and its result as a revelation; at that moment literature gathered the inheritance of religion and organized itself on the model of that which it replaced; the writer became the priest; the purpose of all his gestures was solely to induce the descent of the 'Real Presence' into this consecrated Host. The whole literature of the nineteenth century is a vast incantation, directed towards Miracle."

This transvaluation, which Rivière then deplored, Mr. Murry not only welcomes but exaggerates. . . . I have touched on this point to draw the further implication that 'being on the side of intelligence' means keeping philosophy, religion and poetry each in its proper place, or else doing away with one or another of them altogether.[14]

The roots of the argument are made even clearer in Eliot's "Preface to the 1928 Edition" of *The Sacred Wood.* Wordsworth, Arnold, and Tennyson are all invoked, though not by name:

Poetry is a superior amusement: I do not mean an amusement for superior people. I call it an amusement, an amusement *pour distraire les honnêtes gens,* not because that is a true definition, but because if you call it anything else you are likely to call it something still more false. . . . It will not do to talk of "emotion recollected in tranquillity," which is only one poet's account of his recollection of his own methods; or to call it a "criticism of life," than which no phrase can sound more frigid to anyone who has felt the full surprise and elevation of a new experience in poetry. And certainly poetry is not the inculcation of morals, or the direction of politics; and no more is it religion or an equivalent of religion, except by some monstrous abuse of words. (*SW* viii-ix)

"And religion?" Arnold had written in 1879. "The reign of religion as morality touched with emotion is indeed indestructible."[15] Statements like this must have struck Eliot as a "monstrous abuse of words." In "Arnold and Pater," published five months after *Ash-Wednesday,* he focuses on two words he considered most abused by Arnold: Culture and Religion. Maintaining the tone of the cautious philosopher, he exposes the deficiencies of his opponent's thought:

[The aim of Arnold's books about Christianity] is to affirm that the emotions of Christianity can and must be preserved without the belief. From this proposition two different types of man can extract two different types of conclusion: (1) that Religion is Morals, (2) that Religion is Art. The effect of Arnold's campaign is to divorce Religion from thought. . . . The total effect of Arnold's philosophy is to set up Culture in the place of Religion, and to leave Religion to be laid waste by the anarchy of feeling. . . . The degradation of philosophy and religion, skillfully initiated by Arnold, is competently continued by Pater. (*SE* 434, 436, 437)

"Arnold and Pater" builds to a grand finale, with Richards's Arnoldian program no doubt in mind:

The dissolution of thought in that age [the nineteenth century], the isolation of art, philosophy, religion, ethics and literature, is interrupted by various chimerical attempts to effect imperfect syntheses. Religion became morals, religion became art, religion became science or philosophy; various blundering attempts were made at alliances between various branches of thought. Each half-prophet believed he had the whole truth. The alliances were as detrimental all round as the separations. The right practice of 'art for art's sake' was the devotion of Flaubert or Henry James; Pater is not with these men, but rather with Carlyle and Ruskin and Arnold, if some distance below them. *Marius* is significant chiefly as a reminder that the religion of Carlyle or that of Ruskin or that of Arnold or that of Tennyson or that of Browning, is not enough. It represents, and Pater represents more positively than Coleridge of whom he wrote the words, 'that inexhaustible discontent, languor, and home-sickness . . . the chords of which ring all through our modern literature.' (*SE* 442-43)

This is a striking passage in the subtle way Eliot acknowledges the worth and beauty of Pater's literary perception at the same time that he condemns its foundation. Eliot the critic carefully sets himself apart from the Victorians, and in that very act identifies Eliot the poet with them. That "inexhaustible discontent, languor, and home-sickness" which Pater saw in "our modern literature"—what we now call Victorian literature—certainly characterizes "Prufrock," "Gerontion," and *The Waste Land*.

A few months before *Ash-Wednesday* was published, Eliot ventured a definition of poetry:

For poetry is not the assertion that something is true, but the making that truth more fully real to us; it is the creation of a sensuous embodiment. It is the making the Word Flesh, if we remember that for poetry there are various qualities of Word and various qualities of Flesh.[16]

This definition creates a paradox. As we have seen, Eliot argued for the maintenance of solid boundaries between poetry and religion. But to say that poetry "is the making the Word Flesh" seems to shatter those boundaries. The paradox resolves itself, however, in the realization that Eliot's theory of poetic incarnation, a theory to be developed more fully in *Four Quartets,* in no way implies an illegitimate raid into the religious domain. Poetry is making truths more fully real; "it is the creation of a sensuous embodiment." *Ash-Wednesday* does not assert, nor does it attempt to persuade. The poem *does* make more fully real the stages of the poet's belief; it does embody, through the senses, his realization of the Christian vision. The reader must know a certain amount *about* Christianity, but he does not have to believe in it. Sin, prayer, purgation, doubt and temporary relief from doubt—all of these things become parts of a coherent whole. They are all part of the poet's "Journey to no end" (*AW* II), which is the quest undertaken by "those who doubt, but who have the mind to conceive, and the sensibility to feel, the disorder, the futility, the meaninglessness, the mystery of life and suffering, and who can only find peace through a satisfaction of the whole being" (*SE* 416).

The quest for faith culminates in *Ash-Wednesday,* a poem of recurrent beginnings which suggest that the quest is endless—quite different from what we thought it to be. The movement across a waste plain changes to a spiralling ascent along steps that are images of dying selves. But the poet must be forever repeating the climb, for these old selves never quite die. Renouncing the yearning to be done with doubt, Eliot accepts its complications as a part of the process of religious belief (see chapter 2). With this poem, he no longer defines the quest in terms of a single ultimate goal, but rather as a series of returns, all of them inspired by the continuing awareness of weakness and failure, which constitutes genuine humility. All that matters, all that can be achieved, is a constant diving back into that fire which refines: "*Poi s'ascose nel foco che gli affina.*" "In purgatory," Eliot wrote in 1929, "the torment of flame is deliberately and consciously accepted by the penitent" (*SE* 255). *Ash-Wednesday,* published in April 1930 but composed over three years, is about the torment of the penitent, and about that deliberate and conscious acceptance. No longer does Eliot pursue some kind of transforming spiritual "success." In *Ash-Wednesday,* he settles upon what for him is the liberating acknowledgment that there can be no final earthly success.

From the desolation of the hollow valley has sprung the knowledge that Tennyson embodied in "The Holy Grail": there can be no lasting apprehension of the Grail, and the active pursuit of Grace is a self-deluding impossibility. Eliot touched upon this in "The 'Pensées' of Pascal," published a year after *Ash-Wednesday*:

It is recognized in Christian theology—and indeed on a lower plane it is recognized by all men in affairs of daily life—that free-will of the natural effort and ability of the individual man and also supernatural *grace,* a gift accorded we know not quite how, are both required, in co-operation, for salvation. Though numerous theologians have set their wits at the problem, it ends in a mystery which we can perceive but not finally decipher. (*SE* 413)

It is a mystery, a "gift accorded we know not quite how," and *not* something that can be discovered after sufficient searching for it. All one can do is exercise "that free-will of the natural effort" in the process of turning inward and submitting to the refining fires. "Teach us to care and not to care/Teach us to sit still"—this is the essential prayer, spoken in the first and last sections of the poem. The poet must learn to care supremely for salvation without making the mistake of reducing life to a linear progression towards it, for that leads all too easily to spiritual pride. He must renounce the old version of the quest, and be still.

All of this is hinted at in "What the Thunder said." At the same time that the quest is suddenly crystallized, it is revealed to be, at least to some extent, a delusive failure:

> There is the empty chapel, only the wind's home.
> It has no windows, and the door swings,
> Dry bones can harm no one.

In the graveyard speaks the thunder: its words of new life point the way, which is inward. But they are only a hint half-understood, and the poem ends with a disintegration into fragments, through which the reader must sort to find the new way:

> London Bridge is falling down falling down falling down
> *Poi s'ascose nel foco che gli affina . . .*

One of the fragments, that line from *Purgatorio* XXVI, looks forward to *Ash-Wednesday*. Arnaut Daniel, embracing his suffering for the sake of purgation, dives back "into that fire which refines." His parting words, singing of past folly and future salvation, even supplied Eliot with a few titles, eventually dropped, for Parts II and III of the poem.[17]

Part II of *Ash-Wednesday* was the first to appear in print. Published in December 1927 under the title "Salutation," the poem takes up aspects of the quest described in the earlier poetry in order to redefine it. The hollow valley has become the valley of Ezekiel's vision; the dry bones about the empty chapel of *The Waste Land* are now scattered under a juniper-tree and have words of their own, just as mysterious as the thunder's. The bones sing, but "only/The wind will listen" (*AW* II)—this is still "only the wind's home" (*WL* 389). The spectral desert of "Rock and no water" (*WL* 332) has become a blessing; its emptiness and desiccation are images of what the soul must undergo in order to reach the "End of the endless/Journey to no end" (*AW* II). That phrase, typical of the paradoxical way of thinking Eliot came to use more and more as the only adequate verbal rendering of untranslatable mysteries, describes a new version of the quest. The object of the "journey" is no longer the chimera of unshakable Faith, or the gift of Grace, but rather "the recognition of the reality of Sin," and a humble acceptance of the consequences of that reality.

"Recognition of the reality of Sin"—the phrase comes from "Baudelaire" (1930). Here is the whole passage:

> In the middle nineteenth century, . . . an age of bustle, programmes, platforms, scientific progress, humanitarianism and revolutions which improved nothing, an age of progressive degradation, Baudelaire perceived that what really matters is Sin and Redemption. . . . To a mind observant of the post-Voltaire France . . . the recognition of the reality of Sin is a New Life; and the possibility of damnation is so immense a relief in a world of electoral reform, plebiscites, sex reform and dress reform, that

damnation itself is an immediate form of salvation—of salvation from the ennui of
modern life, because it at last gives some significance to living. (*SE* 427)

Surely Eliot is implying that, from one point of view, very little has
changed in eighty years; what has mattered and will always matter is
man's capacity for self-knowledge. And for the orthodox Christian, this
naturally involves coming to terms with man's fallen nature—of which
doubt is a part. One must empty out all the illusory, nineteenth-century
notions about the irrevocable improvements of evolution and the self-
sufficiency of mankind.

"Salutation" is about the death of the old and the beginning of the
new life. In the wilderness, under a juniper-tree, Elijah asked for death
but received new life instead: "And he arose, and ate and drank, and
went on the strength of that food forty days and forty nights to Horeb the
mount of God."[18] Under a juniper-tree, the remains of the old life, having
undergone a violent purgation, wait patiently. In the words of Psalms 51,
part of the Commination service for Ash Wednesday: "Thou shalt purge
me with hyssop, and I shall be clean: thou shalt wash me, and I shall be
whiter than snow./Thou shalt make me hear of joy and gladness: that the
bones which thou hast broken may rejoice" (7-8). "Salutation" *is* a poem
of rejoicing: a way has been found out of the labyrinth of the apparently
fruitless quest. There is no movement at all, not even the meaningless
circling round the prickly pear—only a hieratic tableau and the disem-
bodied voice offering praise to a Lady who brings peace with her goodness and loveliness and devotion.

"Salutation" contains the seeds of *Ash-Wednesday* as a whole. The
words of purgation also contain the possibility of salvation, as suggested
by another title Eliot considered for Part II: "Jausen lo Jorn," taken from
Arnaut Daniel's words before he dives back into the refining fire (*Purgatorio* XXVI), "And I see *with joy the day* for which I hope, before
me."[19] Ezekiel taught that God loves the sinner. He throws open the door
of repentance and life to all who will enter. God speaks to the house of
Israel, through Ezekiel:

Cast away from you all your transgressions . . . and make a new heart and a new
spirit. . . . For I have no pleasure in the death of him that dieth, saith the Lord God:
wherefore turn yourselves, and live ye. . . .

Therefore, O thou son of man, speak unto the house of Israel; Thus ye speak, saying,
If our transgressions and our sins be upon us, and we pine away in them, how should
we then live? Say unto them, As I live, saith the Lord God, I have no pleasure in the
death of the wicked; but that the wicked turn from his way and live: turn ye, turn ye
from your evil ways; for why will ye die . . . ? (Ezek. 18: 31-32; 33: 10-11)

The poet's salvation depends on the succour of the "Lady of silences" (*AW* II). Symbol of what Eliot described in "Dante" (1929) as "the recrudescence of an ancient passion in a new emotion" (*SE* 262), she must guide him past the reality of his own nature:

> Terminate torment
> Of love unsatisfied
> The greater torment
> Of love satisfied   (*AW* II)

For Eliot, redemption demands the humiliating understanding of precisely why it is necessary.

One ought to remember at this point that Eliot did not write an evangelical tract. His business as a poet, as he stated again and again, was not to argue for the truth of his convictions, but to make poetry. The same year that "Salutation" was published, Eliot wrote in "Shakespeare and the Stoicism of Seneca" that a poet's very life is the struggle "to transmute his personal and private agonies into something rich and strange, something universal and impersonal" (*SE* 137). The function of poetry, he added, "Is not intellectual but emotional . . . it cannot be defined adequately in intellectual terms" (*SE* 138). Of course the Biblical and liturgical references in *Ash-Wednesday* are important. The more the reader knows about the religious significance of the holy day, the more he will understand the emotions of the poem. And the recognition of certain words as parts of traditional prayers will certainly help in understanding a poem about the need for prayer (see the end of chapter 3). But these are all parts of a larger whole, which makes "more fully real to us" the emotions at the heart of the poet's religious experience. These emotions include the poet's struggle against his own nature; they include despair and doubt.

Since *Ash-Wednesday* is somewhat inaccessible to those of us who do not share Eliot's Christian convictions, the tendency has been to think of it as detached from Eliot's previous work. Yet the poem echoes what has come before. "I cannot drink/There, where trees flower, and springs flow, for there is nothing again" (*AW* I) recalls "Nothing again nothing" from "A Game of Chess," suggesting that the penitent soul of *Ash-Wednesday* sees in the earthly garden only a rats' alley and spiritual unfulfillment. Eliot remains the same poet. Preface some of the convoluted statements in Part I with Gerontion's "Think now," or compare "Why should I mourn/The vanished power of the usual reign?" (*AW* I) to "I have lost my passion: why should I need to keep it/Since what is kept must be adulterated?" The lines of Part I are still spoken from a particular point of view; they come from a certain state of mind examining and, perhaps in that very process, condemning itself. The ironic perspective still holds.

The insistent return of "Because," repeated ten times in the first section, suggests the mechanical probing of reason, which works in terms of cause and effect, trying to arrive at explanations but creating only a labyrinth of self-qualifications that leads nowhere.[20] This way of thinking finally gives way to prayer and a patient rejection of what has gone before:

> And I pray that I may forget
> These matters that with myself I too much discuss
> Too much explain

Thus, Part I introduces the idea that prayer can be a way of emptying the mind of distractions that separate the soul from God. These matters include the workings of the intellect: the first twenty-five lines of the poem. This is not to say that *all* of Part I must be understood ironically. The turning to prayer should after all be accepted at face value if the act, repeated in almost every section, is to retain its full significance. Even the cautious formulations of the first twenty-five lines cannot simply be rejected or embraced as "false" or "true." They are part of a genuine state of mind, the limitations of which must be understood by the penitent in the way of purgation.

Part I first appeared in 1928, with the title "Perch 'io Non Spero." These are the first words of a "ballate" by Guido Cavalcanti, which Pound had translated some years before:

> Because no hope is left me, Ballatetta,
> Of return to Tuscany,
> Light-foot go thou some fleet way
> Unto my Lady straightway,
> And out of her courtesy
> Great honour will she do thee.[21]

Cavalcanti, in exile, despairs of seeing his lady again, although all his senses cry for her "Till all my mournful body is . . . shaken." Eliot no longer hopes to know such things. His use of the word "turn" fuses the secular echo of Cavalcanti with scriptural references emphasizing the purgative nature of this new journey.

The notion of the spirit turning away from sin and towards God is essential to the first day of Lent. In the Commination service, there are repeated references to it, many of them based on the verses from Ezekiel quoted above:

Turn ye (saith the Lord) from all your wickedness, and your sin shall not be your destruction. . . . Turn ye then, and ye shall live. . . . O most mighty God . . . who wouldest not the death of a sinner, but that he should rather turn from his sin, and be saved. . . . Turn thou us, O good Lord, and so shall we be turned. Be favourable, O Lord, Be favourable to thy people, Who turn to thee in weeping, fasting, and praying.[22]

In Part III, the word "turn" takes on another sense:

> At the first turning of the second stair
> I turned and saw below
> The same shape twisted on the banister

The poet turns back to see one of his dying selves, a retrospective movement which—and this is precisely the point—comes perilously close to regression. Lancelot Andrewes exploited this double sense of "turn," in a sermon Eliot probably knew:

Repentance itself is nothing but a kind of circling. . . . Which circle consists of two turnings. . . . First a turn wherein we look forward to God and with our whole heart resolve to turn to Him. Then a turn again wherein we look backward to our sins wherein we have turned from God.[23]

For Eliot though, this regressive turning is more than a detached "look backward." It is a yearning back, almost a reliving of the experience, which the sensual quality of the language confirms:

> Blown hair is sweet, brown hair over the mouth blown,
> Lilac and brown hair . . .   (*AW* III)

Suddenly we are in a Swinburnian realm, where hair and mouth become symbols for pleasure and erotic fulfillment.

The poet cannot escape his fallen nature. Although he has renounced in Part I both worldly fulfillment ("I shall not know/The one veritable transitory power") and the blessèd face, he still finds himself entranced, gazing through an emblem of generation, "a slotted window bellied like the fig's fruit," out onto the transitory blessings of those dying generations:

> And beyond the hawthorn blossom and a pasture scene
> The broadbacked figure drest in blue and green
> Enchanted the maytime with an antique flute. (*AW* III)

He does not hope to turn, he cannot hope to turn, but he will turn and turn again: towards the attraction of past moments of pagan ease, and towards God in prayer:

> Lord, I am not worthy
> Lord, I am not worthy
>
> but speak the word only.   *(AW* III)

Except for Part II, each of the sections ends with a fragment of prayer. They are not completed prayers reflecting the discipline of unquestioning belief; rather, they are stray lines or words suggesting the *need* to pray more than anything else. This repeated movement towards prayer shows the need for communion with that which is not human but divine. Taken together, the fragments of prayer reveal a kind of progress. In Parts I and III, "Pray for us sinners . . ." and "Lord I am not worthy" grow from a sense of the poet's and of man's corruption; in Parts IV and VI, "And after this our exile" and "Suffer me not to be separated" look forward to the soul's union with God.

According to St. John of the Cross, "the soul cannot be possessed of the divine union, until it has divested itself of the love of created beings." Eliot uses this as an epigraph for *Sweeney Agonistes*; it appeared first at the head of "Fragment of a Prologue" in the October 1926 *Criterion*. The epigraph should be read in conjunction with other statements Eliot was making during these years. The "love of man and woman," he wrote in 1929, "is only explained and made reasonable by the higher love, or else is simply the coupling of animals" *(SE* 274). The next year, he returned to the same theme: "Baudelaire has perceived that what distinguishes the relations of man and woman from the copulation of beasts is the knowledge of Good and Evil" *(SE* 428-29). Juxtaposing the two statements reveals that Eliot's "higher love" involves the knowledge of Good and Evil, which is to say "the recognition of the reality of Sin" *(SE* 427). Working towards "the divine union" does not simply replace the love of created beings with indifference or loathing, Eliot would insist; rather, it transforms love itself, so that love becomes "the recrudescence of an ancient passion in a new emotion, in a new situation, which comprehends, enlarges, and gives a meaning to it" *(SE* 262). That new emotion is expressed in Part IV, as the poet sees "Through a bright cloud of tears . . . The silent sister veiled in white and blue."

Eliot wrote elsewhere about this metamorphosis in "Poet and Saint . . . ," reviewing a selection of Baudelaire's work translated by Arthur Symons. The review was published in May 1927, just a few months before his "Salutation" to a beautiful Lady in a white gown:

> We can, however, call attention to passages where it seems to us that Mr. Symons has enveloped Baudelaire in the Swinburnian violet-colored London fog of the 'nineties. His paraphrase of 'L'Invitation au Voyage' is significant.

> My child and my star,
> Let us wander afar . . .

Baudelaire wrote

> Mon enfant, ma soeur,
> Songe à la douceur
> D'aller là-bas vivre ensemble.

The word *soeur* here is not, in my opinion, chosen merely because it rhymes with *douceur*; it is a moment in that sublimation of passion toward which Baudelaire was always striving; it needs a commentary out of his Correspondence, for instance the astonishing letter to Marie X . . . cited by Charles Du Bos.[24]

The poet of *Ash-Wednesday* strives toward that same "sublimation of passion." Passion yet unredeemed is felt in his backward gaze through the slotted window to the sweet hair and mouth—even the sound of "slotted" is hard and sexual. Passion redeemed expresses itself in the last lines of the poem:

> Sister, mother
> And spirit of the river, spirit of the sea,
> Suffer me not to be separated
>
> And let my cry come unto Thee.

The word "sister," used twice in the last eleven lines of *Ash-Wednesday,* recalls the passage just quoted from "Poet and Saint. . . ." In the "astonishing" letter that Eliot mentions but does not quote, one sees Baudelaire displaying "the recrudescence of an ancient passion in a new emotion":

> C'est un sentiment vertueux qui me lie à jamais à vous. En dépit de votre volonté, vous serez désormais mon talisman et ma force. Je vous aime, Marie, c'est indéniable; mais l'amour que je ressens pour vous, c'est l'amour du chrétien pour son Dieu; aussi ne donnez jamais un nom terrestre, et si souvent honteux, à ce culte incorporel et mystérieux, à cette suave et chaste attraction qui unit mon âme à la vôtre, en dépit de votre volonté. Ce serait un sacrilège.—J'étais mort, vous m'avez fait renaître.[25]

Eliot thought that Dante expressed the same kind of "recrudescence" in the account of his first meeting with Beatrice in *Purgatorio* XXX. He comments upon the encounter in terms that describe the struggle in *Ash-Wednesday*:

> And in the dialogue that follows we see the passionate conflict of the old feelings with the new; the effort and triumph of a new renunciation, greater than renunciation at the grave, because a renunciation of feelings that persist beyond the grave. In a way, these cantos are those of the greatest *personal* intensity in the whole poem. (*SE* 263)

We see this conflict clearly in Parts III and VI. Part VI, moreover, shows that the passion need not be specifically sexual, as the poet again strives to rise above the tyranny of the senses and sublimate the love of God's creation into the love of God. Against his will, he conjures a seascape, in the form of a confession:

> (Bless me father) though I do not wish to wish these things
> From the wide window towards the granite shore
> The white sails still fly seaward, seaward flying
> Unbroken wings
>
> And the lost heart stiffens and rejoices
> In the lost lilac and the lost sea voices
> And the weak spirit quickens to rebel
> For the bent golden-rod and the lost sea smell

It is a reluctant celebration through memory, since the lilac and the voices and the smell are all "lost." And they are Eliot's own memories, reaching back to the lovely Cape Ann summers when he was a boy. The great "*personal* intensity" of these lines, of Eliot's struggle to renounce the old feelings, is made clearer in light of something he wrote in 1927, in a review now buried in Volume 83 of *The Dial*:

> We all know the mood; and we can all, if we choose to relax to that extent, indulge in the luxury of reminiscence of childhood; but if we are at all mature and conscious, we refuse to indulge this weakness to the point of writing and poetizing about it; we know that it is something to be buried and done with, though the corpse will from time to time find its way up to the surface.[26]

The corpse sprouts in the form of sea memories. Eliot turns towards them and then, following the cyclic movement of the whole poem, turns away:

> Blessèd sister, holy mother, spirit of the fountain,
>   spirit of the garden,
> Suffer us not to mock ourselves with falsehood
> Teach us to care and not to care
> Teach us to sit still
> Even among these rocks,
> Our peace in His will

After the wondrous vision of the Lady in Part IV, after the incantatory questions and responses of Part V, the poet ends *Ash-Wednesday* with the "passionate conflict" that will never end. The prayer "Teach us to care and not to care/Teach us to sit still," uttered before in Part I, expresses the same need, the same discipline still to be achieved. But perhaps something has been gained: the understanding that makes it possible for the poet in Part VI to say and believe "Our peace in His will." Again, these are words of "the greatest *personal* intensity." Eliot wrote in 1929 of Dante's words *"la sua voluntate è nostra pace"*:

> It seems to me *literally true*. And I confess that it has more beauty for me now, when my own experience has deepened its meaning, than it did when I first read it. (*SE* 270-71)

Understanding that "His will is our peace," the poet has achieved, at least for the moment, humility, which Eliot considered "the greatest, the most difficult, of the Christian virtues."[27] Humility enables one to begin again. *Ash-Wednesday* is indeed a poem of beginnings.

We seem to have left the Victorians far behind. Certainly, the experience communicated by *Ash-Wednesday* signals a departure from those caught "wandering between two worlds." The purgative journey, with all its waverings and lapses, takes place entirely within the limits of what I have been calling "faith." One imagines Arnold shaking his head over *Ash-Wednesday,* remarking of its author, as he did of Newman, that "he has adopted, for the doubts and difficulties which beset men's minds today, a solution which, to speak frankly, is impossible" (see chapter 1).

But let us look closely at the lines evoking the lost seascape and the time of Eliot's youth. Those "sea voices," as I have noticed in chapter 3, echo the words of Tennyson's Ulysses: "the deep/Moans round with many voices." Eliot thought the line "too poetical," but he kept returning to it. Throughout much of his poetic career, Eliot would disparage this or that aspect of Tennyson—but he kept returning to him.

Tennyson appears elsewhere in that seascape. Several years before Eliot was born, Algernon Charles Swinburne, himself an occasional disparager of Tennyson, wrote a fierce defense of the Laureate in reply to Hippolyte Taine's elaborate dismissal of Tennyson's work as "drawing-room furniture" (see chapter 5). Swinburne remembered when, many years before, a painter of great renown had "pointed out to me, with a brief word of rapturous admiration, the wonderful breadth of beauty and the perfect force of truth in a single verse of 'Elaine' [one of Tennyson's *Idylls of the King*]—

> And white sails flying on the yellow sea."[28]

When Eliot wanted to convey the unforgotten, unforgettable attraction of sensuous beauty in the reverting conclusion to *Ash-Wednesday,* he evoked the line which Swinburne and that unnamed painter both loved:

> From the wide window towards the granite shore
> The white sails still fly seaward, seaward flying

More than any other Victorian, Alfred Tennyson is in the background of Eliot's work. The second half of this book examines the relationship between these two poets.

Part 2

Eliot and Tennyson

5

Nineteen Hundred and Nine

Introducing the 1928 edition of *Selected Poems of Ezra Pound,* Eliot set out to clarify the meaning of *vers libre,* a term that "now means too much to mean anything at all":

> My own verse is, so far as I can judge, nearer to the original meaning of *vers libre* than is any of the other types: at least, the form in which I began to write, in 1908 or 1909, was directly drawn from the study of Laforgue together with the later Elizabethan drama; and I do not know anyone who started from exactly that point.[1]

For the literary historian, "1908 or 1909" represents a watershed: the point when, as English poetry lay dying of senescence (excepting the figure of Yeats), T. S. Eliot came across an edition of Arthur Symons's *The Symbolist Movement in Literature.* "The year 1909," C. K. Stead has written, "marks perhaps the lowest point of a long decline in the quality of English poetry":

> The "aesthetic" movement of the 'nineties had long since collapsed. . . . The work of the aesthetes had been replaced by that of what Ford calls "the physical force school," a change which corresponded with a violent swing of the political pendulum to the Right. . . . The poetry we find established in 1909 is a poetry of political retrenchment, committed to conserve political and social ideas and institutions doomed to collapse.[2]

Eliot himself wrote, a quarter of a century after his Pound introduction, that "the situation of poetry in 1909 or 1910 was stagnant to a degree difficult for any young poet to-day to imagine."[3]

With poets like W. E. Henley, William Watson, and Henry Newbolt holding the attention of the public, the poetic scene was indeed dreary.[4] But what of the English tradition as a whole? It would be unreasonable to assume that, because of the paucity of decent contemporary verse, the poets of the past were suddenly condemned to a limbo with no channels into the present. And for Eliot to acknowledge that, at a certain time, he

began to draw upon the technical innovations of Laforgue and the Jacobeans, does not mean that Laforgue and the Jacobeans were the only
writers of whom he was aware, or that they were the only writers of
major influence in his poetic development.

One must strive for a more comprehensive view of the literary atmosphere at this time. In doing so, one soon confronts an event ignored by
all the critics, an event that, when examined closely, begins to eat at the
foundations of received opinion concerning Eliot's literary ancestry. 1909
was the centennial of Alfred Tennyson's birth. Exploring the literary
scene of this time enables one to establish the complex, dominating presence of Tennyson during the years when Eliot was himself becoming a
poet.

1909 saw the publication of C. F. G. Masterman's *The Condition of England,* a fine analysis of contemporary English life. Writing in the tradition
of Carlyle, Ruskin and Arnold, Masterman focused his attention on the
new twentieth-century symptoms of what he took to be the pervasive
decay of the quality of life in England.[5] The world he describes is the
world that T. S. Eliot would make his subject in *The Waste Land*. One
chapter is devoted to "The Suburbans," the male population of which
"is sucked into the City at daybreak, and scattered again as darkness
falls" across "miles and miles of little red houses in little silent streets."
Masterman wrote with a sense of the horror beneath the surfaces, which
Eliot would surely have recognized:

> Summer and winter pass over these little lamplit streets, today the lilac and syringa,
> tomorrow the scattered autumn leaves, in an experience of tranquillity and repose.
> But with the ear to the ground there is audible the noise of stranger echoes in the
> labyrinthine ways which stretch beyond the boundaries of these pleasant places; full
> of restlessness and disappointment, and longing, with a note of menace in it; not
> without foreboding to any who would desire, in the security of the suburbs, an un-
> ending end of the world. (p. 61)

Elsewhere he describes the rootless class of the new rich, whose aimless
wanderings curiously parallel Eliot's flow of crowds over London Bridge:

> It fills vast hotels scattered round the coasts of England and ever multiplying in the
> capital. . . . It has annexed whole regions abroad, Biarritz and the Riviera coast,
> Austrian and German watering places, whither it journeys for the recovery of its lost
> health, and for distractions which will forbid the pain of thinking. . . . At best it is an
> existence with some boredom in it. . . . At worst . . . it becomes a nightmare and a
> delirium.   (pp. 26-27)[6]

Once again we are back in *The Waste Land,* with the desiccated conver-
sationalists at the Starnbergersee, or the weeper by the waters of Leman.

A year after the publication of *The Condition of England* there appeared the second edition of another book by Masterman, first published in 1900, called *Tennyson as a Religious Teacher.* In 1968 E. D. H. Johnson wrote that this book remains "the best single study of Tennyson's philosophic ideas in relation to the Victorian religious crisis."[7] In his account of the philosophy or "teaching" of the representative Victorian poet, Masterman refers to Tennyson as "the most widely influential English poet of the nineteenth century."[8] The chapters range from "God" and "Self" to "Evolution" and "Immortality." The book as a whole, title included, indicates the seriousness with which a first-rate mind such as Masterman's, obviously attuned to the changes being wrought in modern society, could still consider Alfred Tennyson—and not merely as poetic craftsman, but as thinker. It also suggests the notion of poet as prophet or sage speaking to the masses, against which the self-conscious rebels of the 'nineties, and the Modernists, reacted.

"A poet is not necessarily a philosopher or a theologian: he is primarily an artist," Masterman wrote. "A writer may indeed outline philosophy in verse—as, for example, Robert Browning—or teach theology in poetry, as Dante and, in a sense, Milton." But "Tennyson made no pretence of essaying so arduous a task: he was an artist in words, of extraordinary power, compelled to gaze at the facts of life through the troubled atmosphere of the thought of his time" (p. 6). Masterman saw Tennyson as a poet first and last, from whom there cannot "rightly be demanded an orderly system of philosophy or theology."

Masterman's book was by no means an isolated phenomenon around the time of Tennyson's centenary. A few words must be said here about what has long been conveniently described as "the reaction against Tennyson." Labels in literary history, when used often enough, become misleading. The death of Queen Victoria did not signal the end of Tennyson's formidable prestige. One must remember that a reaction requires something considerable against which to react. The parodies of the eighteen eighties, the condescensions of the 'nineties, and the dogmatic pronouncements of Yeats, Pound and others clamoring under the banner of a "new poetry" (see chapter 6), all take their place, and indeed only make sense, within the much larger picture of Tennyson's generally acknowledged position as the most popular and greatest of "modern" English poets. It is a picture too often forgotten by the scholars directing their attention only to those literary phenomena that foreshadow future developments.

It is true that by 1909 his poetry had undergone scrutinies which discovered that some of it was bad, uninspired stuff. But this was nothing new. John Killham has observed that "the reaction" was crystallized all the way back in 1864 with the publication of *Enoch Arden,* and that "the reaction against Tennyson [was] in large measure connected with the change in taste occurring in the last three decades of the nineteenth rather than with that of the twentieth century. . . ."[9] This reaction consisted of two major criticisms: that his work was tame, drawing-room stuff, of the kind to provoke the name "School-Miss Alfred"; and that it was too polished or "professional." John D. Jump, in his introduction to *Tennyson: The Critical Heritage*, writes that although *Enoch Arden* "confirmed the almost overwhelming prestige which Tennyson was to enjoy throughout the last third of his life . . . it also helped to stimulate in a minority of readers the objection that his writing was too mannered and artificial."[10] As the years passed, the inevitable parodies appeared, most of which directed their attack against the poet's political and theological views. Jump continues:

> Adverse literary reactions continued to embody themselves in the complaints . . . of elegant tameness and mannered derivativeness. But these complaints came only from a small minority of Tennyson's readers during the last twenty or thirty years of his life. The vast majority steadily acknowledged what F. T. Palgrave called his 'imperial position in Poetry'. . . . By the last years of Tennyson's life his principal foreign public was unquestionably transatlantic. . . . For thirty years after Tennyson's death, his poetry continued in great favour with readers generally. (pp. 15-16)

Those thirty years (1892-1922) extend to the publication of *The Waste Land*. And Killham has noted that in the four decades or so before the Great War "hardly a year passed without a complete edition of Tennyson's poetical works (or a part of one) issuing from English printing-houses. . . ."[11]

So we must be very careful with an assertion like Paull F. Baum's that "the reaction against Tennyson's great popularity became loudly vocal a dozen years after his death when the Victorian age reached its close,"[12] or even with a tossed-off phrase like the more scrupulous Mr. Killham's: ". . . in 1910 at the height of the reaction. . . ."[13] The strictures and general fuss of "the reaction" are nothing less than a confirmation of Tennyson's continuing, dominating *presence* in those years, in both England and America—an inescapable presence for anyone committed to the art of poetry. It was not until the early 'twenties, with new modes of poetry and criticism beginning to establish themselves, with the rampant disillusionment provoked by the slaughter of World War I, and with the publication in 1923 of two biographical studies which seemed to define authoritatively the Laureate's achievement and his failings, that the eclipse of Tennyson as a major poetic force was well under way.

The occasion of his centenary brought forth all the attitudes towards Tennyson. He was far from losing his hold on the public; he was still the subject of serious study, as Masterman's book testifies; and his reputation was easily withstanding, as it had been for over forty years, the noisy cannonade of the reaction. In the world of letters, scholars fiercely defended him, or merely noted with impartiality the impending "obscuration" of his fame, or tried to understand why "the Devil's advocate," to use W. P. Ker's term, was so busy trying to call into question Tennyson's worth.[14] The point to be made is not that there was any clear consensus as to Tennyson's ultimate place in English poetry, but that there was substantial debate: he was still a figure to be reckoned with. According to Edmund Gosse's 1905 edition of *A Short History of Modern English Literature,* the last thirty years of the nineteenth century were "The Age of Tennyson," and that shadow still loomed large.[15]

Earnest tributes were not lacking in 1909. At Oxford, T. Herbert Warren, President of Magdalen College and a knowledgeable scholar who had written an important piece some years before on Tennyson and Dante, lectured on "The Centenary of Tennyson."[16] The British Academy heard Henry Jones's commemorative paper, "Tennyson," in October. And the Leslie Stephen Lecture for 1909, delivered at Cambridge by W. P. Ker, was devoted to Tennyson.

Professor Ker replied to those who were so anxious to expose the inadequacies of Tennyson as 'thinker':

> But there are other kinds of poetic thought besides that which can be discussed in prose. . . . The thought of Tennyson is not so well bestowed in the argumentative poems . . . as in some of those where he uses mythology, the legends of *Tithonus* or the *Holy Grail,* to convey his reading of the world. The difference between the two kinds of thought is very great; and the nobler kind is not discourse but vision. It does not lend itself to discussion; if it is once apprehended there is no more to be said. . . .[17]

This is a far from primitive reading of the poetry, conveyed by a scholar who was one of Ezra Pound's sources for *The Spirit of Romance,* published in 1910. The understanding of myth as a means of conveying the poet's "reading of the world," and the preference for "vision" as opposed to "discourse," come quite close to the positions of Pound and Joyce and Eliot. Ker was presenting to his Cambridge audience a way of seeing the best of Tennyson's poetry that would free it from what they were convinced was a dead, misguided age. Neither they nor many modernist writers, however, were capable of perceiving this: to them, Tennyson *was* the Victorian age, and his poetry would be forever entangled in its weaknesses.

The monumental Eversley Edition of *The Works of Alfred Lord Tennyson* was published in London in 1907-8; the American edition in New York, 1908. These volumes, made authoritative by Tennyson's own notes and his son's editing, were to remain standard until Christopher Ricks's edition came out in 1969. They too contributed to the flurry of reviews and lectures reflecting upon the nature of Tennyson's achievement. The appearance of the Eversley Edition prompted Paul Elmer More to write an essay on the poet, published in *The Nation,* 28 January 1909, and included in the Seventh Series of More's *Shelburne Essays* (1910). The article is worth considering for a moment: it is another example of the first-rate criticism that Tennyson's work was still capable of stimulating; it reflects contemporary attitudes towards the poet; and Eliot, who later acknowledged being aware of More and the Shelburne Essays while still at Harvard, was probably familiar with it.[18]

In order to define Tennyson's greatness with more precision, More first dwells on what he considers to be his weaknesses. The main problem was that Tennyson too often confined and adapted his genius to fit the temper of the times. He represented "a whole period of national life" (p. 64); he was "the official voice of the land" (72), "the mouthpiece of his generation" (74), "the spokesman of the age" (82), expressing its "official philosophy" (84). "Tennyson is the Victorian age" (64), More wrote, and the Victorian age was marred by something fundamentally false:

> The gist of Tennyson's faith, and what made him the spokesman of the age, was in a bold completion of evolution by the theory of indefinite progress and by a vision of some magnificent consummation wherein the sacrifices and the waste and the pain of the present were to be compensated somehow, somewhere, somewhen—who shall say? . . . That reconciliation of faith and science, this discovery of a father near at hand within the inexorable law of evolution, this vision of an eternal state to be reached in the progress of time—all this is what we call the Victorian compromise. (pp. 82, 83)

More then quotes the final stanza of *In Memoriam* to illustrate that compromise. Here is the term that Chesterton would popularize a few years later in the first chapter of his *Victorian Age in Literature,* "The Victorian Compromise and its Enemies"; here is the concept that Eliot would invoke in his own essay on Tennyson. The final three stanzas of *In Memoriam,* he wrote in 1936, "show an interesting compromise between the religious attitude and, what is quite a different thing, the belief in human perfectibility" (*SE* 336). The idea of "the Victorian compromise" is central to an understanding of how the children and grandchildren of the Victorians regarded their forebears.

More related the compromise to what Eliot would call, in "The Dry Salvages," "superficial notions of evolution":

> Because the Victorians could not discover the rational bond between the world of time and evolution and the idea of eternity and changelessness, they would deny that these

two can exist side by side as totally distinct spheres, and by raising the former and lowering the latter would seek the truth in some middle ground of compromise. . . . They placed the faith of religion in some far-off event of time, as if eternity were a kind of enchantment lent by distance. (pp. 86-87)

"It is only by bringing out clearly this aspect of his work"—namely, Tennyson's entanglement with the misconceived "resolutions" worked out by his contemporaries—"that we are enabled to discern . . . another and contrasted phase, which was not of the age but was the unfettered voice of the poet himself" (85-86):

By the side of the official message of Tennyson there comes up here and there through his works an utterly different vein of mysticism, which is scarcely English and certainly not Victorian. It was a sense of estrangement from time and personality which took possession of him at intervals from youth to age. (87)

"With Tennyson," More concludes, "the task is always to separate the poet of insight from the poet of compromise" (94). This attitude—that there were really two Tennysons—was soon to be universally accepted: in Sir Harold Nicolson's words, there were "the black, unhappy mystic of the Lincolnshire wolds" and "the prosperous Isle-of-Wight Victorian."[19] It enabled succeeding generations to embrace some of Tennyson's work without breaking their law of disowning all things "Victorian."

Besides clarifying the nature of Tennyson's presence at the time when Eliot was beginning to write serious poetry, More's essay also foreshadows significant aspects of Eliot's work (see note 18). More's discussion of religious dualism, "which sets the eternal world not at the end of the temporal, but utterly apart from it" (92), parallels T. E. Hulme's concept of discontinuity and Eliot's own convictions. More's picture of Edward FitzGerald—crying out upon " 'the cursed inactivity' " of the nineteenth century, a "determined recluse" who "alone among the busy, anxious Victorians . . . stood entirely aloof from the currents of the hour, judging men and things from the larger circles of time . . . emancipated from the illusions of the present [in] his grave, pathetic wisdom" (74)—brings us to the world of "Gerontion." Moreover, More's bold declaration that *The Holy Grail* has an insight into things spiritual and a precision it would be hard to match in any other English poem" (89) shows a perspicacity well ahead of its time, pointing towards Douglas Bush's 1951 statement that "The Holy Grail," unique among Tennyson's *Idylls,* "is in some sense a Victorian *Waste Land.*"[20]

More's essay takes its place in the array of literary statements acknowledging Tennyson's importance. In 1909 George Saintsbury, a critic whom Eliot respected (*Homage to John Dryden* is dedicated to him), was completing the third and final volume, "From Blake to Mr. Swinburne," of his massive *History of English Prosody from the Twelfth Century to the Present Day,* published the following year. Saintsbury confirmed in great detail what had never really been questioned, even by those of the reaction: Tennyson's remarkable metrical virtuosity. According to Saintsbury, the volumes of 1830 and 1832 revealed the "fresh Phoenix-birth of an English 'poet of the century,' " whose extraordinary accomplishments in countless verse forms were to establish him as a redoubtable craftsman.[21]

May 1909 saw the third reprinting of *The Poems of Alfred Tennyson 1830-1863.* First published three years before, this was Ernest Rhys's Everyman's Library edition, which included an introduction by Rhys. In the Houghton Library's collection of books owned and autographed by Eliot, there is a copy of this book, purchased sometime during his Harvard years.

Rhys—poet, publisher, and former member of the Rhymers' Club— was well acquainted with the avant-garde of English poetry then just beginning to find itself. In the early months of 1909, he established what was to be a long friendship with Ezra Pound. By April of that year, according to Noel Stock's biography of Pound, both of them were involved with "a newly-formed group of poets led by T. E. Hulme" which included F. S. Flint, Florence Farr and Joseph Campbell.[22] That same month, Elkin Matthews published Pound's second book of poems, *Personae.*

In his introduction, Rhys acknowledges that "we are not in a state to measure him finally":

> We are rather in the lee now of his immense reputation, and our only chance of getting back our interest is to remember him not as a mid-Victorian but an early Victorian, and relate "The Lady of Shalott" to the days when he recited "Clerk Saunders" and "Oriana" to the Cambridge Apostles. . . . In this volume the Tennyson that Arthur Hallam knew will be found fully ranged for the first time with the later Tennyson. . . .[23]

Here again is the notion of two Tennysons, only one of whom could be accepted by contemporary readers. The high Victorian was too much of his time; the extravagant, dark figure of Cambridge and London days was more accessible to a public insisting upon, in P. E. More's words, "the something false we designate as Victorian."[24]

But Rhys's essay turns out to be another example of relatively impartial criticism, which does not try to whittle down Tennyson's achievement at all. Rhys even cites Arthur Hallam's laudatory and prophetic 1831 review of Tennyson's *Poems, Chiefly Lyrical.* There are conflicting accounts of how well-known this review was at the time. Richard Le Gallienne called it "famous" in 1893, yet Yeats claimed that "I alone knew

Hallam's essay" when he and his fellow poets were meeting at the Cheshire Cheese.[25] In any event, Rhys knew the value of the review:

> Arthur Hallam's tribute was printed in the same *Englishman's Magazine,* to which Tennyson, as we have seen, contributed too. He gives in his article a list of the Five Excellences of Tennyson's early lyric poems. . . . But the most salient passage in the essay was that in which Hallam attempted to decide the relation of the modern poet to his time, as if to declare the latent qualities of this new poet. (xi, xii)

As most students of Tennyson are aware, those "Five Excellences" include, quoting Hallam now, "his power of embodying himself in ideal characters, or rather moods of character, with such extreme accuracy of adjustment, that the circumstances of the narrations seem to have a natural correspondence with the predominant feeling, and, as it were, to be evolved from it by assimilative force," as well as "his vivid . . . delineation of objects, and the peculiar skill with which he holds all of them *fused,* to borrow a metaphor from science, in a medium of strong emotion."[26] The qualities thus described look forward to the kind of poetry Eliot and Pound wanted to write. In Marshall McLuhan's words, "Had it [Hallam's essay] been understood in 1831 the energies of the Pre-Raphaelites might have found more direct channels to what in English poetry did not occur until the advent of Joyce, Pound, and Eliot."[27] It seems that a few people were beginning to understand or at least notice Hallam's essay eighty or so years after it was written.

The "salient passage" to which Rhys refers struck him because of its application to what poets like Pound and Hulme were just beginning to do as part of their new "movement." Hallam starts off by describing what is in essence the dissociation of sensibility:

> Those different powers of poetic disposition, the energies of Sensitive, of Reflective, of Passionate Emotion, which in former times were intermingled, and derived from mutual support an extensive empire over the feelings of men, were now restrained within separate spheres of agency. . . . In the old times the poetic impulse went along with the general impulse of the nation; in these it is a reaction against it. . . . Our inference, therefore, from this change in the relative position of artists to the rest of the community is, that modern poetry in proportion to its depth and truth is likely to have little immediate authority over public opinion. Admirers it will have; sects consequently it will form; and these strong under-currents will in time sensibly affect the principal stream. (40-41)

Earlier in the essay he elaborated upon this dissociation:

> [Shelley and Keats] are both poets of sensation rather than reflection. . . . Other poets *seek* for images to illustrate their conceptions; these men had no need to seek; they lived in a world of images; for the most important and extensive portion of their life

consisted in those emotions which are immediately conversant with the sensation. (36-37)

It is certainly plausible that Rhys would have shared his knowledge of this striking essay, on a Tennyson far removed from Victorian laureateship, with his friends, who scorned public opinion and talked so much of the Image. And it is more than plausible that the young Harvard poet Thomas Eliot read with care both Mr. Rhys and Mr. Hallam.[28]

A few other literary events around this time should not go unnoticed. Thomas J. Wise's two-volume bibliography, a landmark in Tennyson scholarship, was printed privately in 1908. T. Herbert Warren's comparative studies ("Virgil and Tennyson: A Literary Parallel"; "Tennyson and Dante") were collected in his *Essays of Poets and Poetry Ancient and Modern* (1909). In 1914 appeared A. E. Baker's massive Tennyson Concordance, yet to be replaced. In 1911, Hallam, Lord Tennyson completed *Tennyson and his Friends,* sequel to the *Memoir.* Hallam Tennyson's annotated edition of *In Memoriam* (1906) prompted the Third Edition of A. C. Bradley's excellent *Commentary* (1910). And 1909 marked T. S. Eliot's twenty-first year.

1908-9 was Eliot's final year as a Harvard undergraduate. One day in December 1908, at the Harvard Union library, he picked up the second edition of Arthur Symons's *The Symbolist Movement in Literature.* "I liked his quotations," Eliot related years later, "and I went to a foreign bookshop somewhere in Boston . . . which specialized in French and German and other foreign books and found Laforgue, and other poets."[29] Laforgue presented the opportunity to move beyond the atmosphere of Tennyson and Swinburne and the 'nineties, an atmosphere with which, as Hugh Kenner observes, Eliot had already "filled his mind."[30]

Student poets in Cambridge, Massachusetts still looked to Tennyson and Browning as their "chief models," according to Herbert Howarth:

> A Tennysonian elegance, a fluency in oration and in rhapsody, and sometimes a consciously noble attitude, mark the work of the Harvard poets of this order. And it appears that Harvard in general regarded this order of poet as the most admirable. . . .[31]

Something as blatantly imitative of Tennyson's "Lotos-Eaters" as the anonymous "Song of the Sirens" could easily find its way into the pages of the *Harvard Advocate,* 14 October 1910:

> Come to us, oh ye that weary,
> Mariners of the foam-flecked shoulders!—
> Loose from oars your crooked fingers,
> Furl your sails, and come ashore. . . .

In the same issue one finds G. W. Gray's "At Twilight," which sounds like a string of discarded stanzas from *In Memoriam*:

> The lanes are lost in thickened trees,
> The live leaves whisper overhead,
> And there a lone star, wild and red,
> Peers like some eye that sees and sees.

The subject of "Tennyson at Harvard" suggests a paradox: Tennyson was the compromising arch-Victorian, or the unread, dead Great Poet, or the misread Master—but in all cases his poetry was still impossible to avoid, still a living force. Eliot's Harvard poems, like those of his peers, echo the voice of Tennyson. In order to set them in the right context, we must go further back in Eliot's youth, remembering Eliot's dictum concerning ways in which a poet borrows: "Immature poets imitate; mature poets steal; bad poets deface what they take, and good poets make it into something better, or at least something different" (*SW* 125). Those whom Herbert Howarth has called "the Harvard Tennysonians" (p. 101) were bad poets; Eliot was still an immature one.

Collecting references that are scattered throughout Eliot's essays, one can put together the whole range of his "boyhood enthusiasms" in poetry. There were Kipling's *Barrack-Room Ballads,* especially "Danny Deever"; Byron; the standard martial poetry, such as Macaulay's *Horatius,* Charles Wolfe's "The Burial of Sir John Moore," Burns's "Bruce to his Men at Bannockburn," and Tennyson's "The Revenge"; Sir Edwin Arnold's *The Light of Asia*; and FitzGerald's translation of the Rubáiyát. Later on, there were Shelley, Keats, Swinburne, and Rossetti, especially "The Blessed Damozel." Tennyson is hardly mentioned—but Tennyson's influence is unmistakable in Eliot's *Poems Written in Early Youth*. A young man writing poetry in the first decade of this century would find it impossible to avoid the shadow of Tennyson. It wasn't necessary to "discover" him, or cultivate a special enthusiasm for him. One simply *knew* Tennyson, Tennysonian diction, Tennysonian nuance, Tennysonian themes. Eliot's early poems bear this out. One would do well to remember what Eliot once said about parallel passages from Massinger and Shakespeare: "This is, on Massinger's part, an echo, rather than an imitation or a plagiarism—the basest, because least conscious form of borrowing" (*SW* 126).

When sixteen-year-old Thomas Eliot was called upon to compose a Graduation Day poem, to be recited at Smith Academy, June 1905, he assumed the voice of Tennyson, who throughout his career struggled with the conflicting demands of private vision and social responsibility:

Standing upon the shore of all we know
We linger for a moment doubtfully,
Then with a song upon our lips, sail we
Across the harbor bar—no chart to show,
No light to warn us of rocks which lie below,
But let us yet put forth courageously.[32]

Here are the mariners and their sea, representative of challenge and struggle, which Tennyson created. "Ulysses," "Crossing the Bar," and "The Lotos-Eaters" all lie behind these words. The poem's celebration of Progress sounds eminently Victorian, and recalls the kind of official optimism Tennyson was often compelled to muster:

Great duties call—the twentieth century
More grandly dowered than those which came before,
Summons—who knows what time may hold in store,
Or what great deeds the distant years may see,
What conquest over pain and misery,
What heroes greater than were e'er of yore!
. . . .
And let thy [Smith's] motto be, proud and serene,
Still as the years pass by, the word "Progress!"   (pp. 13, 17)

Eliot's few slight lyrics published in the *Harvard Advocate* manipulate vowel sounds in the manner of Tennyson. Hugh Kenner supplies an example:

The moonflower opens to the moth,
    The mist crawls in from sea;
A great white bird, a snowy owl,
    Slips from the alder tree.[33]

Phrases like "While all the East was weaving red with gray" (p. 19), and "the wild roses in your wreath" (p. 18) are other examples. One also finds Tennysonian images: white mist on the sea, or an impenetrable maiden standing "at evening in the room alone" ("On a Portrait," p. 21).

In these early poems, Eliot's preoccupation with the process and effects of time recalls the same theme in Tennyson's poetry. The time-wrought disappointment of earthly love is the subject of two songs: "If space and time, as sages say" and "When we came home across the hill." In the latter, the natural scene remains unchanged, but the cut roses of passion are destroyed in the very act of seizing them for one's own. Desire consumes itself and leaves death. For Eliot and for Tennyson, time and desire are inextricably bound. April is the cruellest month because it stirs both memory and desire—and memory evokes the failures of de-

sire. Time brings the emptying end of desire and its futile rebirth. There
is a Tennysonian yearning in these early poems: if only we could escape
the world of time, if only we could flee into a garden or an island where
the green fuse does not droop and crumble.

In "Before Morning," printed in 1908, the dawn mixes colors of life
and death—"While all the East was weaving red with gray"—and mingles
"Fragrance of bloom and fragrance of decay." The incantatory language
of this poem pushes the flower image more and more into the realm of
symbol:

> Fresh flowers, withered flowers, flowers of dawn.

Fresh and withered flowers are central images in several of Eliot's
pre-Laforguian lyrics. They become icons of time, and are usually associated with women and the vicissitudes of sexual fulfillment. Their
beauty lies precariously this side of death. Suggesting the bloom of desire
and its bleak aftermath, they recall the atmosphere of the Pre-Raphaelites
and the 'Nineties.

In these poems, the disillusioning act is performed again and again,
as in a nightmare.[34] To paraphrase: "I gave you flowers, their beauty
bespeaks our ecstasy . . . time intervenes . . . the flowers and I are faded,
without life." Finally, in "Circe's Palace" (1908), flowers are transformed
into a symbol of Circe's enervating power:

> Around her fountain which flows
> With the voice of men in pain,
> Are flowers that no man knows.
> Their petals are fanged and red
> With hideous streak and stain;
> They sprang from the limbs of the dead.—
> We shall not come here again.   (p. 20)

Circe turns men into beasts; for Eliot, fleshly desire is bestial. One need
not be reminded of Jung's *vagina dentata* to discern the horror of these
hungry flowers of fertility, which take their life from sapped members of
the dead. "We shall not come here again," mutters the speaker of the
poem. He is Ulysses, referring both to himself and those of his men not
already transformed into panther, peacock, or "sluggish phython"—an
emblem of man's ultimate loss of power brought on by woman's magic.
"The peacocks walk, stately and slow,/And they look at us with the
eyes/Of men whom we knew long ago." This echoes the words of Tennyson's Ulysses: "It may be we shall touch the Happy Isles,/And see the
great Achilles, whom we knew." In both cases, the phrase "whom we

knew" points to a time and state in poignant contrast to the speaker's present situation.

"On a Portrait" was published in the *Harvard Advocate,* 26 January 1909. Remember that Eliot had just discovered Laforgue. For the first twelve lines, this sonnet appears to resemble a Tennysonian set piece on the "high-born maiden."[35] Aloof from the scurrying mass of humanity, she stands "Beyond the circle of our thought." Like the mysterious Mariana (whose story is of course never told), like "Shadowy, dreaming Adeline," the lady remains unknowable, yet with a reality that transcends the "tenuous dreams" surrounding her. The final couplet, however, wrenches this picturesque, reverential perspective by suddenly making us aware of a detached and mocking observer:

> The parrot on his bar, a silent spy,
> Regards her with a patient curious eye.

Implicit in these two lines are all the possibilities of ironic awareness, including that of self-consciousness. It is not too much to say that this image represents a turning point in Eliot's poetry: an attitude that will develop, using the model of Laforgue, into a distinct poetic voice. Exploiting the state of mind behind the fastidious discriminations of Laforgue, and with the varied uses of irony, Eliot could for the first time write poems that were "new" in the English tradition, having apparently little to do with the themes and images of Tennyson or the Pre-Raphaelites or the Decadents. No more songs of flowers and dying love, no more straining to hint at the possible terrors of romantic union in a language meant for expressing its pleasures—now he could retreat for a while behind the Laforguian pose, speaking in precious, urbane terms that have the invaluable function of *distancing* the poet from his emotions. For Eliot's emotions were becoming more and more intractable as he was discovering, in poetry and private life, the terrible emptiness glossed over by romantic ideals.

> Whiter the flowers, Love, you hold,
> Than the white mist on the sea;
> Have you no brighter tropic flowers
> With scarlet life, for me?   (p. 22)

In a sense, then, Laforgue liberated Eliot from the dangerous grip of Tennyson. And most critics, while acknowledging that his juvenilia perhaps did grow from Tennyson's poetic world, would agree that, with Laforgue, Eliot left his Victorian predecessor far behind. What lay ahead was the making, with Pound and a few others, of Modern Poetry in English.

Is it possible to cut poetic ties so easily? Eliot once said that "a writer's art must be based on the accumulated sensations of the first twenty-one years."[36] Can the poet erase a major precursor with the ease of announcing him to be old-fashioned? No. Tennyson would remain, in many ways, with the Harvard graduate student soon to settle in England and embark upon a career in letters. The exploration of Eliot's early critical prose, which is the task of chapter 6, illuminates this enduring, furtive relationship.

6

Strategies of Defense: Eliot's Early Criticism, 1916–1923

—And who is the best poet, Heron? asked Boland.
—Lord Tennyson, of course, answered Heron.
—O, yes, Lord Tennyson, said Nash. We have all his poetry at home in a book.
    At this Stephen forgot the silent vows he had been making and burst out:
—Tennyson a poet! Why, he's only a rhymester!
—O, get out! said Heron. Everyone knows that Tennyson is the greatest poet.

Joyce, *A Portrait of the Artist as a Young Man*

I do not care to pose as a champion of Tennyson.

Eliot, 1918

Hugh Kenner has pointed out that the years 1917-21 were for Eliot a time when he "carried out what must be the most arduous, the most concentrated critical labor of which detailed record exists: nothing less than a rethinking, in the specific terms exacted by conscientious book reviewing, of the traditional heritage of English letters."[1] Some of the most famous essays written around this time were a major catalyst in the headlong decline of the literary status of Victorian poetry in the 'twenties and 'thirties. But a closer look at Eliot's early criticism, collected and uncollected, reveals an attitude towards the Victorians, and towards Tennyson in particular, that is really quite complex. Although Eliot was not above condescending to his arch-Victorian predecessor, he refused to join his peers in their outright dismissal of Tennyson's work. What emerges on Eliot's part is an ambivalent, wavering point of view, and a subtle strategy of defense: unmistakable signs of "the anxiety of influence." His references to poets like Tennyson and Kipling indicate a profound familiarity with their work, coupled with a need to distance it, evaluate it, sometimes misrepresent or belittle it—and finally, to come to terms with it.

Extending Kenner's chronological bounds by several years, the following pages survey Eliot's early criticism and focus on the scattered remarks concerning Tennyson, his age, and his contemporaries. There are some important factors to keep in mind. From 1916 through 1918 Eliot was teaching Victorian literature to adults, in both extension lectures and tutorials associated with the University of London and the London County Council. The syllabuses for these (and other) courses were published in 1974 by Ronald Schuchard, who wrote:

> The courses on modern literature point to an unbroken continuity between Eliot and the Victorians that many scholars have long suspected but inadequately confirmed. In contrast to his supposed negative opinions, they further indicate how complex are his separate aesthetic and moral attitudes toward nineteenth-century authors.[2]

Something else to remember is Eliot's method of assuming different roles for different audiences, a method analyzed by Hugh Kenner (see his invaluable chapter, "Criticism," in *The Invisible Poet*). This was significant at a time when one's judgment of the Victorians often depended on the literary circle to which one belonged. Kenner observes that for Middleton Murry's *Athenaeum,* or *The Times Literary Supplement,* Eliot's "fundamental critical strategy" was "a close and knowing mimicry of the respectable" (p. 99). For the small audience of *The Egoist,* an audience not unfamiliar with Yeats and Pound and Joyce, he intensified his polemic and sharpened his tone:

> What we want is to disturb and alarm the public: to upset its reliance upon Shakespeare, Nelson, Wellington, and Sir Isaac Newton. . . . To point out that every generation, every turn of time when the work of four or five men who count has reached middle age, is a *crisis*.[3]

Finally, one must always be careful about Possum's jokes. It is often difficult to decide exactly to what degree his declarations are qualified or even totally undermined by an ironic point of view. Take for example his review of a forgettable book on Thomas Hardy, for the *Manchester Guardian* of 23 June 1916:

> This is an excellent book of its kind. It resembles, in form, a doctor's thesis at an American university, and in substance a good set of Extension lectures.

Further information exposes this innocent-looking statement as mockery; the self-effacing words "of its kind" turn out to be razor sharp. Elsewhere Eliot complained of a University Extension audience's preference for debased, superficial "appreciations" as opposed to criticism.[4] And just a few months after the Hardy piece, reviewing for the *New Statesman* a collection of essays by Stephen Leacock, now talking to a presumably more sophisticated audience than the *Guardian*'s, Eliot wrote:

> He draws a truthful picture of the American graduate student, the prospective Doctor of Philosophy: his specialization in knowledge, his expansion in ignorance, his laborious dulness, his years of labor and his crowning achievement—the thesis. . . . This labour is fatal to the development of intellectual powers. It crushes originality, it kills style. Few, very few of these "original contributions" are well written or even readable. . . .[5]

So, something that "resembles, in form, a doctor's thesis at an American university, and in substance a good set of Extension lectures" really has very little to recommend it.

What follows, then, is a selective, year-by-year compilation of remarks that have to do with Eliot's strategy of defense regarding his Victorian predecessors, particularly Tennyson, Swinburne, and Kipling. Surveying his early prose in this manner also enables one to observe the development of Eliot's poetic, a process often more clearly articulated in the articles that remain uncollected than in the widely known pieces. To avoid the clutter of excessive footnotes, I sometimes cite only the date and appropriate page numbers of periodicals. The reader will have no trouble tracking down the source if he supplements this information with Donald Gallup's *T. S. Eliot: A Bibliography* (1969).

1916

"In my earlier criticism," Eliot wrote in "To Criticize the Critic" (1961), "both in my general affirmations about poetry and in writing about authors who had influenced me, I was implicitly defending the sort of poetry that I and my friends wrote" (*TCC* 16). His practical poetic would reach full expression in the "dissociation of sensibility" theory, which emphasized the fusion of sensation and thought and preferred evocation to reflection. Traces of this theory already appear in 1916. A crazy epic poem by Charles M. Doughty fails because, unlike the images of Dante, its realities are not made real enough: "In 'Hyperion' the weariness is made actual; here it is stated."[6] Mr. Lee Masters's poetry is deficient "because he does not fix before you the contact and cross-contact of souls, the breath and scent of the room. His mind is reflective, not evocative."[7] These criteria were evolving out of the nineteenth-century background, the "ruminating" poetry of Tennyson and Browning and Wordsworth. Eliot *had* to set up over-simplified oppositions in order to free himself and his friends from past achievement, and make his work "new."

The Victorians were of course the handiest of foils. Comparing H. D.'s translations of ancient Greek to Gilbert Murray's, Eliot mentions a poet to whom he will refer again and again:

> H. D. is a poet. She has at least avoided the traditional jargon prescribed for translators: she has turned Euripides into English verse which can be taken seriously, verse of our own time, as modern as was Swinburne's when it appeared. Her verse is a perversion of the opposite extreme. Swinburne is too fluid, H. D. too abrupt.[8]

Swinburne's fluid world of words had its effect on Eliot, both in his early insistence upon the fusion of language and object (see for instance "Swinburne as Poet," *SW* 149), and in his own sounding chants:

> Blown hair is sweet, brown hair over the mouth blown,
> Lilac and brown hair . . . (*AW* III)

1917

Eliot continues to use Swinburne as point of departure or of comparison. The "erudite complexities of Swinburnian metre," he writes in "Reflections on *Vers Libre*," represent an impressive mastery of technique, but that is all. In his pamphlet on Ezra Pound, he contrasts Pound's scrupulous attention to every word with the looseness of Shelley or Swinburne, "whose adjectives are practically blanks." Mr. Pound has illuminated the relation between poetry and music, which "is very different from what is called the 'music' of Shelley or Swinburne, a music often nearer to rhetoric (or the art of the orator) than to the instrument":

> For poetry to approach the condition of music (Pound quotes approvingly the dictum of Pater) it is not necessary that poetry should be destitute of meaning. Instead of slightly veiled and resonant abstractions, like:
>
> > Time with a gift of tears,
> > Grief with a glass that ran—
>
> of Swinburne, or the mossiness of Mallarmé, Pound's verse is always definite and concrete, because he has always a definite emotion behind it. (*TCC* 170)

The Victorian poet-orators, Eliot implies, learned how to adjust cunningly to the expectations of their audience; the real instrument of poetry, however, can only be true to its own nature. In this passage are the main components of what will become Eliot's "Victorian foil": a misconceived relation between poetry and music; rhetoric; and meaningless abstractions. Only by categorizing the Victorian poetic achievement in such a manner could Eliot release himself and his peers from its magnitude.

Eliot invokes "the object" in many of his essays around this time. The term symbolizes a new approach "by which contemporary verse has tried to escape the rhetorical, the abstract, the moralizing. . . ."⁹ The objects are, naturally, to be observed: just the right word for the new poetry, implying the primacy of vision and the absence of intruding moralization (the full title of Eliot's first book of poetry was *Prufrock and Other Observations*). In "Reflections on *Vers Libre*," Eliot writes that the *Spoon River Anthology* "is reflective, not immediate; its author is a moralist, rather than an observer" (*TCC* 187). These qualities again evoke the dichotomy of old and new, dead and vital, created by the Modernists. And the old poetry is Victorian.

In the same essay, Eliot compares the author of *Spoon River Anthology* to George Crabbe, who is "the more intense of the two." A short piece called "The Rev. G. Crabbe, LL.B.," by Ezra Pound, also appeared in 1917. Both men appreciated Crabbe's realism and admired his use of prosaic material; it was a reflection of what they were trying to do, Eliot more so than Pound, in their own verse. Pound's essay immediately launches into what was to become, in the Modernist credo, the standard attack on the principal representative of the Victorians. I quote at some length to illustrate the extent to which this sentiment could be carried:

> Byron liked him [Crabbe], but the British Public did not. The British public liked, has liked, likes and always will like all art, music, poetry, literature, glass engraving, sculpture, etc. in just such measure as it approaches the Tennysonian tone. It likes Shakespear, or at least accepts him in just so far as he is 'Tennysonian'. It has published the bard of Avon expurgated and even emended. There has never been an edition of 'Purified Tennyson'.
>   . . . It was that lady-like attitude toward the printed page that did it—that something, that ineffable 'something', which kept Tennyson out of his works. When he began to write for Viccy's [Queen Victoria's] ignorant ear, he immediately ceased to be the 'Tennyson so muzzy that he tried to go out through the fireplace', the Tennyson with the broad North accent. . . . He became the Tate Gallery among poets.
>   The afflatus which has driven great artists to blurt out the facts of life with directness or with cold irony, or with passion, and with always precision . . . this urge, this impulse (or perhaps it is a different urge and impulse) leads Tennyson into pretty embroideries.¹⁰

Eliot would of course do his share in trying to bury the Victorian poets, but not in the same bluff manner. From the first, he was more willing to give credit where credit was due; he was never quite taken in by his peers' proclamations of revolution. In the *"Vers Libre"* essay I have noted, Eliot quietly points out that Arnold's "Strayed Reveller" illustrates the same kind of "escape from rhyme" appropriated by the *vers librists*. He criticizes the fashionable dismissal of all things Victorian by satirizing the pose of a lady, "renowned in her small circle for the accuracy of her stop-press information on literature," who cries " 'But one cannot read the Victorians at all!' " And in "The Borderline of Prose," which attempts to clarify the relations of verse and prose, Eliot cites passages from three Victorian writers—Ruskin, Newman, and F. H. Bradley, all "masters of the English language"—as examples of that kind of excellent prose, with a sure sense of prose rhythm, far above the blurred "poetic" exercises of the "long-forgotten 'Nineties."[11]

Reviewing for the *Egoist* Pound's edition of John Yeats's letters, Eliot straddles the question of the Victorians. On the one hand, safe in the land of generalities, he commends John Yeats's distinction of true poetry versus rhetoric: "He differs from the usual Englishman in his dislike for the edifying, in his preference of vision to exhortation." Edification and exhortation were, of course, the property of the Victorian poets. Yet when he is faced with a specific Victorian poet, Eliot considers fairly: Matthew Arnold "is a true poet and only incidentally a teacher."[12]

For *The Egoist,* Eliot would often become the fastidious sophisticate criticizing national dullness, a role that was part of the English avant-garde. Debts to English predecessors of the past fifty or sixty years could hardly be acknowledged, even if Eliot had wanted to. An example of this occurs near the end of Part II of "Reflections on Contemporary Poetry" (*Egoist,* October 1917), when Eliot considers a book on John Davidson written by H. Fineman.

Keep in mind that in 1961 Eliot wrote a brief preface for a selection of Davidson's poems, which begins:

> I feel a peculiar reverence, and acknowledge a particular debt, towards poets whose work impressed me deeply in my formative years between the ages of sixteen and twenty. Some were of an earlier age—the late sixteenth and early seventeenth centuries—some of another language; and of these, two were Scots: the author of *The City of Dreadful Night,* and the author of *Thirty Bob a Week.* It is because I am given an opportunity of expressing, once again, my gratitude to John Davidson, that I write this preface.[13]

In 1917, at age thirty, Eliot was not in a position to be so direct. Davidson was of the Rhymers' Club, the Rhymers' Club was of the 'Nineties, and the phenomenon of the 'Nineties was in 1917 considered by many to be either terribly adolescent or terribly old-fashioned. In any case, the poets of the 1890s were children of the high Victorians, and therefore tainted.

The tone and strategy of Eliot's 1917 remarks are revealing, especially in light of what he was free to acknowledge in 1961. He carefully avoids having to "estimate the value of John Davidson" (p. 133), which is what he says the book tries to do, and which Eliot was so ready to do with so many other authors more distantly removed either by time or language. That, in fact, was his standard method, known to reviewers before and since: seize the subject of the book under review and, instead of dwelling on the book's strong and weak points, run off with the subject. In this case, however, Eliot resorts to a few flippant remarks on "University criticism" (the book was published by the University of Pennsylvania Press). He then reels off a final paragraph thick with condescension and allusions, the effect of which is to keep the reader fairly intimidated and unaware of the fact that not much is being said about John Davidson, who was a late Victorian and therefore barred from the ranks of the poets worthy of discussion:

> Davidson, Mr. Fineman says, "Proceeds to erect a new dwelling-place for the imagination on the basis of things that are real to modern man." This is really Davidson's cardinal sin, as well as his virtue; he too often is interested in the dwelling-place rather than in the tenant, who is the same through all ages; I doubt whether Villon would have taken the electron so seriously. Still, there is Dante's astronomy . . . but that was not a very recent theory. A careful study of the nineteenth-century poetry based on "things real to modern man" would be interesting, beginning with Princess Ida and her fluid haze of light; perhaps Mr. Fineman will do it, after studying the method involved in such an extended piece of criticism, say, as Sainte-Beuve's *Life of Chateaubriand*.   (p. 134)

Thus Eliot avoids having to admit any kind of admiration for a poet "whose work [had] deeply impressed" him some years before.

"Princess Ida" represents, by the way, one of Eliot's earliest references to Tennyson. He had in mind of course *The Princess* and its scientific disquisitions in verse—in particular, the account of Laplace's nebular theory:

> 'This world was once a fluid haze of light,
> Till toward the centre set the starry tides,
> And eddied into suns, that wheeling cast
> The planets: then the monster, then the man;
> Tattooed or woaded, winter-clad in skins,
> Raw from the prime, and crushing down his mate;
> As yet we find in barbarous isles, and here
> Among the lowest.'[14]

Here was the Tennyson whom the avant-garde could attack with impunity, and who, according to Yeats, ruined his art with an unwholesome "brooding over scientific opinion."[15] "Things real to modern man" change from decade to decade; the poet who pays too much attention to them, to the surface of his time, has his audience too much in mind: the result is oration, not poetry. So runs the argument. The mere mention of *The Princess* was enough to provoke smiles that discounted Tennyson's poetry as a whole. But what is worth noticing here is Eliot's familiarity with the passage.

The last of the three-part "Reflections on Contemporary Poetry" considers Harriet Monroe's and Alice Corbin Henderson's anthology, *The New Poetry* (1917), which does indeed contain an impressive array of poets who were "new" at the time: Lawrence, Frost, H. D., Aldington, Williams, Stevens, Pound, Eliot himself (the first three sections of "Portrait of a Lady"), and others. The introduction, written by Harriet Monroe and discussed by Eliot at some length, demands our attention for a moment. It shows how this new generation of poets was defined in relation to the Victorians, and how extreme were the declarations of rebellion.

"What is the new poetry?" Miss Monroe asks, "and wherein does it differ from the old?"[16] The "truly modern poet" rejects "all the rhetorical excesses through which most Victorian poetry now seems 'over-apparelled' . . ." (p. v). But the difference goes deeper than questions of form:

> The new poetry strives for a concrete and immediate realization of life; it would discard the theory, the abstraction, the remoteness, found in all classics not of the first order. It is less vague, less verbose, less eloquent, than most poetry of the Victorian period. . . . [I]t becomes intensive rather than diffuse. It looks out more eagerly than in; it becomes objective. (p. vi)

Miss Monroe presents Yeats and Synge as the great liberators, who "had little patience with the 'over-apparelled' art of Tennyson and his imitators":

> They found it stiffened by rhetoric, by a too conscious morality leading to pulpit eloquence, and by second-hand bookish inspirations. . . . The surprises and irregularities, found in all great art because they are inherent in human feeling, were being ruled out of English poetry, which consequently was stiffening into forms too fixed and becoming more and more remote from life. As Mr. Yeats said in Chicago:
> "We were weary of all this. We wanted to get rid not only of rhetoric but of poetic diction. We tried to strip away everything that was artificial, to get a style like speech, as simple as the simplest prose, like a cry of the heart."
> It is scarcely too much to say that "the new poetry"—if we may be allowed the phrase—began with these two great Irish masters. Think what a contrast to even the simplest lyrics of Tennyson the pattern of their song presents, and what a contrast their direct outright human feeling presents to the somewhat culture-developed optimism of Browning, and the science-inspired pessimism of Arnold. Compared with these Irishmen the best of their predecessors seem literary. (p. ix)

How does Eliot respond to all of this? Monroe's introduction, he writes, "makes many excellent points which are worth making," but it "leads me to wonder whether a whole generation can arise together and insurrect. . . . Perhaps the word ["insurrect"] is invidious, but there is certainly a hit at the Victorian age *in toto*."[17] It turns out that Eliot is not at all comfortable with this propagandist "hit."

He implies that Monroe's polemical fervour—her speaking as if "the new movement" were as coherent and organized as a battle maneuver—is rather foolish. She is creating a useful fiction, for "in literature especially, the innovations which we can consciously and collectively aim to introduce are few, and mostly technical." It is up to the few really first-rate poets, Eliot says, slowly to bring about major changes, and their efforts cannot be subsumed under the banner of any school; neither is it accurate to disclaim one's predecessors in such a facile manner.

But Eliot goes on to blur these assertions with a clutter of conditionals, for he must appear faithful to the "movement":

> Certainly if a spontaneous revolution is possible, if it is possible for a whole generation, and not merely an isolated individual here and there, to arise as one man to wring the neck of rhetoric, one would expect, as is indeed the case, that the various volunteers should come variously armed. (p. 151)

A few readers might have recognized the slogan Eliot invokes, which goes back to the Rhymers' Club: a small detail reflecting the larger continuity of tradition. Yeats mentions the slogan and its source in "Friends of My Youth," a lecture he delivered in March 1910:

> We had among us Lionel Johnson, Arthur Symons, Ernest Dowson, John Davidson, and others. Ten of us made up the club, but many more gathered in the Cheshire Cheese at that time, and what had brought them to the same mind as myself, by a different path, was largely French influences. Just as Tennyson and Swinburne in England, so Victor Hugo had filled his work with heterogeneous interests [with Tennyson it was "the introduction of scientific speculations," with Swinburne "the revolutionary fire of Mazzini"]. Verlaine led the revolt. One of his pages we used to quote contained these words: "Take rhetoric and wring its neck!"[18]

Eliot returns to the term "rhetoric" at the conclusion of his "Reflections." Again he expresses dissatisfaction with Monroe's oversimplifying credo. I must quote at some length, for it is impossible to paraphrase Eliot when he is being arch:

> But as for the escape from rhetoric—there is a great push at the door, and some cases of suffocation. But what is rhetoric? The test seems unsatisfactory. There is rhetoric even among the new poets. Furthermore, I am inclined to believe that Tennyson's

verse is a "cry from the heart" [quoting the Yeats lecture cited by Monroe]—only it is the heart of Tennyson, Latitudinarian, Whig, Laureate. The style of William Morris is a "style like speech" [same source], only it is the speech of Morris, and therefore rather poor stuff. The "Idylls of the King" sound often like Tennyson talking to Queen Victoria in heaven; and the "Earthly Paradise" like an idealized Morris talking to an idealized Burne-Jones.   (p. 151)

"But what is rhetoric?" he asks. Several years later (July 1919) Eliot would analyze the term in " 'Rhetoric' and Poetic Drama," concluding that there is proper as well as improper poetic "rhetoric"—another sign of his unwillingness to embrace without question the anti-Victorian "movement" in English poetry, in this case by critically examining one of its principal catchwords.[19]

Before moving to 1918, a word about the *Idylls,* which we have just seen Eliot so casually dismiss. They represented, to Eliot and others at the time, Tennyson at his least successful. In Eliot's pamphlet on Ezra Pound, justifying Pound's learned excursions into other ages and the consequent demands placed on the reader, he writes:

Very few people know the Arthurian legends well, or even Malory (if they did they might realize that the *Idylls of the King* are hardly more important than a parody, or a 'Chaucer retold for Children'); but no one accuses Tennyson of needing footnotes, or of superciliousness toward the uninstructed.   (*TCC* 166)

We have come a long way from this statement to John Rosenberg's assertion that "the *Idylls of the King* is one of the four or five indisputably great long poems in our language."[20] The misreading of the *Idylls,* far more than any other work of Tennyson's, was carried to great extremes—even by someone as acute as Eliot, who was less ready than many to denigrate the Victorians *in toto.* How strikingly the vision of the *Idylls* applies to the England of 1917, engaged in her own "last dim battle." And how shortsighted to dismiss the poem, as Eliot does, because Tennyson modified its source. For accuracy's sake, it is necessary to note that Eliot was not always above reading Tennyson badly.

1918

Nineteenth-century English writers, nineteenth-century English characteristics and modes of thought—more and more, these are the subjects of Eliot's remarks. Eliot deliberately places himself in conscious relation to his Victorian predecessors as he continues his assimilation of the Tradition, now focusing on England's more immediate past. His judgments of that past and its literature are the result of studied consideration; they are a far cry from the careless ignorance of some of his peers. He took Tennyson and the Victorians seriously enough to *criticize* them, rather than relegating them to the shelves of the unread.

He reviews the letters of Thomas Woolner, the famous Victorian sculptor, and finds them valuable for the insights they give into the Pre-Raphaelite Brotherhood, Tennyson, and Carlyle. Although Eliot never quite abandons an attitude of superiority in this review, he obviously enjoys the look backward, whether dwelling on the image of Matthew Arnold as dandy, or recounting the ceremonious unveiling of a Woolner statue to the accompaniment of "Rule Britannia."[21]

But this was written for the *New Statesman.* For *The Egoist,* he was still one of the avant-garde, which adoped a stance of vehement reaction against Victorian poetry: its discursive, rhetorical mode, its image of the poet as public philosopher and moralist, its carelessness with words. One of the major purposes of Eliot's criticism at this time was to *startle* his readers. To accomplish this, he often sacrificed fairness and accuracy for effect. Eliot was in the problematic position of speaking as one of the rebels, yet refusing to swallow whole their conception of what they were rebelling against.

Several reviews written in the spring of 1918, all for the *Egoist,* are especially revealing of Eliot's attitude toward English literature of the previous century. In "Professional, Or . . ." (*Egoist,* April), he responds to a *TLS* article denouncing "Professionalism in Art":

> The opposite of the professional is not the dilettante, the elegant amateur, the dabbler who in fact only attests the existence of the specialist. The opposite of the professional, the enemy, is the man of mixed motives. Conspicuously the Victorian epoch is anti-professional; Carlyle as an historian, Ruskin as an economist; Thackeray who could write such good prose as the Steyne episode, and considered himself a kindly but penetrating satirist; George Eliot who could write *Amos Barton* and steadily degen-erate. Decadence in art is caused by mixed motives. The art of the Victorians is spoiled by mixed motives, and Oscar Wilde finally added ingredients to the mixture which made it a ludicrous emetic. (p. 61)

This view parallels Arthur Hallam's essay and Yeats's inheritance and promulgation of its ideas. The pure poet, who "merely puts into his poetry his highly developed perceptions, merely gives you so much life as it presents itself to a rare and delicate organization" (Yeats's paraphrase of Hallam's argument, in "Friends of My Youth") is opposed to the impure poet, like Wordsworth, who "mixed in poetry popular maxims, popular morality, all the evangelism of the day." "When you come to Tennyson," Yeats adds, "there is theology, humanitarianism: all kinds of things were mixed into the pure substance of poetry."[22] Eliot, however, does not include Tennyson in his damning list of Caryle, Ruskin, Thackeray, and George Eliot. As we shall soon see, Eliot considered Tennyson as one of the professionals, who, whatever his weaknesses, devoted himself fully to his language.

Eliot goes on to say that the spirit of anti-professionalism has infected both English poetry and English criticism. It manifests itself in the abhorrent journalese of Chesterton (whose *Victorian Age in Literature* Eliot was repeatedly attacking during these months), in the Polite Essays of the polite appreciator Alice Meynell, and in "the annual scourge of the Georgian Anthology" (May, p. 69). The Georgian poets, Eliot maintains, are inbred amateurs, mere dabblers in verse, who have not studied the work of their predecessors or of men writing in other languages as these things must be studied (June/July, p. 84). Consequently they can do nothing but echo Wordsworth at his most didactic or Keats at his weakest (March, p. 43). And it is a mistake to think that these amateurs have anything in common with someone to whom they have too often been compared:

> I cannot see the resemblance to Tennyson which people often remark in Georgian poetry. I do not care to pose as a champion of Tennyson, and Mr. Chesterton's approval makes one uneasy about him. But Tennyson was careful in his syntax; and, moreover, his adjectives usually have a definite meaning; perhaps often an uninteresting meaning; still, each word is treated with proper respect. And Tennyson had a brain (a large dull brain like a farmhouse clock) which saved him from triviality. The subject given (airy fairy Lillian) he took it lightly, but as a serious study in technique. Mr. [James] Stephens takes a trivial subject ponderously; only the technique is without seriousness. . . . Tennyson to the Rev. Frederick Dennison Maurice is better than Mr. Sassoon to Mr. Graves [referring to Sassoon's "A Letter Home," addressed to Robert Graves, in *Georgian Poetry 1916-1917*]. (March, p. 43)

This passage may serve as a symbol of Eliot's ambivalent attitude towards Tennyson during these years: a mixture of uneasy but honest respect, waspish condescension, and considerable knowledge of the subject, revealed in his reference to Tennyson's flawless verse epistle "To the Rev. F. D. Maurice."

Reviewing in the April *Egoist* a collection of essays by Alice Meynell, Eliot is engaged by only one: "Some Thoughts of a Reader of Tennyson":

> In the present tidy small volume she wins our hearts when she says that Tennyson is "more serious than the solemn Wordsworth," or when she denounces Swinburne. (Compare her analysis of Tennyson with that of Chesterton in his *Victorian Age.*) But on the whole she has not the single critical motive. She is an amateur of letters. Like Mr. Chesterton, she has not in the end criticized the author at all. When she writes of Tennyson:
>
>> Unaware of a separate angel of modern poetry is he who is insensible to the Tennyson note—the new note that we reaffirm even with the notes of Vaughan, Traherne,

Wordsworth, Coleridge, Blake, well in our ears—the Tennyson note of splendour, all-distinct. He showed the perpetually transfigured landscape in transfiguring words. He is the captain of our dreams. Others have lighted a candle in England, he lit a sun.

. . . it is what a University Extension audience would like; but it is not criticism.   (p. 61)

Again, Tennyson is admitted to the ranks of the "serious." He is one of the professionals.

The state of English criticism is denounced just as soundly as contemporary poetry for its dilettante nature. "But we must learn to take literature *seriously,*" Eliot writes in the April *Egoist* (p. 61), and this involves working at genuine literary criticism as opposed to the genre of "literary studies" (May, p. 70) or the flashy journalese written by the pseudo-critics: "the forces of death with Mr. Chesterton at their head" (May, p. 69). Without real criticism, the dead writers will remain dead:

The Englishman, completely untrained in critical judgment, looks complacently back over the nineteenth century as an accumulation of Great Writers. England puts her Great Writers away securely in a Safe Deposit Vault, and curls to sleep like Fafner. There they go rotten; for if our predecessors cannot teach us to write better than themselves, they will surely teach us to write worse; because we have never learned to criticize Keats, Shelley, and Wordsworth (poets of assured though modest merit), Keats, Shelley, and Wordsworth punish us from their graves with the annual scourge of the Georgian Anthology.   (p. 69)

Here, as elsewhere, Tennyson is spared the rod. Indeed, it is Wordsworth, not Tennyson, who becomes for Eliot the archetypal nineteenth-century anti-poet: "To remain with Wordsworth is equivalent to ignoring the whole of science subsequent to Erasmus Darwin" (June/July, p. 84). Only once does Eliot speak of the two poets as one, in "A Note on Ezra Pound," written for *To-day* (September 1918) in order to sell Pound to a wider public. He could not afford to make distinctions in this case, but had to set up Ezra Pound against the nineteenth century as a whole:

English verse in general may be said to have deteriorated. What we commonly find among contemporary poets is a mentality which has remained in the age of Wordsworth or in the age of Tennyson, with a technique which is actually inferior to that of either of these. Whatever we may think of these or other figures of the past century, each of them did contribute (for what it is worth) something or other; Wordsworth and Tennyson were indeed adequate to at least some sides of the mind of their time; the more intelligent of their contemporaries could read them with serious self-respect. But while the mind of man has altered, verse has stood still. . . .   (pp. 3-4)

"Each of them did contribute (for what it is worth) something or other"—about as hedging and opaque a remark as one could make! Thus Eliot avoids the kind of categorical condemnations of Tennyson pronounced by

Pound and Monroe and others, without having to appear in the awkward position of posing as Tennyson's champion. It would take another twenty years or so before he could do that.

1919 and the Example of Kipling

This year marks the beginning of Eliot's second period of critical writing, according to his own classification in the retrospective essay, "To Criticize the Critic":

> After 1918, when *The Egoist* had come to an end, I was writing essays and reviews for two editors in whom I was fortunate, for they both gave me always the right books to review: Middleton Murry in the short-lived *Athenaeum,* and Bruce Richmond in *The Times Literary Supplement.* (*TCC* 17-18)

1919 was the year of *The Athenaeum*: out of the thirty-four entries listed by Donald Gallup as Eliot's contributions to periodicals for this year, twenty-five are in Murry's journal. Its audience was larger than *The Egoist*'s, its tone more temperate. As one can see by the number of entries, 1919 was also a year of remarkable critical productivity for Eliot. Henceforth I shall have to be more selective in this survey, focussing mostly on remarks that pertain directly to Tennyson, or indirectly, through the example of Kipling.

Eliot's "Kipling Redivivus" (*Athenaeum,* 9 May 1919) deserves close attention. It "has never been reprinted and does not need to be," says Mr. Kenner, and perhaps he is right—but it does provide valuable insights into Eliot's strategy for dealing with those outcast Victorian poets who, whatever their status among the new poets, heavily influenced his work.[23]

Mr. Kipling's work, Eliot begins, suffers from the wrong kind of rhetoric. Kipling, like Swinburne, has not "the sound-value of music" but "the sound-value of oratory" (297). To exemplify this he quotes from the well-known first Chorus of *Atalanta in Calydon* ("When the hounds of spring are on winter's traces") and from "Danny Deever" ("What are the bugles blowin' for? said Files on Parade"). Theirs is "the poetry of oratory," which *persuades* "not by reason, but by emphatic sound" (297). Like the public speaker, they have an idea to impose; "and they impose it in the public speaker's way, by turning the idea into sound, and iterating the sound" (297):

> And, like the public speaker's, their business is not to express, to lay before you, to *state,* but to propel, to impose on you the idea. And, like the orator, they are personal: not by revelation, but by throwing themselves in and gesturing the emotion of the moment. . . .

> Nothing is better, I well think
> Than love; the hidden well-water
> Is not so delicate a drink.
> This was well seen of me and her

(to take from one of Swinburne's poems ["The Leper," 1-4] which most nearly resembles a statement); or

> The end of it's sitting and thinking
> And dreaming hell-fires to see—[Kipling's "The Ladies," 53-54]

these are not statements of emotion, but ways of stimulating a particular response in the reader.   (298)

That, as we have seen Eliot maintain before, is the cardinal sin: to have an audience in mind and push across concepts instead of concentrating entirely on creating a point of view or "world," like Shakespeare, Dante, Villon, Conrad, or James.

The abstractions pushed across by Kipling and Swinburne, Eliot maintains, are callow and unreal: "Had Mr. Kipling taken Liberty and Swinburne the Empire [instead of the reverse], the alteration would be unimportant" (298). So, he adds, Kipling's manner remains only a unique eccentricity; it cannot make his verse a unified whole. One element of his "style or manner . . . which demands attention," though, is its fusion of cynicism and sentimentalism:

> The sentiment of Tennyson and Mrs. Browning is obsolete, it is no longer a living force; it is superseded by Mr. Kipling's. Tennyson, we must insist, could never have written
>
> > Love at first sight was her trouble,
> >   She didn't know what it were;
> > But I wouldn't do such, 'cause I liked her too much—
> >   And I learned about women from 'er; ["The Ladies," 45-48]
>
> nor could he have written
>
> > Gentlemen-rankers off on a spree,
> > Damned from here to eternity,
> > O God, have mercy on such as we:
> >   Ba Ba Ba. ["Gentlemen-Rankers," 11-14]
>
> Mr. Kipling may have winked at Tennyson down the road. But Tennyson did not wink back.   (298)

Eliot's attitude seems quite clear. He cannot accept the Victorian *donnée* of the poet as Prophet, Public Moralist, and Public Speaker. He certainly was writing a different kind of poetry. Despite Eliot's charac-

teristic insistence upon paying serious attention to poets like Kipling and
Swinburne, whom others had either ignored or dismissed as "Victorian,"
and despite his admission that "Mr. Kipling is very nearly a great writer"
(298), the essay still gives the impression that its author is discussing
figures who could not have less to do with his own work. The tone of cold
appraisal and the arch wisecracks contribute to this impression. But if we
go back to some of Eliot's own references, something else emerges, which
indicates the contradiction at the base of Eliot's relation not only to Kipling, but also to Arnold, Tennyson, and Swinburne.

Eliot refers to no less than fourteen of Kipling's poems in this essay,
including some of the Barrack-Room Ballads that he had known since
childhood (see above, chapter 5), such as "Danny Deever," "Mandalay,"
"Gentlemen-Rankers," and "The Ladies." Almost all of the poems are
cited as illustrations of one defect or another: the affinity with "orator or
preacher," the lack of a cohering point of view, the bombast of the popular
"prophet," or plain bad writing. Yet many of these same poems would
eventually find their way into Eliot's 1941 *Choice of Kipling's Verse* as
examples of his high and unique artistry.[24] Of course, Eliot changed in
twenty years; but he was also in a much better position to display such
admiration in 1941 than in 1919. The new poetic he was gradually artic-
ulating in the years before 1922 had no place for poets like Kipling; at the
same time, these were poets with whom he had grown up, and in whose
verse he was saturated. It is apparent, in the way they vary slightly from
the actual text, that some of the poems in "Kipling Redivivus" ("Gentlemen-Rankers," "The Ladies," Swinburne's "The Leper") are quoted
from memory. What was true in the case of Kipling was also true for
Tennyson and even Swinburne: Eliot's official strictures were often at
odds with his affinity for these poets. For the sake of the cause, and for
his own liberation as a poet, Eliot publicly condemned them to an en-
closed vacuum with no channels into the present. The trick worked for
decades.

Consider, for example, some of the poems he belittles in "Kipling
Redivivus." "Danny Deever" shows "a consummate gift of word, phrase,
and rhythm" according to his 1941 essay, which also praises the poem's
interplay of regularity and variance of pace (the technique stressed in
"Reflections on *Vers Libre*"), as well as its evocation of horror, culminating in the "exactly right" word *whimper*.[25] In "Mandalay," another
poem singled out for blame in 1919, one finds the same vision of English
streets that gave Eliot "the shudder" in *In Memoriam* VII (*SE* 333):

> I am sick o' wastin' leather on these gritty pavin'-stones,
> An' the blasted English drizzle wakes the fever in my bones;

> Tho' I walks with fifty 'ousemaids outer Chelsea to the Strand,
> An' they talks a lot o' lovin', but wot do they understand?   (35-38)

Compare this to Eliot's "Morning at the Window":

> And along the trampled edges of the street
> I am aware of the damp souls of housemaids
> Sprouting despondently at area gates.   (*CPP* 16)

"Gentlemen-Rankers" describes the horror, and its particular circumstances, that would haunt Eliot for so long:

> When the drunken comrade mutters and the great guard-lantern gutters
>   And the horror of our fall is written plain,
> Every secret, self-revealing on the aching whitewashed ceiling,
>   Do you wonder that we drug ourselves from pain?   (27-30)

Compare this to the third of Eliot's "Preludes":

> You dozed, and watched the night revealing
> The thousand sordid images
> Of which your soul was constituted;
> They flickered against the ceiling.   (*CPP* 12-13)

The displacement Kipling manages in something like "the aching white-washed ceiling"—the blurring of subject and object—would become a characteristic device in Eliot's early verse.

Still later in his career, addressing the Kipling Society in 1958, Eliot could be more specific about his debt to Kipling:

> . . . Kipling has accompanied me ever since boyhood, when I discovered the early verse—"Barrack Room Ballads"—and the early stories—"Plain Tales from the Hills." There are boyhood enthusiasms which one outgrows; there are writers who impress one deeply at some time before or during adolescence and whose work one never re-reads in later life. But Kipling is different. Traces of Kipling appear in my own mature verse. . . . I once wrote a poem called "The Love Song of J. Alfred Prufrock": I am convinced that it would never have been called "Love Song" but for a title of Kipling's that stuck obstinately in my head: "The Love Song of Har Dyal." Many years later I wrote a poem called "The Hollow Men": I could never have thought of this title but for Kipling's poem "The Broken Men."[26]

There is more to be noticed, however, than a mere derivation of titles. Prufrock's love song takes on a new measure of irony when set against its forebear.

"The Love Song of Har Dyal" appears in the short story "Beyond the Pale," one of Kipling's *Plain Tales from the Hills* (1888), which Eliot greatly admired and knew from youth.[27] "Beyond the Pale" tells the story of an Englishman's brief, furtive liaison with a fifteen-year-old Hindu widow. An "aimless wandering" (238) "deep away in the heart of the [Indian] City" (237) brings him one day through an alley to "a dead-wall pierced by one grated window" (237). Behind the window lives the beautiful girl, whom he cannot see. Half-playfully, they whisper to each other some verses from one of the poems in the *Arabian Nights*, "The Love Song of Har Dyal." Her voice stops suddenly and mysteriously; he leaves and returns the next night. As the gongs of the City toll, the young voice resumes "The Love Song," "at the verse where the Panthan girl calls upon Har Dyal to return" (241). It is these stanzas that Eliot includes in his Kipling anthology:

> Alone upon the housetops, to the North
> I turn and watch the lightning in the sky,—
> The glamour of thy footsteps in the North,
> *Come back to me, Beloved, or I die!*
>
> Below my feet the still bazaar is laid
> Far, far, below the weary camels lie,—
> The camels and the captives of the raid.
> *Come back to me, Beloved, or I die!*
>
> My father's wife is old and harsh with years,
> And drudge of all my father's house am I.—
> My bread is sorrow and my drink is tears,
> *Come back to me, Beloved, or I die!*

The Englishman gains entry. This marks the beginning of his "double life" (241), wild and dream-like. In the day-time he "drove through his routine of office-work" or "put on his calling-clothes and called on the ladies of the Station" (242); at night would come the walk through the City, past slums and "dead walls" (242), to the maiden, Bisesa. Their love is intense, but one night the girl becomes "quite unreasonably disturbed" (245). She desperately insists that he return no more. After a time, however, he does come back, and sees the girl hold out her arms through the window into the moonlight:

> Both hands had been cut off at the wrists, and the stumps were nearly healed.   (245)

From the dark someone thrusts at the Englishman and cuts through his *boorka,* the cloak he had been using for disguise:

> The stroke missed his body, but cut into one of the muscles of the groin, and he limped slightly from the wound for the rest of his days.   (245-46)

He never sees Bisesa again. "He had lost her in the City where each man's house is as guarded and unknowable as the grave. . . ." (247). The window is walled up, and the Englishman returns to a life of dead regularity.

"The Love Song of Har Dyal" and the tale centering around it, describing passions great and mysterious, were not only a source for "Prufrock" but also an ironic foil. Prufrock wanders through streets of the City; Prufrock's destination has something to do with a woman, or women; Prufrock leads a double life, taking toast and tea, and then lingering in the chambers of the sea. But his City is not of the exotic East; he passes by cheap hotels and restaurants, not strange marketplaces and water buffalo wallowing in blue slime. He dreams of sea-girls, but calls on the ladies instead, dressed not in an "evil-smelling *boorka*" (242) but in morning coat, mounting collar, necktie rich and modest. His mind flutters about bare arms and trailing skirts, but he will only circle the moment of crisis—circle and back off. In the realm "beyond the pale," two braceleted white arms end in stumps, a terrible symbol of human passion fulfilled; in Prufrock's salon, the unsettling revelation of braceleted white arms is—that they are downed with light brown hair. The refrain of Har Dyal's love song—"Come back to me, Beloved, or I die!"—bespeaks great longing and desire; the refrain in "Prufrock," also a woman to her beloved, belongs to an altogether different world:

> "That is not it at all,
> That is not what I meant, at all."

It is more than just Kipling's title that shows in "The Love Song of J. Alfred Prufrock." Kipling's story and accompanying verses, firmly set in Eliot's consciousness, inform the whole poem.

As he develops his own revaluations of the English poetic tradition, Eliot continues to display an *awareness,* biased yet acute, of Tennyson's achievement. This is in accord with his belief that "in the long run . . . the continuity of the language has been the strongest thing; so that however much we need French or Italian literature to explain English literature of any period, we need, to explain it, the English inheritance still more."[28]

In "Some Notes on the Blank Verse of Christopher Marlowe," Eliot articulates one of the basic assumptions underlying his view of Tennyson at this time: that this formidable craftsman failed when it came to the expression of sophisticated emotions:

It [a study of blank verse] would show, I believe, that blank verse within Shakespeare's lifetime was more highly developed, that it became the vehicle of more varied and more intense art-emotions than it has ever conveyed since; and that after the erection of the Chinese Wall of Milton, blank verse has suffered not only arrest but retrogression. That the blank verse of Tennyson, for example, a consummate master of this form in certain applications, is cruder (*not* "rougher" or less perfect in technique) than that of half a dozen contemporaries of Shakespeare; cruder, because less capable of expressing complicated, subtle, and surprising emotions.   (*SW* 87)

Describing Marlowe's innovations in verse technique, he returns to Tennyson. *Tamburlaine,* Eliot tells us, gave blank verse "a new driving power," enabling it to escape from the confinements imposed by the rhymed couplet and "the elegiac or rather pastoral note of Surrey, to which Tennyson returned" (*SW* 91). The nature of this achievement is revealed by contrasting one of the great speeches in *Tamburlaine I* with a passage from Thomas Kyd; this passage in turn is compared and judged "not really inferior" to the four concluding lines of Tennyson's "Dora":

> So these four abode
> Within one house together; and as years
> Went forward, Mary took another mate;
> But Dora lived unmarried till her death.

Thus, we are supposed to see the "retrogression" of blank verse which Eliot had previously described. Of course the argument is sophistic. "Dora" was for Tennyson a peculiar experiment in Wordsworthian simplicity, marred, in J. H. Buckley's words, by "a too laborious reduction of language and emotion . . . in simple assertive sentences intended perhaps to achieve the elemental effect of a Biblical parable."[29] It is hardly a characteristic quotation. What is to be noticed here is Eliot's need to misrepresent Tennyson in order to get him out of the way—to categorize him as the skillful manufacturer of prettified vacuities. It is as if all Tennyson wrote were the "English Idyls" (of which "Dora" is one).

Reviewing Charles Whibley's *Literary Studies* in "The Local Flavour," Eliot again links Tennyson, in a quietly derogatory way, to the founder of English blank verse:

> On Surrey's blank verse he [Whibley] is feeble; he does not even give Surrey the credit of having anticipated some of Tennyson's best effects.   (*SW* 36)

Tennyson emerges, then, as the technically perfect master of empty "effect."

One of the effects that struck Eliot deeply was the exquisite conclusion of "Come down, O maid," one of the songs added to *The Princess* in 1850:

> 'Sweeter thy voice, but every sound is sweet;
> Myriads of rivulets hurrying through the lawn,
> The moan of doves in immemorial elms,
> And murmuring of innumerable bees.'

Here is the poet of unsurpassed technical skill whom Eliot never failed to acknowledge; here is an unforgettable illustration of what he could do with the sounds of words. "For simple rhythm and vowel music," Hallam Tennyson wrote, "my father considered this . . . as among his most successful work."[30] Eliot entitled his anonymous review of the new literary journal *Coterie,* "Murmuring of Innumerable Bees" in the *Athenaeum* of 3 October 1919; one cannot be sure precisely what this was supposed to imply. Were the poets in this issue of *Coterie* (Chaman Lall, Aldous Huxley, Edith Sitwell, Richard Aldington, among others) no more significant than a murmuring mass of insects? Must they work towards the sensory sensitivity exemplified in "Come down, O maid" as a whole? Whatever the answer, Eliot was having a good time playing possum:

> The verse-producing units circulating on the surface of Great Britain may be reduced roughly to four generations: the first, the aged, represented by the great name of Hardy, but including several figures in process of oblivescence [sic]; the middle-aged, included Mr. Yeats and a small number of honoured names; the ageing, including the Georgian poets[;] and the curious shapes of Mr. Eliot and Mr. Pound: all these ages have already lined their nests or dug their graves. We could, at will, pronounce a fitting obituary over any one of these writers except the first mentioned.   (p. 972)

Years later, in "From Poe to Valéry" (1948), Eliot would again invoke Tennyson's lines, comparing them to Poe's careless usage. Eliot declares that Tennyson, "of all English poets since Milton, had probably the most accurate and fastidious appreciation of the sound of syllables" (*TCC,* 31-32). But that was written in 1948. In 1919, it was far more convenient to regard Tennyson as the poet of "Dora." It was far more comfortable to recall his plays, which Eliot does in reviewing a recent production of *The Duchess of Malfi*:

> The dullest, the most theatrically inept, of acting plays will be readable if it only has a few good lines, but the closet drama is wholly unreadable. Between the lines, even the second best lines, of "The Duchess of Malfi" and the best lines of a play by Tennyson or Browning or Swinburne there is an absolute difference.[31]

1920

The concept of Tennyson as moralistic wizard of words who sang only the "proper" sentiments, goes back at least to the famous conclusion of

Hippolyte Taine's *Histoire de la Littérature Anglaise* (1863-64; trans. H. van Laun, 1871). Taine's work made a substantial impact on subsequent English literary criticism. One thinks especially of Taine's introduction, in which he details his method: applying the principles of scientific investigation to the study of literature by examining both author and work in terms of historical and psychological forces. "Les trois forces primordiales" are racial inheritance ("la race"); physical, social, and political environment ("le milieu"); and something he calls "le moment."[32] Taine's influence on Eliot is clear in *The Sacred Wood,* with its manner of scientific scrupulousness and objectivity.

Eliot first came across Taine's *Histoire* studying under Irving Babbitt, fall term 1909, in the course "Literary Criticism in France, with Special Reference to the Nineteenth Century." In his early prose, Eliot refers to Taine several times. One of those references includes Tennyson.

The *Athenaeum* of 6 August 1920 published a letter by Eliot in which he answers a reader's objections to his distinction between criticism and philosophy made in "The Perfect Critic," published the month before. The frontier between the two endeavors, Eliot admits, cannot be clearly defined, but one example might serve to clarify matters:

> I have in mind a rather celebrated passage towards the end of Taine's "History of English Literature" (I have not the book by me) in which he compares Tennyson and Musset. Taine is a person for whom I have considerable respect, but this passage does not seem to me to be good as criticism; the comparative vision of French and English life does not seem to me to issue quite ingenuously out of an appreciation of the two poets; I should say that Taine was here philosophizing. . . . (p. 190)

In this "celebrated passage," which runs quite a few pages, Taine depicts Tennyson as a poet perfectly representative of Victorian England—and Taine's Victorian England is truly a marvel of the Frenchman's imagination. "Pleasantness" is its very foundation; all is ordered, wholesome, and complacent:

> Such is this elegant and common-sense society, refined in comfort, regular in conduct, whose dilettante tastes and moral principles confine it within a sort of flowery border, and prevent it from having its attention diverted.[33]

"Does any poet suit such a society better than Tennyson?" Taine asks, and proceeds with what can be called the classic distortion of Tennyson's work, which would find greater and greater credence in the years to come. I quote at length because Taine's conception of Tennyson, although perhaps, in Eliot's words, "not . . . good as criticism," still influenced Eliot's own attitude towards the Laureate:

Without being a pedant, he is moral; he may be read in the family circle by night; he does not rebel against society and life; he speaks of God and the soul, nobly, tenderly, without ecclesiastical prejudice; . . . he has no violent and abrupt words, excessive and scandalous sentiments; he will pervert nobody. We shall not be troubled when we close the book; we may listen when we quit him, without contrast, to the grave voice of the master of the house, who repeats the evening prayers before the kneeling servants. . . . He has not rudely trenched upon truth and passion. He has risen to the height of noble and tender sentiments. He has gleaned from all nature and all history what was most lofty and amiable. . . . His poetry is like one of those gilt and painted stands in which flowers of the country and exotics mingle in artful harmony their stalks and foliage, their clusters and cups, their scents and hues. It seems made expressly for these wealthy, cultivated, free business men, heirs of the ancient nobility, new leaders of a new England. It is part of their luxury as of their morality; it is an eloquent confirmation of their principles, and a precious article of their drawing-room furniture.   (pp. 272-73)

In "Blake" (originally "The Naked Man," *Athenaeum,* 13 February 1920), Eliot assumes his official, poetically defensive posture towards Tennyson. Remarking upon the harmful conformity imposed by accumulation of conventional knowledge, he sounds very much like Taine:

Tennyson is a very fair example of a poet almost wholly encrusted with parasitic opinion, almost wholly merged into his environment. Blake, on the other hand, knew what interested him, and he therefore presents only the essential, only, in fact, what can be presented, and need not be explained. . . . He approached everything with a mind unclouded by current opinions.   (*SW* 154-55)

But the fact that Blake's philosophy was so personal results in formlessness, a fault "most evident, of course, in the longer poems—or rather, the poems in which structure is important" (*SW* 155-56). Of course, Eliot was having difficulties finding a form for his own long poem, but he seems to have hit upon the principle of organization he would use in *The Waste Land*:

You cannot create a very large poem without introducing a more impersonal point of view, or splitting it up into various personalities.   (*SW* 156)

The weakness of Blake's long poems, Eliot concludes, "is that Blake became too much occupied with ideas" (156). In the first version of this essay, Eliot added one more sentence:

But even these poems evince an intelligence more powerful, in its way, than that of, let us say, either Tennyson or Browning.[34]

Another in the series of protective potshots, this one distinguished by its lilting, teasing delay in identifying the target: more powerful,/in its way,/than that of,/let us say. . . . Eliot, however, was not at all comfortable with this statement: in *The Sacred Wood* it does not appear. Thus we are provided with yet another illustration of Eliot's confused ambivalence with regard to Tennyson.

The long poem—its conditions, various possible structures, regrettable absence in contemporary poetry—was something which would occupy Eliot for years to come. His poetic career is defined by the presence of three long poems, the last of which recalls the most famous of Tennyson's long poems (see chapter 7). In "The Possibility of a Poetic Drama," published originally in the November 1920 *Dial*, Eliot resumes his contemplation of form and the long poem, begun in the Blake essay. "The Elizabethan Age in England," he writes, "was able to absorb a great quantity of new thoughts and new images . . . because it had this great form of its own [i.e., drama] which imposed itself on everything that came to it." But the nineteenth century, with its own great stock of "fresh impressions," "had no form in which to confine them":

> Two men, Wordsworth and Browning, hammered out forms for themselves—personal forms, *The Excursion, Sordello, The Ring and the Book, Dramatic Monologues*; but no man can invent a form, create a taste for it, and perfect it too. Tennyson, who might unquestionably have been a consummate master of minor forms, took to turning out large patterns on a machine. . . . These poets were . . . obliged to consume vast energy in this pursuit of form, which could never lead to a wholly satisfying result. (*SW* 62-63)

This reference to Tennyson recalls a previous one: "the blank verse of Tennyson . . . a consummate master of this form in certain applications . . ." (in the Marlowe piece: see above, p. 110). A consummate master of "minor" forms, a consummate master of blank verse "in certain applications"—always the begrudging acknowledgment of supreme skill, and always the qualification that seems to relegate Tennyson to the museum shelf of the second- and third-rate, rather than admit him to the ranks of the great.

The context of the above reference ("Tennyson . . . took to turning out large patterns on a machine") suggests that Eliot had *In Memoriam* in mind as the product of Tennyson's "machine" in this case. The same reference echoes a remark Eliot read in A. C. Benson's *Edward Fitz-Gerald,* which so influenced the writing of "Gerontion."[35] Discussing FitzGerald's relationship with Alfred Tennyson, Benson quotes from a letter FitzGerald wrote to Frederic Tennyson in 1850:

> . . . I cannot care for his *In Memoriam.* . . . His poem I never did greatly affect: nor can I learn to do so: it is full of finest things, but it is monotonous, and has that air of being evolved by a Poetical Machine of the highest order.[36]

Eliot saw fit to criticize Tennyson's poem in another piece written at this time, "A Note on the American Critic," which reviews the critical stance of Paul Elmer More. More has "failed to put his finger on the right seriousness of great literary art"; "the seriousness which we find in Villon's *Testament* and which is conspicuously absent from *In Memoriam* . . ." (*SW* 43). Reading through Eliot's prose, one finds no other significant mention made of *In Memoriam* until 1936, when he would return to the poem without the need to belittle it.

1921-1923

Writing for the first number of Wyndham Lewis's *The Tyro,* Eliot refers condescendingly to "Tennyson's broad-shouldered genial Englishman" as part of the gallery of literary types making up "the chief myth which the Englishman has built about himself."[37] Again echoing Taine, he pronounces that, unlike Baudelaire, who made the essential attempt to establish a point of view toward good and evil, Tennyson only "decorated the morality he found in vogue." "Browning," Eliot continues, "really approached the problem [of good and evil], but with too little seriousness, with too much complacency; thus the 'Ring and the Book' just misses greatness—as the revised version of 'Hyperion' almost, or just, touches it." And we have just noted how Eliot found this moral seriousness "conspicuously absent from *In Memoriam*."

We see that Eliot was certainly contemplating, and perhaps rereading, long poems from the preceding century as he struggled with his own. In "Prose and Verse," an essay he contributed to the April 1921 *Chapbook,* he returns to the subject:

> Poe demands the static poem; that in which there shall be no movement of tension and relaxation, only the capture of a single unit of intense feeling. We are, most of us, inclined to agree with him: we do not like long poems. This dislike is due, I believe, partly to the taste of the day, which will pass, and partly to the abuse of the long poem in the hands of distinguished persons who did not know how to employ it. . . . [Successful long poems] have, in different degrees, the movement toward and from intensity which is life itself. Milton and Wordsworth, on the other hand, lack this unity, and therefore lack life; and the general criticism on most of the long poems of the nineteenth century is simply that they are not good enough.[38]

"John Dryden" is one of three 1921 essays on seventeenth-century poetry that define the next phase in Eliot's attitude towards the English tradition. He thought enough of the essays—"Andrew Marvell," "John Dryden," and "The Metaphysical Poets," all published originally in *TLS*—to have them reprinted in 1924 by Hogarth Press under the title *Homage to John Dryden,* and to include them, still grouped together, in *Selected Essays.*

All three of these essays describe the merits of poets like Dryden and Marvell and Donne by repeatedly setting them off against the failures of nineteenth-century poetry, specifically Victorian. Eliot discovered for himself an effective means for getting the Victorians out of his way: blame them for not being seventeenth-century poets, and present their poetry in a way that makes it seem like the sorry antithesis of seventeenth-century unification of sensibility. This strategy culminates in "The Metaphysical Poets," which contains the "rumination" passage, the one usually quoted to illustrate Eliot's attitude towards Tennyson and the Victorians in general: "But Keats and Shelley died, and Tennyson and Browning ruminated."

Tennyson and Browning are especially victimized in "The Metaphysical Poets" (October 1921). Eliot picks up on a concept of literary degeneration that he had begun to formulate in "Andrew Marvell" (March 1921):

> You cannot find it [wit: "a tough reasonableness beneath the slight lyric grace"] in Shelley or Keats or Wordsworth; you cannot find more than an echo of it in Landor; still less in Tennyson or Browning; and . . . Mr. Hardy is without it and Mr. Yeats is outside of the tradition altogether. (*SE* 293-94)

The two Victorians are irrevocably linked in "The Metaphysical Poets"; that "or" becomes an automatic "and." To illustrate "the difference between the intellectual poet and the reflective poet" (287), Eliot juxtaposes lines from Chapman's *The Revenge of Bussy D'Ambois* with an unidentified passage taken from "Bishop Blougram's Apology":

> No, when the fight begins within himself,
> A man's worth something. God stoops o'er his head,
> Satan looks up between his feet—both tug—
> He's left, himself, i' the middle; the soul wakes
> And grows. Prolong that battle through his life! (693-97)

Of course Eliot does Browning an injustice by making off with this quotation as if it were not part of something entirely different from the world and intents of the verse of *Bussy D'Ambois*. This is Blougram speaking to Mr. Gigadibs!, not Browning "reflecting" or exhorting his readers. The words are an effect of the Bishop's blazing, furiously rationalizing mind: "For Blougram, he believed, say, half he spoke" (line 980). But Eliot is not concerned with objective evaluation:

> It is perhaps somewhat less fair, though very tempting (as both poets are concerned with the perpetuation of love by offspring), to compare with the stanzas already quoted from Lord Herbert's Ode the following from Tennyson:

One walked between his wife and child,
With measured footfall firm and mild,
And now and then he gravely smiled.
  The prudent partner of his blood
  Leaned on him, faithful, gentle, good,
  Wearing the rose of womanhood.
And in their double love secure,
The little maiden walked demure,
Pacing with downward eyelids pure.
  These three made unity so sweet,
  My frozen heart began to beat,
  Remembering its ancient heat.   (*SE* 287)

Here Eliot has singled out the bathetic tableau near the end of "The Two Voices," placing it against the final three stanzas of Lord Herbert's "An Ode Upon a Question Moved, whether Love Should Continue Forever." The difference between the two, Eliot argues, reveals "something which had happened to the mind of England between the time of Donne or Lord Herbert of Cherbury and the time of Tennyson and Browning" (287). He presents Tennyson at his worst to make the point.

Eliot is interested in placing his poetic ancestry in the seventeenth century and in distancing himself from his more immediate forebears. He explains that "Tennyson and Browning are poets, and they think; but they do not feel their thought as immediately as the odour of a rose" (287). "We may express the difference" between the two sensibilities, Eliot expounds, "by the following theory:"

> The poets of the seventeenth century, the successors of the dramatists of the sixteenth, possessed a mechanism of sensibility which could devour any kind of experience. . . . [But in] the seventeenth century a dissociation of sensibility set in, from which we have never recovered; and this dissociation, as is natural, was aggravated by the influence of the two most powerful poets of the century, Milton and Dryden. Each of these men performed certain poetic functions so magnificently well that the magnitude of the effect concealed the absence of others. The language went on and in some respects improved. . . . But while the language became more refined, the feeling became more crude. The feeling, the sensibility, expressed in the *Country Churchyard* (to say nothing of Tennyson and Browning) is cruder than that in the *Coy Mistress.*
>
> The second effect of the influence of Milton and Dryden followed from the first, and was therefore slow in manifestation. The sentimental age began early in the eighteenth century, and continued. The poets revolted against the ratiocinative, the descriptive; they thought and felt by fits, unbalanced; they reflected. In one or two passages of Shelley's *Triumph of Life,* in the second *Hyperion,* there are traces of a struggle toward unification of sensibility. But Keats and Shelley died, and Tennyson and Browning ruminated.   (*SE* 287-88)

"Tennyson and Browning"—the phrase sounds over and over, in the manner of an incantation. Eliot is trying to exorcize his principal Victorian spooks.

In "Contemporary English Prose" (*Vanity Fair,* July 1923), Eliot goes through the same motions:

> Curiously enough, the most original talents in our literature of the greater part of that [nineteenth] century were prose talents; neither Tennyson nor even Browning—I speak with deliberation—can occupy the place of importance of Ruskin, Newman, Arnold or Dickens.   (p. 51)

"Je n'avance ceci qu'après mûre délibération," he wrote in the original French text of this review, published at the end of 1922 in the *Nouvelle Revue Française*. Indeed, *all* of his early remarks concerning Tennyson were spoken "with deliberation," as Eliot was maneuvering past the Victorian monolith.

Once past the monolith—once he was confident in the possession of his own poetic voice—he could begin to regard Tennyson with a more objective eye. This important change is reflected in Eliot's "Whitman and Tennyson," a review of a book on Walt Whitman published in the 18 December 1926 issue of *The Nation & Athenaeum*. He begins in a typical manner, ranging from *Martin Chuzzlewit,* Andrew Jackson and Carl Sandburg to *Les Fleurs du mal,* in order to achieve a more accurate "critical appreciation" (426) of Whitman's poetry in the context of its place and time. "But perhaps more important than these contrasts," Eliot continues, "is the similarity of Whitman to another master, one whose greatness he always recognized and whose eminence he always acknowledged generously—to Tennyson" (426). Eliot spends the rest of the essay developing the thesis that

> Between the ideas of the two men, or, rather, between the relations of the ideas of each [man] to his place and time, between the ways in which each held his ideas, there is a fundamental resemblance.   (p. 426)

"Both were born laureates," Eliot says:

> . . . [B]oth . . . made satisfaction almost magnificent. It is not the best aspect of their verse; if neither of them had more, neither of them would be still a great poet. But Whitman succeeds in making America as it was, just as Tennyson made England as it was, into something grand and significant. You cannot quite say that either was deceived, and you cannot at all say that either was insincere, or the victim of popular cant.

This is not at all the same as saying that "Tennyson is a very fair example of a poet almost wholly encrusted with parasitic opinion . . ." (1920). Of course, Eliot still considers Tennyson in terms that place him in an altogether different world, far from modern poetry. But one still discerns a change in tone from the earlier attitude. Acknowledging that Tennyson is "still a great poet," Eliot no longer needs to speak of him so defensively.

Apparently pleased with his unusual coupling of two poets conventionally viewed as opposites, he returns to it in a discussion of Poe some months later ("Israfel," *The Nation & Athenaeum*, 21 May 1927):

> In England the romantic cult was transformed by the enormous prestige of Tennyson; in America by Tennyson also and later by Whitman, the American Tennyson. . . . (p. 219)

This prompted one reader, a J. H. McNulty, to write a letter, published in the June 4 issue, conveying his "bewilderment" at the asserted likeness. Mr. McNulty politely inquired, "May I ask if the phrase is a slip, or a joke . . .?" (p. 302). Beneath the letter is printed Eliot's equally polite reply, referring him to "Whitman and Tennyson," and briefly summarizing that essay. He ends with a statement that comes as something of a surprise to one who is familiar with his earlier judgments on the insignificance of Tennyson's mind compared to his technical skill:

> It is, in fact, as a verse maker that he [Whitman] deserves to be remembered; for his intellect was decidedly inferior to that of Tennyson.

Eliot was slowly moving past the willful rejection of Tennyson; he was slowly moving away from the need to invoke him again and again only to confirm his irrelevance. Ten years after the Whitman review, at about the time he was beginning his final long poem, Eliot finally confronted his predecessor face to face in an introduction he wrote for a selection of Tennyson's verse. The next chapter bases its comparison of Eliot and Tennyson on this essay.

7

Time-ridden Voices

For a few days [in 1928] he pondered over whether he might compose a complex idyllic poem about Eton—"a mixture of Tennyson and T. S. Eliot."

Michael Holroyd, *Lytton Strachey: A Biography*

I do not ask to be reassured about my essays on minor Elizabethan dramatists, but am always interested to hear what other critics of poetry think, for instance, about what I have written on Tennyson. . . .

Eliot, 1961   (*TCC* 23)

My father invariably believed that humility is the only true attitude of the human soul. . . .

Hallam Tennyson, *A Memoir*

Poems of Tennyson, with an introduction by T. S. Eliot, was published in 1936 by Thomas Nelson and Sons, London, as one of the "Nelson Classics." The volume contains "Early Poems," "English Idyls and other Poems," *The Princess, In Memoriam,* and *Maud.* The Nelson company had already come out with an edition of the *Idylls* (1929), and a third volume of *Later Poems* (1936), introduced by B. Ifor Evans, completed the series.

"Tennyson," Eliot begins, "has three qualities which are hardly found together except in the greatest poets: abundance, variety, and complete competence."[1] Note the equivocal tone: are we to assume then that Tennyson is among the "greatest," or has Eliot deliberately refrained from being more straightforward in order to imply that, even with these gifts, Tennyson still falls short of the mark? One thinks of all those earlier references to Tennyson, in which praise, when it did come, was almost inevitably coupled with qualification. The old attitude died hard, but Eliot was honest enough to work towards abandoning its distortions. When he revised his introduction for inclusion in *Essays Ancient and Modern* (1936), he changed the opening to read:

> Tennyson is a great poet, for reasons that are perfectly clear. He has three qualities which are seldom found together except in the greatest poets: abundance, variety, and complete competence.[2]

That added assertion now beginning the essay acts as a startling sign that Eliot no longer had to cloud his appraisal of Tennyson with defensiveness.

For the first few pages of the introduction, Eliot seems to be having some trouble deciding upon its proper tone and direction. He focuses at once on Tennyson's technical skills, which, as we have seen, he was always ready to notice. They are all part of his confident mastery of the poet's craft: "We may not admire his aims: but whatever he sets out to do, he succeeds in doing . . ." (328). There is his "astonishing" metrical accomplishment, which shows itself in his knowledge of Latin and Greek versification, and in his extending, "much more than he has been given credit for, the range of active metrical forms in English" (ix). There is "the auditory gift: the finest sense of verbal music of any English poet since Milton" (ix). The metrical and auditory innovations of Tennyson's early poems were just as significant as the more radical changes of Blake, Wordsworth, and Coleridge. To illustrate this, Eliot quotes from the sixth stanza of "Mariana":

> All day within the dreamy house,
>   The doors upon their hinges creaked;
> The blue fly sung in the pane; the mouse
>   Behind the mouldering wainscot shriek'd,
> Or from the crevice peer'd about.

Eliot singles out "The blue fly sung in the pane" as a line which "is enough to tell us that something important has happened" (330).

Another line from this passage also had its effect. Like the sea voices of "Ulysses," the image and sound of "the mouse/Behind the mouldering wainscot" remained in Eliot's poetic consciousness, finally emerging in *Four Quartets* as an allusive symbol of empty household desolation:

> there is a time for building
> And a time for living and for generation
> And a time for the wind to break the loosened pane
> And to shake the wainscot where the field-mouse trots   (*EC* I)
>
> Dust in the air suspended
> Marks the place where a story ended.
> Dust inbreathed was a house—
> The wall, the wainscot and the mouse.   (*LG* II)

"Mariana" provides the starting point for a lengthy and unsteady digression, the whole of which Eliot cut from the revised version of his introduction. It is worth quoting at length:

> This poem, *Mariana*, exemplifies a poetic gift which has never been sufficiently recognized: that of being able to make the object real by arousing several senses at once; here the old house is not only seen, but heard, touched, and even smelt. Tennyson has been praised for the accuracy of his vision; and within limits this is just. He is not a *seer* as is Blake, or Wordsworth, or Coleridge: a seer is a man who sees through things in seeing them, and who makes people look at things at which they had never looked. Tennyson finds the right words to evoke what he has seen; but what he sees is what other people see. His was not the eye to elicit significance from insignificant detail; nor had he Wordsworth's passionate craving for intimacy for nature [sic] and the life of nature. Most of the time he looks out from a spacious library on to a lawn from which rises a noble oak tree. He varies only from the English landscape to the romantic classical landscape, from the park of Sir Walter Vivian to the slopes of Mount Ida. But he knew English landscape of other kinds and under other aspects than that of peaceful dignity: the windy moors or the stormy seashore of *Locksley Hall*. And because he is no *seer*, what he sees is an English landscape more typical than that of any other English poet. You can test this when you know Tennyson's poetry well enough: wherever you go in England, except in cities or suburbs, or among factories or slums; wherever there is unspoilt country, you will see the England of Tennyson rather than of any other poet.
>
> We may begin reading Tennyson with a few of his more popular poems: first the airy exercises in versification, then some of the English landscapes and the classical landscapes. But Tennyson is a major poet. That is, there is something more than can be got from any one poem or any selection of poems, and this something is what is worth finding. The poetry of Tennyson is a whole work; and to read it and understand it is an important part of experience. We have to read a good deal of him, and we have to read his long poems. (x-xi)

Tennyson almost sounds like a failed Imagist here, a poet who was able "to make the object real," who found "the right words to evoke what he has seen," but who could not—and this was the essential quality of Imagism—"elicit significance from insignificant detail." In this passage, Eliot moves from the faintly condescending evocation of the Tennysonian library, lawn, and noble oak tree, to the subject that takes up the body of the essay: Tennyson's long poems. Both topics—landscape in poetry, and the long poem—foreshadow the principal concerns Eliot would face in building his own long poem, *Four Quartets*. It becomes evident that in turning to Tennyson, he was turning to a poet whose work could guide him, through both positive and negative example, in composing the *Quartets*.

One can see why Eliot discarded this passage. The idea of Tennyson's failing "to elicit significance from insignificant detail" is directly contradicted by the lines from "Mariana" just quoted, lines which convey a whole world of loneliness and ennui in their precise depiction of physical detail. And the suggestion that Tennyson's conjuring skills were confined to "unspoilt country" hardly makes sense in light of Eliot's own admiring citation, later in the essay, of the great seventh lyric of *In Memoriam*: "Dark house, by which once more I stand/Here in the long unlovely street. . . ." Much of the passage, moreover, echoes the old stance of complacent superiority, which Eliot was forsaking. What the passage and its eventual excision reveal is the very process of Eliot's revaluation—his testing and refining of concepts regarding Tennyson's work. It also shows Eliot eagerly advancing upon material that applied to his own poetic endeavor, dimly apprehended in 1936 with "Burnt Norton" just about finished, awaiting its placement in a larger pattern.

Eliot classified himself as the type of literary critic "whose criticism may be said to be a by-product of his creative activity" (*TCC* 13). There is no doubt, in the essay we are considering, that when Eliot tackles the question of Tennyson's long poems, he becomes more fully engaged, dropping the tentativeness of the first few pages and writing with precision and a sure sense of what should be said. In the revised version, there are relatively few changes from this point on, compared to the major overhaul wrought on the first part.

Eliot begins by getting out of the way the long poems of Tennyson that, he believes, do not succeed. "The *Idylls of the King* do not enter into this review as they are not included in the present volume, but their merits and defects are similar to those of *The Princess*" (xii). The versification of these long poems is, as usual, "masterly," but their form does not work. Under the false guise of narratives, they are really picturesque idylls. To support the point that "for narrative Tennyson had no gift at all," Eliot resorts to a favorite comparison of his:

> For a static poem, and a moving poem, on the same subject, you have only to compare his *Ulysses* with the condensed and intensely exciting narrative of that hero in the XXVIth Canto of Dante's *Inferno*. Dante is telling a story. Tennyson is only stating an elegiac mood. The very greatest poets set before you real men talking, carry you on in real events moving. Tennyson could not tell a story at all. (331)

In focusing on "Ulysses" in this way, Eliot was actually placing himself close to his Victorian predecessor. I have already pointed out in chapter 3 how Tennyson's auditory image of the moaning sea voices was for Eliot an unforgettable representation of the seascape he knew from youth: the image is echoed in poems ranging from the original "Death by Water" to *Ash-Wednesday* and "The Dry Salvages." And Eliot's own poetry in general, at least through *The Waste Land,* could certainly be characterized as static presentations of elegiac mood rather than exciting stories. After all, the original "Death by Water," his own attempt at an ocean voyage narrative modelled on Dante's, was eventually discarded. Perhaps Eliot was aware that in describing Tennyson's limitations he was also describing his own.

"But in *Maud* and *In Memoriam,*" Eliot goes on to say, "Tennyson is doing what every conscious artist does, turning his limitations to good purpose" (332). These two works "are each a series of poems, given form by the greatest lyrical resourcefulness that a poet has ever shown" (330-31). "Lyrical resourcefulness" was also one of Eliot's gifts, although he was always more sparing with it than Tennyson. Always the "conscious artist," Eliot turned his parallel limitations to good purpose in the *Quartets,* each one of which is "a series of poems, given form" by alternating lyrical moments with a more relaxed, conversational kind of verse. Remember that as far back as 1921, Eliot had said that "no long work can maintain the same high tension throughout," and that the long poem should have "the movement toward and from intensity which is life itself"[3] (see chapter 6, p. 115).

Building up to what is for him Tennyson's most significant achievement, *In Memoriam,* Eliot explains that *Maud* also suffers from "a fundamental error of form" (332). Just as *The Princess* "is more than an idyll and less than a narrative," so *Maud* is neither fully dramatic nor fully lyrical in form (332-33). In the dramatic mode, the poet would identify himself with the lover; in the lyrical mode, the poet would identify the lover with himself. But Tennyson does neither, Eliot asserts, and consequently his "real feelings . . ., profound and tumultuous as they are, never arrive at expression" (333).

The more one listens to Eliot's strictures apparently directed at *Maud,* the more it sounds as if he is describing his own work. W. K. Wimsatt, in one of the earliest and still one of the best critical accounts of Eliot's relationship to Tennyson, has shown how *Maud,* "as a monodrama of frustration and melancholy . . . is one of the many precursors of *Prufrock* and is a minor analogue."[4] The essay, "*Prufrock* and *Maud*: from Plot to Symbol" (1952), demonstrates that "the main features of Tennyson's lyric monodrama, its themes of hesitation, removal, and frustration, its brooding melancholy, and its technique of pathological soliloquy" sound very much "like antecedents to the poetry of Eliot and especially to *Prufrock*" (201). Wimsatt also finds images in *Maud* that are "most suggestive of Eliot," and he divides these images into three groups:

(1) certain garden images of innocence and ecstasy occurring apropos of the protagonist's halcyon moments as a hopeful and then accepted lover; (2) certain confused

images of a death in life, of a dream world, and of yet another realm of death, running through the immediately succeeding darker phase of the action; (3) miscellaneous images of weariness, suspicion, and fear occurring at various points.   (201)

The setting and sound of "Birds in the high Hall-garden," Wimsatt tells us, convey "an intimation of mysterious ecstasy much like that which may be found in several passages of Eliot's poetry" (202). But he fails to point out a specific echo identifying the joy felt in the manorial garden of "Burnt Norton" with the joy in the Hall-garden:

> Birds in our wood sang
>   Ringing through the valleys,
> Maud is here, here, here
>   In among the lilies.
>
> Go, said the bird, for the leaves were full of children,
> Hidden excitedly, containing laughter.
> Go, go, go, said the bird . . .

After discussing *Maud,* Eliot devotes the rest of his introduction to Tennyson's most famous poem. He considered this the heart of the essay, for the revised essay bears the title "In Memoriam." But before examining these remarks, one must turn to another lyric in *Maud,* not mentioned at all by Eliot, which nonetheless says more about his close relation to Tennyson than any of the others: "O that 'twere possible" (II, iv). Swinburne called it a "haunting and overpowering . . . divine lament"; Tennyson himself assented to Benjamin Jowett's opinion that it contained his most touching lines.[5] Written originally in 1833-34, the lyric underwent many changes before finding its place in *Maud,* the poem which grew around it (see *Poems,* ed. Ricks, pp. 598-602, 1082*n*). I should like to quote the lyric entire, since it forms a basis for comparing aspects of Eliot and Tennyson.

I

> O that 't were possible
> After long grief and pain
> To find the arms of my true love
> Round me once again!

II

> When I was wont to meet her
> In the silent woody places
> By the home that gave me birth,

We stood tranced in long embraces
Mixt with kisses sweeter, sweeter
Than anything on earth.

III

A shadow flits before me,
Not thou, but like to thee.
Ah, Christ, that it were possible
For one short hour to see
The souls we loved, that they might tell us
What and where they be!

IV

It leads me forth at evening,
It lightly winds and steals
In a cold white robe before me,
When all my spirit reels
At the shouts, the leagues of lights,
And the roaring of the wheels.

V

Half the night I waste in sighs,
Half in dreams I sorrow after
The delight of early skies;
In a wakeful doze I sorrow
For the hand, the lips, the eyes,
For the meeting of the morrow,
The delight of happy laughter,
The delight of low replies.

VI

'T is a morning pure and sweet,
And a dewy splendor falls
On the little flower that clings
To the turrets and the walls;
'T is a morning pure and sweet,
And the light and shadow fleet.
She is walking in the meadow,
And the woodland echo rings;
In a moment we shall meet.
She is singing in the meadow,
And the rivulet at her feet
Ripples on in light and shadow
To the ballad that she sings.

VII

Do I hear her sing as of old,
My bird with the shining head,
My own dove with the tender eye?
But there rings on a sudden a passionate cry,
There is some one dying or dead,
And a sullen thunder is roll'd;
For a tumult shakes the city,
And I wake, my dream is fled.
In the shuddering dawn, behold,
Without knowledge, without pity,
By the curtains of my bed
That abiding phantom cold!

VIII

Get thee hence, nor come again,
Mix not memory with doubt,
Pass, thou deathlike type of pain,
Pass and cease to move about!
'T is the blot upon the brain
That *will* show itself without.

IX

Then I arise, the eave-drops fall,
And the yellow vapors choke
The great city sounding wide;
The day comes, a dull red ball
Wrapt in drifts of lurid smoke
On the misty river-tide.

X

Thro' the hubbub of the market
I steal, a wasted frame;
It crosses here, it crosses there,
Thro' all that crowd confused and loud,
The shadow still the same;
And on my heavy eyelids
My anguish hangs like shame.

XI

Alas for her that met me,
That heard me softly call,
Came glimmering thro' the laurels
At the quiet evenfall,
In the garden by the turrets
Of the old manorial hall!

XII

Would the happy spirit descend
From the realms of light and song,
In the chamber or the street,
As she looks among the blest,
Should I fear to greet my friend
Or to say 'Forgive the wrong,'
Or to ask her, 'Take me, sweet,
To the regions of thy rest'?

XIII

But the broad light glares and beats,
And the shadow flits and fleets
And will not let me be;
And I loathe the squares and streets,
And the faces that one meets,
Hearts with no love for me.
Always I long to creep
Into some still cavern deep,
There to weep, and weep, and weep
My whole soul out to thee.

Like Eliot's, Tennyson's poetry is dense with recollections, conscious or unconscious, of other works.[6] The rhythms and sounds of phrases were absorbed and stored in his poetic consciousness until they emerged, sooner or later, as part of a new poem. Ricks notes the resemblance of the opening lines of "O that 'twere possible" to another well-known lyric:

Westron winde, when wilt thou blow,
    The smalle raine downe can raine?
Christ if my love were in my armes,
    And I in my bed againe.

The last four lines of the third stanza are in Swinburne's view a "gentler echo to the Duchess of Malfi's exceeding bitter cry:"

O that it were possible we might
But hold some two days' conference with the dead!
From them I should learn somewhat, I am sure
I never shall know here.   (IV.ii.20-23)

Swinburne's phrase for the process seems just right: Webster's verse is "rekindled in the ear of our memory."[7] The conjured presence of the older lines, whether they be words of the Duchess or the call of the Hall-garden birds in "Burnt Norton," causes an illumination—a kind of flaring up in our minds that casts greater light and shadow over the "new" lines and makes them immeasurably richer.

In "O that 'twere possible" one finds a characteristic Tennysonian theme: the desire to somehow transcend the whole process of time and lose oneself in death-like oblivion. Eliot took up this theme as early as "Prufrock," where the word "time" tolls like the fatal angelus of "The Dry Salvages," announcing not the time for prayer but only the heavy presence of time itself. Time stretches before the speaker in "Deserts of vast eternity" littered with cups and coffee spoons.

In "Rhapsody on a Windy Night," time crawls forward in a tormenting progression of "twisted things" (*CPP* 14) cast out by memory: "Half-past one . . . Half-past two . . . Half-past three. . . ." Gerontion shrinks from the confused corridors of time that make up history; the presence of the Cumaean Sibyl, trapped in time like Tithonus, is felt throughout *The Waste Land*; *The Hollow Men* leaves us with one version of time's conclusion:

> This is the way the world ends
> This is the way the world ends
> This is the way the world ends
> Not with a bang but a whimper

" 'I would that I were dead' ": so the Sibyl's words, part of the epigraph to *The Waste Land,* are rendered in the Loeb edition of Petronius's *Satyricon,* first published in 1913.[8] The translator was remembering the words of another figure frozen in the endless time of a living death:

> the mouse
> Behind the mouldering wainscot shriek'd,
> Or from the crevice peer'd about.
> Old faces glimmer'd thro' the doors,
> Old footsteps trod the upper floors,
> Old voices called her from without.
> She only said, "My life is dreary,
> He cometh not," she said;
> She said, "I am aweary, aweary,
> I would that I were dead!"

The yearning embodied in the Sibyl's recurrent reply underlies not only "Mariana," but also "Tithonus," "Ulysses," "The Lotos-Eaters," "Tiresias," and "O that 'twere possible." Although the need to evade or overcome the terrible burden of time has occupied many poets in many ages, the way it presents itself in Eliot's poetry recalls Tennyson, and suggests an essential resemblance between the two.

As I noted before, Eliot makes no mention of "O that 'twere possible." Reverting to Harold Bloom's terms, one would say that Eliot had no choice but to ignore it, for the lyric encroaches far too much into his own poetic territory—to confront it would be to admit that he was Tennyson's successor. But Eliot did approach the lyric, albeit indirectly, several years before writing his introduction to Tennyson. In 1931, he concluded the essay "Thomas Heywood" with a telling quotation from *A Woman Killed with Kindness*. It was a passage that obviously struck him quite deeply:

> He [Heywood] would in any age have been a successful playwright; he is eminent in the pathetic, rather than the tragic. His nearest approach to those deeper emotions which shake the veil of Time is in that fine speech of Frankford which surely no man or woman past youth can read without a twinge of personal feeling:
>
> > O God! O God! that it were possible
> > To undo things done; to call back yesterday. . . .[9]

Here is Frankford's speech in full. No longer deceived, he has just been smitten by the kind of irrefragable knowledge for which there can be no forgiveness:

> O God! O God! that it were possible
> To undo things done; to call back yesterday;
> That Time could turn up his swift sandy glass,
> To untell the days, and to redeem these hours;
> Or that the Sun
> Could, rising from the west, draw his coach backward,
> Take from the account of time so many minutes,
> Till he had all these seasons call'd again,
> Those minutes and those actions done in them,
> Even from her first offence; that I might take her
> As spotless as an angel in my arms.
> But O! I talk of things impossible,
> And cast beyond the moon.[10]

Verbal parallels aside, both the longing to overturn Time and the nostalgic return to a lost world of innocence place Heywood's lines squarely with Tennyson's "O that 'twere possible." The poetry of both Tennyson and Eliot evokes the "veil of Time" and "those deeper emotions" that tear it aside, at least for a moment.

In "O that 'twere possible," after the introductory four lines (all that are needed in the way of exposition), the speaker remembers the communion achieved with his beloved:

> When I was wont to meet her
> In the silent woody places
> By the home that gave me birth,
> We stood tranced in long embraces
> Mixt with kisses sweeter, sweeter
> Than anything on earth.

It is an act of looking back, from the painful present into the past: the verbs are in the past tense, unlike those in the vision of stanza VI. "We stood tranced" suggests a preternatural state between sleeping and waking, involving an apparent suspension of time, even of consciousness. This is precisely parallel to that past moment which stamps itself so vividly on the consciousness of *The Waste Land*:

> Your arms full, and your hair wet, I could not
> Speak, and my eyes failed, I was neither
> Living nor dead, and I knew nothing,
> Looking into the heart of light, the silence.

Even in *Ash-Wednesday,* the spirit turns away from God to a lost moment that time cannot destroy: "The white sails still fly seaward, seaward flying." But neither Eliot nor Tennyson can sustain the vision of the fulfilling, timeless moment. Madame Sosostris jolts us out of the trance and back into the present world of haruspication and desperation; similarly, Tennyson's speaker, returning over and over to the meeting in the wood, cannot maintain the timeless moment. The pressure of the present brings him back: "A shadow flits before me,/Not thou. . . ."

This interplay between the grim present and the timeless moment attained through memory operates most clearly in stanzas V through VII. "Half the night I waste in sighs, . . . In a wakeful doze I sorrow. . . ." The emphasis here is on the creeping passage of time and the speaker's imprisonment in the present. But the last four lines of the fifth stanza effect a magical transition into another world; verbs disappear, as does the self, now lost in something larger:

> For the hand, the lips, the eyes,
> For the meeting of the morrow,
> The delight of happy laughter,
> The delight of low replies.

In the next stanza, we are in a world of innocence and light, where time does not exist. "She is walking . . . She is singing in the meadow" (Tennyson uses the more immediate present progressive tense, instead of the simple present). Time, however, and the suffering it brings, intervene:

> But there rings on a sudden a passionate cry,
> There is someone dying or dead,
> And a sullen thunder is roll'd;
> For a tumult shakes the city,
> And I wake, my dream is fled.

The contrast between these two states is increased by the contrast in setting: from pastoral to dismal urban landscape. It is not until this point that Tennyson identifies the speaker's actual surroundings as "the city." The initial description was ambiguous, presenting a nightmarish collage of sight and sound:

> When all my spirit reels
> At the shouts, the leagues of lights,
> And the roaring of the wheels.

These lines make manifest the disordered sensibility of the speaker, who is unable to make sense out of or in any way unify the bombardments of the present. It is a vision of hell, where nothing connects with nothing, and all are bound on the turning wheel.[11]

Tennyson's handling of urban images anticipates Eliot's cityscapes. We have already noted that the seventh lyric of *In Memoriam* affected Eliot deeply: he wrote that "it gives me the shudder that I fail to get from anything in *Maud*" (333). But there are city passages in "O that 'twere possible" that must have had their effect on Eliot. Recall what he said about Baudelaire in "What Dante Means to Me" (1950):

A great poet can give a younger poet everything that he has to give him, in a very few lines. It may be that I am indebted to Baudelaire chiefly for half a dozen lines out of the whole of *Fleurs du Mal*; and that his significance for me is summed up in the lines:

> Fourmillante Cité, cité pleine de rêves,
> Où le spectre en plein jour raccroche le passant. . . .

I knew what *that* meant, because I had lived it before I knew that I wanted to turn it into verse on my own account.   (*TCC* 126-27)

In the Tennyson lyric we are examining, amidst the swarming city full of dreams, "le spectre en plein jour raccroche" the maddened lover:

> Thro' the hubbub of the market
> I steal, a wasted frame;
> It crosses here, it crosses there,
> Thro' all that crowd confused and loud,
> The shadow still the same;

> And on my heavy eyelids
> My anguish hangs like shame.
>
> ....
>
> But the broad light glares and beats,
> And the shadow flits and fleets
> And will not let me be . . .

We are in Prufrock's realms, where "The yellow fog . . . rubs its back upon the window-panes," and "the yellow smoke . . . slides along the street":

> Then I rise, the eave-drops fall,
> And the yellow vapors choke
> The great city sounding wide;
> The day comes, a dull red ball
> Wrapt in drifts of lurid smoke
> On the misty river-tide.

The last stanza of "O that 'twere possible" is "The Love Song of J. Alfred Prufrock" in miniature. Its cadences mark off three sections:

> But the broad light glares and beats,
> And the shadow flits and fleets
> And will not let me be;

The doubled-edged implications of that last line (will not leave me alone; will not let me exist) contain the same kind of irony as "No! I am not Prince Hamlet, nor was meant to be. . . ."

> And I loathe the squares and streets
> And the faces that one meets,
> Hearts with no love for me.

Compare this to:

> And indeed there will be time
> For the yellow smoke that slides along the street . . .
> There will be time, there will be time
> To prepare a face to meet the faces that you meet;

Prufrock, in his refined self-pity, thinks of little else besides the hearts that have no love for him.

> Always I long to creep
> Into some still cavern deep,
> There to weep, and weep, and weep
> My whole soul out to thee.

Like Prufrock, Tennyson's speaker would find relief from his isolation in fantasy. Like Prufrock, he drifts to sea-chambers.

In "O that 'twere possible," time brings death, the great barrier separating the speaker from his beloved. In Heywood's lines, the great barrier is sin, again brought by time: "Those minutes and those actions done in them." This difference represents the different directions taken by Tennyson and Eliot from the same impulse: the need to transcend unredeemed time. Eliot found rest in a creed that asserted the fallen nature of man and the consequent necessity for redemption; Tennyson, especially in *In Memoriam,* worked towards a belief focusing more on the divine immortality of the soul.

"O that 'twere possible" was, as Ricks notes, "plainly precipitated by the death of Hallam" (*PT* 598), an event which plunged Tennyson into the most serious spiritual crisis of his life. Tennyson's lyric took over twenty years to reach a satisfactory final form as part of *Maud,* by which time the private source of the poem was no longer recognizable, buried deep within this strange tale of an impassioned, haunted lover. The painstaking development of the lyric reflects the struggle which, according to Eliot, "alone constitutes life for a poet—to transmute his personal and private agonies into something rich and strange, something universal and impersonal" (*SE* 137).

This rich, strange sea-change, at the heart of Eliot's poetic, describes the prolonged genesis not only of "O that 'twere possible" but also of *In Memoriam.* Tennyson began composing lyrics almost immediately after news of Hallam's death, but it would take seventeen years for these fragments to be hammered into their final shape. In the process, the poem grew from an intensely private experience into what was generally regarded as the great public poem of the nineteenth century. Eliot talked about this singular phenomenon in his essay on Tennyson:

> Apparently Tennyson's contemporaries, once they had accepted *In Memoriam,* regarded it as a message of hope and reassurance to their rather fading Christian faith. It happens now and then that a poet by some strange accident expresses the mood of his generation, at the same time that he is expressing a mood of his own which is quite remote from that of his generation.   (334).

Here Eliot is linking *In Memoriam* to his own poem, *The Waste Land,* accepted by the critics and reading public as the ultimate statement of modern futility—far from the poet's mood of religious yearning. It was much easier for Eliot's readers to respond to seduction scenes than to vague, veiled intimations of a spiritual quest; similarly, it was easier for the Victorian public to focus on the apparent resolutions and peals of affirmation, than on the darker struggle which unfolds in *In Memoriam*.

Like Tennyson's poem, *The Waste Land* had its source in private crisis: bewildering acedia, disastrous marriage, breakdown. And it too remained for years "a hoard of fragments," in Lyndall Gordon's words, as Eliot saved shards of verse for a long poem he could not well foresee.[12] *In Memoriam* grew from some despairing attempts at self-consolation to the nineteenth century's grand theodicy; *The Waste Land* started, in Eliot's words, as "a personal . . . grouse against life,"[13] but became a cultural document encompassing nothing less than all of civilization. The genesis of both works reveals a sea-change from fragmentation to somewhat problematic unity—from the private to the public sphere. Perhaps Tennyson's statement on *In Memoriam,* which is not as bald as it sounds, sums up best this aspect of the two works: "It is a very impersonal poem as well as personal."[14]

The parallel geneses of *In Memoriam* and *The Waste Land* suggest that their authors shared a common poetic strategy. The expression of the poet's emotion was central to Eliot's theory of poetry. But he insisted that this expression be indirect and, in a sense, magical: images and situations are used which are appropriate for and somehow evoke or release the right feelings. The poet's emotion "seizes the object in order to express itself"; if this correlation works, the emotion will have its life in the poem and not be dependent on the reader's knowledge of the poet's private life.[15] What is involved is no less than a process of purgation— Eliot believed that Tennyson's emotions "attained no ultimate clear purgation" (332). Whether or not one accepts this view, it can be said that both poets, reacting against excessive Romantic conceptions of the truly poetical utterance, sought modes of displacement and objectification by which they could transmute their private agonies into things rich and strange. To this end, they made use of personae, such as the mask of the old man, and they discovered variations of the mythical method, in which myth becomes a means for an impersonal ordering of the poet's feelings.[16] Tithonus, Eliot's and Tennyson's Tiresias, and the dim figure in "Gerontion" are all old men waiting. They share a peculiar vantage point that entails both insight and paralysis—both knowledge and the inability to act upon that knowledge. They are trapped in and out of time, a predicament with which both poets identified. Through the mask, they could express their feelings with impunity.

Eliot turned to Grail romance in the attempt to structure a poem that he could not fully control. In the *Idylls,* the use of Arthurian myth enabled Tennyson to manipulate "a continuous parallel between contemporaneity and antiquity," and provided "a way of controlling, of ordering, of giving a shape and a significance to the immense panorama of futility and anarchy which is contemporary history." These are Eliot's words, describing Joyce's "mythical method" in *Ulysses*.[17] Tennyson exploited both medieval and classical myth in his effort to cope with the emotions provoked by Hallam's death. "Ulysses," "Tithonus," "Tiresias," and the "Morte d'Arthur" are all products of the poet's need to attain the kind of purgation Eliot described.

Did Tennyson's use of myth have an effect on Eliot? We have already seen that he was quite blind to the scope of the *Idylls,* asserting that they were little more than a sad debasement of Malory. But of course he knew other examples of Tennyson's mythological poems. In his syllabus for "Modern English Literature" (1916), which was the basis for "a three-year Tutorial Class at Southall," the first subject is Tennyson, and the poems listed for reading are as follows: "The Lady of Shalott," "The Lotos-Eaters," "Mariana," "Morte d'Arthur," "Ulysses," "Locksley Hall," "The Two Voices," "The Palace of Art," *Maud, In Memoriam,* and *Idylls of the King.*[18]

It is interesting that he should have included "Morte d'Arthur" separately, apart from the *Idylls.* Eliot remembered well the poem's account of a "wounded King" (line 112) whose kingdom was destroyed. The king's last moments were spent at "A broken chancel with a broken cross/That stood on a dark strait of barren land" (9-10), atop "bare black cliff" and "barren chasms" (187-88). The destination of Eliot's questing consciousness in *The Waste Land* is an empty chapel among the mountains, "In the faint moonlight . . . only the wind's home," where the grass "is singing/Over the tumbled graves" and over dry bones (386-91). Sir Bedivere and his King arrive at a "ruined shrine":

> And in the moon athwart the place of tombs,
> Where lay the mighty bones of ancient men,
> . . . the sea-wind sang. . . .   (45-48)

From Eliot's "endless plains" rises a "sound high in the air/Murmur of maternal lamentation" (367-68). Arriving at the verge of land and life, Arthur and his knight hear

> A cry that shivered to the tingling stars,
> And, as it were one voice, an agony
> Of lamentation, like a wind, that shrills
> All night in a waste land. . . .   (199-202)

"It is, in my opinion, in *In Memoriam,* that Tennyson finds full expression" (333). So Eliot begins his extensive discussion of the poem he had dismissed sixteen years before as "conspicuously" lacking "the right seriousness of great literary art" (*SW* 43). As I have already noted, Eliot's subsequent remarks constitute what he considered to be the heart of the essay. They suggest that Tennyson in general, and *In Memoriam* in particular, were potent forces in the creation of *Four Quartets*. In treating his major Victorian precursor with a new objectivity, he was returning to his roots; in carefully examining *In Memoriam,* he was reviewing forms, images, and themes that he would employ in his own long poem.[19]

A few critics have glanced briefly at some of the parallels between *In Memoriam* and *Four Quartets*.[20] None of them, however, has noticed that Eliot wrote *two* essays on Tennyson that form a perfect frame around the composition of the *Quartets*. These two essays indicate Tennyson's influence and provide a sound basis for comparing the two poems. In addition to the 1936 introduction we are still studying, he delivered a broadcast for the Eastern Service of the B.B.C. called " 'The Voice of his Time': T. S. Eliot on Tennyson's 'In Memoriam.' " This was in January of 1942, about nine months before the initial publication of "Little Gidding." The broadcast was published in *The Listener,* 12 February 1942. More will be said about this talk later; right now, I want only to establish its presence as a justification for exploring the relationship between these two long poems.

It is evident that Eliot began the process of *consciously* assimilating Tennyson sometime before 1936. The aptly titled *Five-Finger Exercises,* published in the *Criterion* of January 1933, were modest practice sessions for the far more rigorous performance of the *Quartets*. "*When* will Time flow away?" the question which concludes "Lines to a Persian Cat," sums up one of the principal concerns of *Four Quartets*. The exercises gave Eliot the opportunity to work with landscape and manipulate sound, especially internal rhyming and assonance, much in the manner of the Tennysonian lyric:

> The songsters of the air repair
> To the green fields of Russell Square. (*CPP* 91)

> Yet the field was cracked and brown
> And the tree was cramped and dry. (*CPP* 91)

The opening of "Lines to a Duck in the Park" first quotes verbatim and then plays Tennysonian variations on the third line of "The splendor falls on castle walls," one of Tennyson's songs from *The Princess* (in 1936 Eliot called these songs "among the greatest of all poetry of their kind"[21]):

> The long light shakes across the lake,
> The forces of the morning quake,
> The dawn is slant across the lawn . . . (*CPP* 92)

Eliot then echoes a line from "The Holy Grail"[22]:

> Here is no eft or mortal snake
> But only sluggish duck and drake.

In the wilderness, Sir Percivale's bedmates were the "eft and snake" (569).

In his 1936 discussion of *In Memoriam,* Eliot turns first, as he always did with Tennyson, to what the latter accomplished as craftsman:

> Its technical merit alone is enough to ensure its perpetuity. While Tennyson's technical competence is everywhere masterly and satisfying, *In Memoriam* is the most unapproachable of all his poems. Here are one hundred and thirty-two passages, each of several quatrains in the same form, and never monotony or repetition. (333)

"Unapproachable" seems a double-edged word to use for praise. The technical accomplishment cannot be approached, it says, let alone surpassed—but the word also connotes forbidding inaccessibility. Indeed, in that version of the essay printed in *Essays Ancient and Modern,* "most unapproachable" has been changed to "less unapproachable" (p. 182): someone, perhaps the printer, must have been confused about the gist of the term. (It was changed back to "most" in *Selected Essays,* 1950.) The word well symbolizes the awful obstacle Tennyson posed for poets of Eliot's generation, at the time they were endeavoring to establish themselves—or rather, the obstacle he *would* have posed, had he been taken seriously. For a poet who was as conscious as Eliot was about the importance of "this contrast between fixity and flux, this unperceived evasion of monotony, which is the very life of verse" (1917: "Reflections on *Vers Libre,*" *TCC* 185), what could *In Memoriam* be (in 1917) besides a massive monument to that young poet's own inadequacy? His only choice was to ignore it, or misread and dismiss it, which is what Eliot had done.

But now he was coming back to the poem, and one of the things that fascinated him most was its form, which fuses one hundred and thirty-three parts into an undiluted whole:

> We may not memorize a few passages, we cannot find a 'fair sample'; we have to comprehend the whole of a poem which is essentially the length that it is. . . . It is unique: it is a long poem made by putting together lyrics, which have only the unity and continuity of a diary, the concentrated diary of a man confessing himself. It is a diary of which we have to read every word. (333-34)

Thus for once Tennyson avoids having to impose the confining continuity of narrative, which was a form, Eliot believed, he could not handle. Instead, he employs a collage-like structuring not dissimilar to Eliot's method: an assembly of diverse fragments is ordered according to what Eliot called in the 1942 talk "a logic of the emotions."[23] *Four Quartets* is organized along the same principle, and it too resembles, more and more as one moves through it, "the concentrated diary of a man confessing himself." Eliot, like Tennyson, takes account of his life, his time, and his craft:

> So here I am, in the middle way, having had twenty years—
> Twenty years largely wasted, the years of *l'entre deux guerres*
> Trying to learn to use words. . . . (*EC* V)

Eliot proceeds to place *In Memoriam* in the context of the age in which it was written, a characteristic procedure of his criticism. The Victorians accepted Tennyson's poem "as a message of hope and reassurance to their rather fading Christian faith"; indeed, Tennyson himself, "on the conscious level" of statements recorded in the *Memoir,* "consistently asserted a convinced, if somewhat sketchy, Christian belief" (334). But Eliot sees in *In Memoriam* a much darker, profoundly religious struggle with doubt and despair, far more religious than the quality of the poem's proclaimed faith. He was finally willing to acknowledge here that Tennyson had given masterful expression to one of the principal subjects of his own poetry. "Below the level of consciousness" (334), "a good way below the surface" (336) are the intensely expressed feelings of "a much more interesting and tragic Tennyson" (334), who could not quite convince himself about the validity of the "compromise between the religious attitude and, what is quite a different thing, the belief in human perfectibility" (336). "Temperamentally," Eliot writes, "he was opposed to the doctrine that he was moved to accept and to praise" (336).

Eliot is careful to spell out and illustrate this doctrine of "the Victorian compromise," a phrase coined by P. E. More and popularized by Chesterton.[24] He believes that much of *In Memoriam* falls victim to it:

> His [Tennyson's] desire for immortality never is quite the desire for Eternal Life; his concern is for the loss of man rather than for the gain of God. . . . The hope of immortality is confused (typically of the period) with the hope of the gradual and steady improvement of this world . . . the faith of Tennyson's age in human progress would have been quite as strong even had the discoveries of Darwin been postponed by fifty years. And after all there is no logical connexion: the belief in progress being current already, the discoveries of Darwin were harnessed to it: [Here he quotes the final three stanzas of *In Memoriam*.] (334-35)

This "belief in human perfectibility" not only denies the discontinuity separating man from God, which was an essential aspect of Eliot's belief, but also becomes time's thrall: it places all its faith in the process of time, and consequently denies, or rather shirks the notion and implications of Eternity. Once again we see Eliot rehearsing concerns in this essay that would find their way into *Four Quartets*. In "The Dry Salvages" II, the poet explores a slowly realized new pattern of the past involving the moments of "sudden illumination"—the intimations of eternity. With this understanding, the past "ceases to be a mere sequence—"

> Or even development: the latter a partial fallacy
> Encouraged by superficial notions of evolution,
> Which becomes, in the popular mind, a means of disowning the past.

These "superficial notions of evolution" lead not only to Tennyson's terrifying vision of "Nature, red in tooth and claw," but also to what Eliot considered far more serious: the self-deceiving consolation found in the creed of inevitable progress, which is indeed a means of disowning the past.

The world of time, that which lies outside it, and that which connects the two, are all part of the meanings of both *In Memoriam* and *Four Quartets*. Hallam's death precipitates a consciousness in Tennyson's mind of the obliterating changes wrought by time. Will not the bleak progression of years overwhelm all traces even of the poet's love for his friend?

> But I should turn mine ears and hear
>
> The moanings of the homeless sea,
>   The sound of streams that swift or slow
>   Draw down Aeonian hills, and sow
> The dust of continents to be;
>
> And Love would answer with a sigh,
>   "The sound of that forgetful shore
>   Will change my sweetness more and more,
> Half-dead to know that I shall die."[25]

In his black moods, when "the nerves prick/And tingle; and the heart is sick," Tennyson envisons "Time, a maniac scattering dust" (50). He sees "Within the green the mouldered tree,/And towers fallen as soon as built" (26), much like Eliot's vision in the first part of "East Coker," where "Houses rise and fall, crumble" into dust. Foreshortening time, Tennyson and Eliot see only cycles of destructive change: "The houses are all gone under the sea" (*EC* II); "There where the long street roars hath been/The stillness of the central sea" (*IM* 123). Within the endless tract of "the waste sad time/Stretching before and after" (*BN* V), the rhythms of life lead both poets to the reality of "Dung and death" (*EC* I), which is the terminus for everyone—for him who "binds the sheaf,/Or builds the house, or digs the grave," and for "those wild eyes that watch the wave/In roarings round the coral reef" (*IM* 36).

In both *In Memoriam* and *Four Quartets,* the sea becomes a symbol for the endless, incalculable time reaching past history into mystery. "The moanings of the homeless sea" (*IM* 35), which evoke in Tennyson's mind countless aeons, recall the auditory image in "Ulysses": "the deep/Moans round with many voices." "The sea has many voices," Eliot writes in the first part of "The Dry Salvages," "Many gods and many voices." To both poets, the voices of the sea speak of a "time not our time":

> . . . a time
> Older than the time of chronometers, older
> Than time counted by anxious worried women
> Lying awake . . .   (*DS* I)

Tennyson describes an anxious mother "praying God will save/Thy sailor,—"

> . . . while thy head is bowed,
> His heavy-shotted hammock-shroud
> Drops in his vast and wandering grave.   (6)

He imagines Hallam's hands "fathom-deep in brine," tossing "with tangle and with shells" (10). The ground swell, the sea as an image of death, "is all about us;"

> It tosses up our losses, the torn seine,
> The shattered lobsterpot, the broken oar
> And the gear of foreign dead men.   (*DS* I)

But death, of course, has no single dominion; it saturates the land as well. Earth, death, and time are fused by Tennyson in the superb second lyric:

> Old Yew, which graspest at the stones
>   That name the under-lying dead,
>   Thy fibres net the dreamless head,
> Thy roots are wrapt about the bones.
>
> The seasons bring the flower again,
>   And bring the firstling to the flock;
>   And in the dusk of thee, the clock
> Beats out the little lives of men.

Eliot remembers these grasping roots of yew in the fourth part of "Burnt Norton," echoing also an image from Tennyson's poem of impending decay, "A spirit haunts the year's last hours" ("Heavily hangs the broad sunflower/Over its grave i' the earth so chilly"):

> Will the sunflower turn to us, will the clematis
> Stray down, bend to us; tendril and spray
> Clutch and cling?
>
> Chill
> Fingers of yew be curled
> Down on us?

Towards the end of his essay, Eliot has this to say:

> Tennyson lived in a time which was already acutely time-conscious: a great many things seemed to be happening, railways were being built, discoveries were being made, the face of the world was changing. That was a time busy in keeping up to date. It had, for the most part, no hold on permanent things, on permanent truths about man and God and life and death. (337)

A "time-conscious" time, "busy in keeping up to date": Eliot is describing the time-obsessed world he depicts in *Four Quartets,* a world of horoscopes and psychoanalysis, where "Men's curiosity searches past and future/And clings to that dimension" (*DS* V). The Victorian railways are now the London underground, but there are still

> . . . the strained time-ridden faces
> Distracted from distraction by distraction
> Filled with fancies and empty of meaning. . . .

The world still moves

> In appetency, on its metalled ways
> Of time past and time future. (*DS* III)

Here, there is no hold on "permanent truths":

> Or as, when an underground train, in the tube, stops too long between stations
> And the conversation rises and slowly fades into silence
> And you see behind every face the mental emptiness deepen
> Leaving only the growing terror of nothing to think about. . . . (*EC* III)

For both Tennyson and Eliot, the way of transcending this time-ridden world lies in time, in moments of mystical awareness. This mysticism is the first characteristic Eliot singles out of that "very much more interesting" Tennyson whom he found in *In Memoriam*:

> His biographers have not failed to remark that he had a good deal of the temperament of the mystic—certainly not at all the mind of the theologian. He was desperately anxious to hold the faith of the believer, without being very clear about what he wanted to believe: he was capable of illumination which he was incapable of understanding. (334)

Eliot himself "had a good deal of the temperament of the mystic"; indeed, much of *Four Quartets* is based on the mystical writings of St. John of the Cross, Dame Juliana of Norwich, and the anonymous author of *The Cloud of Unknowing*. He was also "capable of illumination" which could only be partially understood:

> For most of us, there is only the unattended
> Moment, the moment in and out of time,
> The distraction fit, lost in a shaft of sunlight,
> The wild thyme unseen, or the winter lightning
> Or the waterfall, or music heard so deeply
> That it is not heard at all, but you are the music
> While the music lasts. These are only hints and guesses,
> Hints followed by guesses. . . .   (*DS* V)

These timeless moments of grace, when the white lotos blooms through the "heart of light" (*BN* I) and time itself becomes the illusion, remain accessible only through memory:

> But only in time can the moment in the rose-garden,
> The moment in the arbour where the rain beat,
> The moment in the draughty church at smokefall
> Be remembered; involved with past and future.
> Only through time time is conquered.   (*BN* II)

In *In Memoriam* also, "Only through time time is conquered." For a while, memory is only the poet's anodyne, as he clutches shadowy images of his dead friend:

> Sleep, kinsman thou to death and trance
>   And madness, thou hast forged at last
>   A night-long Present of the Past
> In which we went through summer France.
>
> Hadst thou such credit with the soul?
>   Then bring an opiate trebly strong,
>   Drug down the blindfold sense of wrong
> That so my pleasure may be whole. . . .   (71)

But there finally comes the "moment in and out of time" when, in Douglas Bush's words, "the poet feels the immediate presence of his dead friend and through the power of love has a glimpse of a reality behind the flux."[26] The moment comes through the effects of memory, as Tennyson reads through Hallam's letters ("those fallen leaves which kept their green") in the still night:

> So word by word, and line by line,
>   The dead man touched me from the past,
>   And all at once it seemed at last
> The living soul was flashed on mine,
>
> And mine in this was wound, and whirled
>   About empyreal heights of thought,
>   And came on that which is, and caught
> The deep pulsations of the world,
>
> Aeonian music measuring out
>   The steps of Time—the shocks of Chance—
>   The blows of Death. At length my trance
> Was cancelled, stricken through with doubt.   (95)

We have seen the word "trance" before: it appears at the timeless moment of union in "O that 'twere possible." In the ninety-fifth lyric of *In Memoriam,* the poet is once more in touch with "those deeper emotions which shake the veil of Time." At length the trance is "cancelled, stricken through with doubt." Tennyson, like Eliot, knew that "human kind/Cannot bear very much reality" (*BN* I).

Of course, the two poets do not interpret these moments in precisely the same way. Eliot connects them with the Logos:

> The hint half guessed, the gift half understood, is Incarnation.
> Here the impossible union
> Of spheres of existence is actual,
> Here the past and future
> Are conquered, and reconciled. . . .   (*DS* V)

Tennyson's moment enables him to apprehend a less specified Reality that somehow makes Time, Chance, and Death harmonious parts of a larger whole. But both poets are aware that the very process of rational "interpretation" can be, at best, only partially successful. Tennyson finds it difficult "to frame/In matter-moulded forms of speech . . . that which I became" (95). Eliot acknowledges that "We had the experience but missed the meaning," and all that can be done is to make an "approach to the meaning" (*DS* II) through the inadequate medium of words.

This parallel consideration of words points to yet another resemblance between *In Memoriam* and *Four Quartets,* for both poems are about the poetic craft itself. E. D. H. Johnson has demonstrated how Tennyson's elegy involves "the search for an aesthetic creed," as the poet works through progressive conceptions of poetry.[27] What he finally achieves is, in J. C. C. Mays's words, "confidence in [artistic] form, and . . . ability to sustain it by faith."[28] At first, Tennyson struggles between the need for self-expression and the realization that the very nature of poetic form imposes restrictions upon expression:

> I sometimes hold it half a sin
>   To put in words the grief I feel;
>   For words, like Nature, half reveal
> And half conceal the Soul within.
> . . . .
> In words, like weeds, I'll wrap me o'er,
>   Like coarsest clothes against the cold:
>   But that large grief which these enfold
> Is given in outline and no more.   (5)

Words are like coarsest clothes, or like "shabby equipment always deteriorating/In the general mess of imprecision of feeling" (*EC* V). In "Burnt Norton" and "East Coker," the first half of Part V shows dissatisfaction with the poet's raw material.

Every attempt "to learn to use words" is "a different kind of failure"; the poet's "raid on the inarticulate" too easily turns into a rout of "Undisciplined squads of emotion" (*EC* V). Still, words are all that a poet has. As Tennyson employs them and realizes their power, and as *In Memoriam* gains direction and a sense of the poet's purpose, he attains stability of mind, revitalized faith, and a renewed confidence in his art. Similarly, the fifth section of "Little Gidding" turns not on the thought of decaying words but on language that is thoroughly "right": "The complete consort dancing together." For Eliot, the use of words—the songs, the verbal explorations, the tentative formulations of each poem—remains the only way to approach the meaning or recapture, however feebly, the moments of "sudden illumination":

> And approach to the meaning restores the experience
> In a different form, beyond any meaning
> We can assign to happiness. (*DS* II)

Words and memory can combine to restore the experience in the rose-garden, that "different form" being poetic form. And Eliot's confidence in words is never stronger than in the splendid, symphonic close of "Little Gidding," where the "complete consort" of words does indeed restore, with remarkable economy, the experience of the whole of *Four Quartets*.

In the original version of the essay, Eliot ended his treatment of *In Memoriam* with the following note of reservation:

> I believe that *In Memoriam* is a poem which every one should experience, live through, and pass beyond with gratitude to the author.   (xviii)

To "pass beyond" the poem means, I suppose, to approach the kind of religious conviction that Eliot found lacking in Tennyson. "He did not go far enough," Eliot seems to be saying; "we must pick up where he left off." Revising the essay, however, he dropped the above sentence and added these words:

> Tennyson seems to have reached the end of his spiritual development with *In Memoriam*; there follows no reconciliation, no resolution. . . . And having turned aside from the journey through the dark night, to become the surface flatterer of his own time, he has been rewarded with the despite of an age that succeeds his own in shallowness.   (337-38)

Once again, Eliot is linking *In Memoriam* (as he understood it) to his own long poem, which describes "the journey through the dark night" leading to God:

> Descend lower, descend only
> Into the world of perpetual solitude,
> World not world, but that which is not world,
> Internal darkness, deprivation
> And destitution of all property,
> Desiccation of the world of sense,
> Evacuation of the world of fancy,
> Inoperancy of the world of spirit;
> This is the one way, and the other
> Is the same. . . .   (*BN* III)

Confronting "Internal darkness, deprivation," "perpetual solitude," "Inoperancy of the world of spirit," Tennyson moves through the blackness towards what he names in the Epilogue as "That God, which ever lives and loves," towards the final affirmation:

> And all is well, though faith and form
> Be sundered in the night of fear . . .   (127)

Past the dark "night of fear," Eliot concludes:

> And all shall be well and
> All manner of thing shall be well.   (*LG* V)

Both poets base their apprehension of God not on human reason but on "deeper emotions":

> If e'er when faith had fallen asleep,
> I heard a voice 'believe no more'
> And heard an ever-breaking shore
> That tumbled in the Godless deep;
>
> A warmth within the breast would melt
> The freezing reason's colder part,
> And like a man in wrath the heart
> Stood up and answered 'I have felt.'

In the draughty church, in the rose-garden, Eliot also *feels* the presence of Eternity. *In Memoriam* and *Four Quartets* both pierce "the cloud of unknowing" that lies between man and God—not with the intellect, but with the poet's intuition and the evidence of what he has felt.

Sometime during the latter part of 1941, Herbert Read approached Eliot with the idea of his contributing to a series Read was organizing for the Eastern Service of the B.B.C. called "Masterpieces of English Literature." The whole series, which would be broadcast once a week from October 1941 through February 1942, was based on the books prescribed for the B.A. and M.A. examinations of the Universities of Calcutta, Lahore, Madras and Bombay. Contributors included Stephen Spendor on *Adonais* and E. M. Forster on *The Return of the Native*. Eliot agreed to do two talks. The first, broadcast on 25 November 1941 and published in the December 18 *Listener,* dealt with *The Duchess of Malfi*; the second, called " 'The Voice of His Time,' " broadcast on 20 January 1942 and also published in the *Listener* (12 February), was on *In Memoriam*.[29]

Four Quartets was not far from completion at this time. "The Dry Salvages" had been published in September of 1941, and "Little Gidding" would appear in October 1942. The latter was Eliot's final major poem. After its publication, his literary career would continue in the roles of dramatist and critic. 1942 was a fitting time, then, to confront once more his formidable Victorian predecessor, whose great elegy was in so many ways the nineteenth-century counterpart to his own culminating *Quartets*.

The tone of Eliot's talk is far from the cautious, qualified praise of the 1936 essay. It is expansive, warmly respectful, and even humble:

> My point is that he felt and expressed, before it had come to other men, what was to be the emotional attitude towards evolution of his and the next generation. It is an attitude of vague hopefulness which I believe to be mistaken. But that does not matter: what matters is that Tennyson felt it and gave it expression.   (212)

This is not at all the Eliot who in 1936 had spent quite a few words analyzing the inadequacies of Tennyson's and the Victorians' "attitude of vague hopefulness." He speaks of Tennyson almost as if he were presenting a rather unpopular companion whom he has known well and long, and whose friendship he is now eager to acknowledge:

> I want to put before you Tennyson as I see him, without his trappings of success: a much more sympathetic character. There are several other aspects of Tennyson than that of the Bard of Queen Victoria. One appears in the later poems which he wrote in his native Lincolnshire dialect: the shaggy farmer, fond of his pipe and his glass of port, convivial and not without a shrewd and biting humour. There is the really great classical scholar, with a strong affinity, not to the Greek, but to the Latin poets: for this side of him you should read the two beautiful poems to Virgil and to Catullus, among his later work. There is the craftsman who had the finest ear for verse, in my opinion, of any English poet since Milton. And there is the aspect of him which I wish to present in these few minutes: the poet of melancholia, passion, and despair.   (211)

It is true that the nature of Eliot's address was different from that of the 1936 essay: he was talking informally to an invisible audience of students in India, rather than writing a long, scrupulous letter of introduction to be read by the literate reading public in England. (" 'The Voice of His Time' " was never heard in England: when the possibility of rebroadcasting Read's series of talks on the British Home Service was discussed, it was decided that they were intended "for a serious audience of students and not for our middle-brow audience."[30]) Still, Eliot knew that his talk would probably be printed, since the right to publish in *The Listener* was included in the broadcasting contract. It appears that the circumstances of the talk were just right for Eliot to make his pact with Tennyson; he could settle back without the self-consciousness of the literary pundit, which too often restricted his criticism "to What Precisely/And If and Perhaps and But."[31] The words of Ezra Pound's "A Pact," his reconciliation with Walt Whitman, are most appropriate here:

> I am old enough now to make friends.
> ....
> We have one sap and one root—
> Let there be commerce between us.[32]

Conscious or unconscious commerce between Eliot and Tennyson, as I have been trying to show, was hardly a new phenomenon in 1942—but the pact *was* new.

Eliot's 1942 account of *In Memoriam* suggests more strongly than ever before its close relation to *Four Quartets*; he comes very close to describing his own poem:

> Tennyson took a long time over the poem: perhaps there were superfluous passages, or stretches below his sustained level—if so, he eliminated and improved. The structure is designed with great care. Each section (some are very short and some longer) is a complete poem in itself—that is to say, represents a particular mood realised in its appropriate imagery: but the moods represented by the sections follow according to a logic of the emotions to form a continuous meditation on life and death.   (212)

This is certainly more considered than what he had to say about the poem's structure six years before (the lyrics "have only the unity and continuity of a diary, the concentrated diary of a man confessing himself" [*SE* 333-34]). During the years of creative effort that led to *Four Quartets*, the methods and materials of *In Memoriam* were alive in Eliot's mind. By 1942 he understood that the structure of *In Memoriam* is indeed "designed with great care," employing the same kind of "logic of the emotions" that ordered the parts of his own "continuous meditation on life and death."

Eliot proceeds to illustrate the poem's formal coherence by rehearsing many of the highlights that hold it together, all having to do with the recollection of Hallam: Tennyson's return to his friend's house (7); thoughts of the ship bringing back Hallam's body (9); the image of Hallam's burial site by the river Severn (19); remembering the Cambridge years (22); the first Christmas lyrics (28 ff.); thoughts of Tennyson's sister, Hallam's betrothed (85); actual return to Cambridge (87 ff.); Tennyson addressing his brother, who was journeying to Vienna, place of Hallam's death (98); birth of the New Year, with Hallam's birthday coming soon after (106-7); and the final lyrics which, in Eliot's eyes, represented the poet's failing attempt to be reconciled to the loss of his friend. Eliot also notes the seasonal cycle of *In Memoriam*, quoting from one of the early autumn lyrics (15), and observing, "Every season and every place brings another aspect of grief" (212). One of the basic structural components of *Four Quartets* is, of course, its pattern of seasons and places.

The pattern of season and place enabled Tennyson to vary and organically develop the moods and ideas of his poem. Recurring Christmases, recurring springs (mixing memory and desire: "Is it, then, regret for buried time/That keenlier in sweet April wakes . . .?" [116]), the poet's returns to places where he had been with Hallam—all these things form part of a spiralling movement upwards in which old landscapes, of scene or mind, are revisited with progressively renewed perception. It is really a kind of musical organization, the kind that Eliot used in *Four Quartets*. A month after the *In Memoriam* broadcast, in his lecture on "The Music of Poetry," he articulated the analogy which *In Memoriam* had helped him to see:

> But I believe that the properties in which music concerns the poet most nearly, are the sense of rhythm and the sense of structure. . . . The use of recurrent themes is as natural to poetry as to music. There are possibilities for verse which bear some analogy to the development of a theme by different groups of instruments; there are possibilities of transitions in a poem comparable to the different movements of a symphony or a quartet; there are possibilities of contrapuntal arrangement of subject-matter.[33]

The "contrapuntal arrangement of subject-matter" in *In Memoriam* provided Eliot with an important model for the building of long poems. Beginning the conclusion of his talk, Eliot said:

> Those who nowadays wish to praise Tennyson as a poet often praise him as a great master of language, of imagery and of music, a poet who should never have meddled with deeper matters, with philosophical or religious ideas. (212)

Here he is describing the earlier Eliot, who spoke so highly of Tennyson's technical competence while always finding fault with his conceptions of "man and God and life and death" (*SE* 337). Here he is describing the Eliot who once smiled over Tennyson's "large dull brain like a farmhouse clock" and associated his poetry with bovine rumination. Now, however, after years of re-evaluation inspired by his own closely related poetic endeavor, Eliot had gained a new perspective on Tennyson's work, especially on *In Memoriam*. Coming to terms with the influence of time past, he was able to make his pact, not only with Tennyson but with all the Victorians. The conclusion continues:

> I cannot agree, for I think this his greatest and most moving poem. It is usual to consider Matthew Arnold as the great spokesman in poetry of the religious uncertainties of the nineteenth century, and of their partial and temporary resolution. I do not mean to abate Arnold's significance, when I say that I think that 'In Memoriam' is not only a greater technical achievement than any of Arnold's poems, but a more complex and comprehensive expression of an historic phase of thought and feeling, of the grandeur and the tragedy of the Victorian age. (212)

"Little Gidding" was published about eight months after " 'The Voice of His Time.' " In part II of the poem there appears what Eliot called "a hallucinated scene after an air-raid" (*TCC* 128). "In the uncertain hour before the morning," smoke still rising from the ruins, the speaker encounters the "familiar compound ghost" of "some dead master. . . Both intimate and unidentifiable."

Eliot modelled the passage on Canto XV of the *Inferno,* in which Dante, led by Virgil, is amazed to meet his old mentor, the great Florentine Brunetto Latini, amidst a troop of lost souls. The ghost evokes many of Eliot's literary forebears: not only Dante, but Virgil, Mallarmé, Yeats, and others. Derek Traversi has characterized the scene as "an intimate self-confrontation":

> What the poet meets in his great predecessors is, in a very real sense, nothing other than *himself.* . . . The great writers who are remembered in the course of the passage are there in so far as they have been incorporated into his own work, and become accordingly a part of himself. What we are witnessing here is the recreation of an effort at self-assessment, an attempt both to look back upon and to evaluate the results of a life-time dedicated to the writing of poetry. . . .[34]

The passage is among the most moving that Eliot ever wrote. In an unearthly world seared by the fires of destruction, the poet listens to his strange, embittered companion recite the withering torments of old age. There are "the cold friction of expiring sense," "the conscious impotence of rage/At human folly," "And last, the rending pain of re-enactment/Of all that you have done, and been. . . ." Stephen Spender has pointed out that Matthew Arnold made a similar "report on old age" in "Growing Old."[35] "What is it to grow old?" Arnold asks:

> Is it to feel our strength—
> Not our bloom only, but our strength—decay?
> Is it to feel each limb
> Grow stiffer, every function less exact,
> Each nerve more loosely strung?
> . . . .
> It is to suffer this,
> And feel but half, and feebly, what we feel.
> . . . .
> It is—last stage of all—
> When we are frozen up within, and quite
> The phantom of ourselves,
> To hear the world applaud the hollow ghost
> Which blamed the living man.

Arnold, the mournful poet turned eminent public man, who in Spender's words "haunted Eliot throughout his life," is certainly one of the figures in the composite spirit. The ghost declares with quiet scorn that for restless spirits like himself, "passage" from infernal fires into the streets of London now "presents no hindrance," for it is a passage "Between two worlds become much like each other.'' Arnold's enduring line from ''Stanzas from the Grande Chartreuse'' echoes thus, in our minds, stirring a wealth of associations that, as Eliot explained in 1942, was part of ''the music of poetry.''[36] In 1941, he wrote:

> . . . a poet who has treated problems of his time will not necessarily go out of date. Arnold's *Stanzas from the Grande Chartreuse* voice a moment of historic doubt, recorded by its most representative mind, a moment which has passed, which most of us have gone beyond in one direction or another; but it represents that moment forever.[37]

Arnold's timeless moment of doubt, suspended ''between faith and disbelief''[38] and representing one stage of Eliot's quest (see chapter 2), takes its place in the poet's dawn colloquy.

The ghost finishes his disclosure:

> The day was breaking. In the disfigured street
> He left me, with a kind of valediction,
> And faded on the blowing of the horn.

These concluding lines present a remarkable confluence of allusions. ''And faded on the blowing of the horn,'' which is the air-raid siren signalling the All Clear, refers us to another supernatural scene that takes place ''In the uncertain hour before the morning,'' this time at a sentry-post of Elsinore Castle, Denmark:

> *Bernardo*
> It was about to speak when the cock crew.
>
> *Horatio*
> And then it started, like a guilty thing
> Upon a fearful summons. I have heard
> The cock, that is the trumpet to the morn,
> Doth with his lofty and shrill-sounding throat
> Awake the god of day, and at his warning,
> Whether in sea or fire, in earth or air,
> Th' extravagant and erring spirit hies
> To his confine; and of the truth herein
> This present object made probation.
>
> *Marcellus*
> It faded on the crowing of the cock.   (I.i.147-57)

The breaking day and ''the disfigured street'' of ''Little Gidding'' recall the stark close of Tennyson's seventh lyric of *In Memoriam,* lines that Eliot loved and praised in his 1942 talk as ''giv[ing] expression once for all'' to ''an experience which comes to everyone, sooner or later . . .'':

> Dark house, by which once more I stand
>   Here in the long unlovely street,
>   Doors, where my heart was used to beat
> So quickly, waiting for a hand,
>
> A hand that can be clasped no more—
>   Behold me, for I cannot sleep,
>   And like a guilty thing I creep
> At earliest morning to the door.
>
> He is not here; but far away
>   The noise of life begins again,
>   And ghastly through the drizzling rain
> On the bald street breaks the blank day.

Once again we are at "the uncertain hour." But here there is no accompanying spirit, although the poet yearns for Hallam's. Grief and despair have made Tennyson himself the ghost: he creeps "like a guilty thing," which is Horatio's phrase for the ghost of Hamlet's father. The universal experience of loss and consequent desolation, supremely expressed by Tennyson not only in this lyric but elsewhere in his work, is something that Eliot wanted to convey in the "Little Gidding" dialogue with his disenchanted master.

In the "brown baked features" of the ghost, does Eliot recognize the eyes of Tennyson? Listen to how he concludes his 1936 essay on *In Memoriam*:

> By looking innocently at the surface [of Tennyson] we are most likely to come to the depths, to the abyss of sorrow. Tennyson is not only a minor Virgil, he is also with Virgil as Dante saw him, a Virgil among the Shades, the saddest of all English poets, among the Great in Limbo, the most instinctive rebel against the society in which he was the most perfect conformist. (*SE* 337)

The gloomy, "exasperated" ghost of "Little Gidding" does include Tennyson, whom Eliot "had known, forgotten, half recalled" throughout his poetic career. Among the Great in Limbo, Eliot's Victorian master wanders into "streets I never thought I should revisit," streets he had crept through over a hundred years before, mourning his dead friend. In "Little Gidding," the saddest of all English poets is greeted by one of his descendants. "Too strange to each other for misunderstanding," the two poets walk together.

Appendix

Eliot's Courses at Harvard, 1906-1910

1906-1907   Elementary German
English Literature: Dean Briggs
Government I (Constitutional Government)
Greek Literature
Medieval History

1907-1908   French 2a
German Prose and Poetry
Greek Literature
Greek Prose Composition
History of Ancient Art
History of Ancient Philosophy

1908-1909   Comparative Literature 6a: "The Literary History of England and its Relations to that of the Continent from the Beginning to Chaucer"
Comparative Literature 6b: ". . . from Chaucer to Elizabeth"
English 12 (Composition): Charles T. Copeland
History of Modern Philosophy: George Santayana
The Roman Novel: Clifford H. Moore
Survey of Latin Poetry
Tendencies of European Literature of the Renaissance: M. A. Potter

In the spring of 1909, Eliot took his A.B. The next year he studied for an M.A.

1909-1910   Comparative Literature 18: "Studies in the History of Allegory": William Allan Neilson
Drama in England from the Miracle Plays to the Closing of the Theatres: George Pierce Baker
English 1: Chaucer: Nielson and Robinson
English 24: Poets of the Romantic Period: Nielson
French 17: Literary Criticism in France with special Reference to the Nineteenth Century: Irving Babbitt
Philosophy 10: "The Philosophy of History: Ideals of Society, Religion, Art and Science in their Historical Development": George Santayana

This list is based on the information Herbert Howarth has collected in *Notes on Some Figures Behind T. S. Eliot.*

Notes

Preface

1. Ronald Schuchard, "T. S. Eliot as an Extension Lecturer, 1916-1919," *Review of English Studies,* 25 (August 1974), 303-4.

2. Cited by R. E. Lobb in his 1974 Princeton University diss., *T. S. Eliot and the English Critical Tradition,* p. 54.

3. W. Jackson Bate, *The Burden of the Past and the English Poet* (New York: Norton, 1972), p. 21.

4. T. S. Eliot, "Israfel," *Nation & Athenaeum,* 41 (21 May 1927), 219.

Chapter 1

1. See Herbert Howarth, *Notes on Some Figures Behind T. S. Eliot* (Boston: Houghton Mifflin, 1964), pp. 27-28.

2. Ibid., p. 28. See also Bernard Bergonzi, *T. S. Eliot* (New York: Collier, 1972), p. 4.

3. "The Devotional Poets of the Seventeenth Century: Donne, Herbert, Crashaw," *Listener,* III.63 (26 March 1930), p. 552. This is one of a series of six talks Eliot gave, surveying English poetry from Donne to Dryden. They are recorded in March and April issues of *The Listener* (see Gallup, p. 224, for details). The talks coincide, in terms of time and subject matter, with *Ash-Wednesday,* and provide an interesting gloss on that poem.

4. Howarth, p. 30.

5. The scrapbook is filed in Box I, envelope 10 of the Eliot Family Papers, Houghton Library. The following remarks on Charlotte Eliot's poetry are based on poems in this scrapbook.

6. See Howarth, *Notes,* pp. 22-35, and Lyndall Gordon, *Eliot's Early Years* (New York: Oxford University Press, 1977), pp. 2-6 et passim.

7. "Force and God," *The Unitarian,* August 1887. Scrapbook, Eliot Collection, Houghton Library.

8. "The Present Hour," Scrapbook, Houghton Library.

9. "Charade of the Seasons," Scrapbook, Houghton Library.

10. Charlotte Eliot, *Savonarola A Dramatic Poem,* intro. T. S. Eliot (London: R. Cobden Sanderson, n.d.), p. x.

11. For this picture of Eliot's impressions of Europe in 1914, see the Eliot-Conrad Aiken letters in the Huntington Library, San Marino, California. I am indebted to Lyndall Gordon for this information.

12. *The Festival Theatre Review,* II.37 (5 May 1928), n. pag., Scrapbook, Houghton Library.

13. Matthew Arnold, *Philistinism in England and America,* ed. R. H. Super (Ann Arbor: The University of Michigan Press, 1974), p. 507. For information on the lecture tour, see pp. 505-7.

14. Ibid., p. 165. Super notes that Arnold is quoting from "Peace in Believing," one of Newman's *Parochial Sermons* (London and Oxford, 1842), VI, 400-401.

15. Ibid., pp. 165-66. Super notes that Arnold is quoting, with omission, "Worship, a Preparation for Christ's Coming," *Parochial Sermons* (London and Oxford, 1840), V, 2-3. "Emerson," first published in 1884, was included in *Discourses in America* (1885).

16. "The Hollow Men," *CPP,* pp. 58, 57.

17. Lyndall Gordon makes this point in *Eliot's Early Years,* passim.

Chapter 2

1. "A Note on Poetry and Belief," *Enemy,* 1 (January 1927), pp. 17, 16.

2. Ronald Schuchard, "T. S. Eliot as an Extension Lecturer, 1916-1919," *Review of English Studies,* NS 25 (August 1974), p. 293.

3. "Portrait of a Lady" (1910), *CPP* 10. Unless otherwise indicated, dates following the poems indicate when they were written.

4. "La Figlia Che Piange" (1916), *CPP* 20.

5. "The Love Song of J. Alfred Prufrock" (1910-11), *CPP* 4.

6. Lines 85-86. Henceforth references to Arnold's poetry will be cited by line number. The edition used is Kenneth Allott, ed., *The Poems of Matthew Arnold* (London: Longmans, 1965).

7. Walter E. Houghton, *The Victorian Frame of Mind* (New Haven: Yale University Press, 1957), p. 1.

8. In Mill's *The Spirit of the Age;* cited by Houghton, p. 1.

9. Thomas Carlyle, "Characteristics," in *Critical and Miscellaneous Essays,* Vol. III (London: Chapman and Hall Limited, 1899), pp. 31-32. In his note to 11. 85-88 of "Grande Chartreuse," Kenneth Allott refers to this passage, and adds: "The idea of the age as a spiritual No Man's Land was a commonplace in A.'s circle—see Tom A.'s letter to Clough 16 April 1847, 'Our lot is cast in an evil time; we cannot accept the present, and we shall not live to see the future. It is an age of transition; in which the mass are carried hither and thither by chimeras, while to the few . . . is left nothing but sadness and isolation' (*Correspondence* of A.H.C. i 180)."

10. Lyndall Gordon, "*The Waste Land* Manuscript," *American Literature,* 45 (January 1974), pp. 570, 562.

11. Although "crisis of faith" may be a hackneyed phrase (one thinks of Holley Martins, the hack writer of westerns in Graham Greene's *The Third Man,* and the lecture he is trapped into delivering for the edification of a literary club: "The Crisis of Faith in the Modern Novel"), it is still occasionally handy.

12. These "fragments" are the ten or so miscellaneous poems attached to the original drafts of *The Waste Land*; see the *Facsimile and Transcript,* pp. 90-123. The "Song" is on pp. 98-99.

13. See D. D. Paige, ed., *The Letters of Ezra Pound 1907-1941* (New York: Harcourt, Brace, 1950), pp. 169-71.

14. The poetry is contained in a bound notebook, with over fifty pages of holograph drafts, and in a folder of miscellaneous manuscripts, both holograph and typescript. The unpublished poems cannot be quoted.

15. "Rhapsody on a Windy Night" (1911), *CPP* 16.

16. "Preludes" III (1911), *CPP* 12-13.

17. See Ronald L. Bush's Princeton dissertation, "The Genesis of Ezra Pound's Cantos" (1974), Ch. 5: "Stages of Revision."

18. "Eyes that Last I Saw in Tears" (pub. 1924), *CPP* 90.

19. See *Facsimile and Transcript,* p. 98. For the *Tyro* published version of the poem, Eliot used the original "Waiting that touch."

20. I. A. Richards, "A Background for Contemporary Poetry," *Criterion,* 3 (July 1925), p. 520*n.*

21. "A Note on Poetry and Belief," p. 16.

22. From a "note in the Yale MS." See Allott, ed., *Poems of Matthew Arnold,* p. 220*n.*

23. Curtis Dahl, "The Victorian Wasteland," in Austin Wright, ed., *Victorian Literature: Modern Essays in Criticism* (New York: Oxford University Press, 1961), p. 36. This article originally appeared in *College English,* 16 (1955), pp. 341-47.

24. "To the Duke of Wellington" (pub. 1849), 11. 11-13.

25. Edward FitzGerald was one of those elderly Victorian gentlemen. A. C. Benson writes, in the biography of FitzGerald that influenced the writing of "Gerontion": "as the years went on, the hopefulness decreased, the pessimism grew upon him . . . . the bent of his whole mind was towards scepticism . . . . he saw clearly that he himself and minds like his own, acute, questioning, unsatisfied minds, must be condemned to doubt. . . ." See A. C. Benson, *Edward Fitzgerald* (1905; rpt. London: Macmillan, 1925), pp. 184-86 et passim.

26. "A Note on Poetry and Belief," pp. 16-17.

27. *Facsimile and Transcript,* pp. 30-31.

28. Douglas Bush, *Mythology and the Romantic Tradition in English Poetry* (1937; rpt. Cambridge, Mass.: Harvard University Press, 1969), pp. 509-10.

29. "Isolation. To Marguerite" (pub. 1857), 1. 26.

30. "A Summer Night" (pub. 1852), 11. 37-41.

31. The critics have taken note of this. See for instance Grover Smith, *T. S. Eliot's Poetry and Plays,* 2nd ed. (Chicago: University of Chicago Press, 1974), p. 12, and B. C. Southam, *A Guide to the Selected Poems of T. S. Eliot* (New York: Harcourt, Brace, 1969), p. 37: "Throughout the 'Portrait' Eliot seems to suppose the readers' acquaintance with 'The Buried Life', on which he provides a kind of modern commentary, a re-writing of Arnold's serious dramatic monologue as a *conversation galante,* a complex statement, with shifting tones of irony, quite different from the relative simplicity of Arnold's singleness of tone and feeling."

32. Robert Langbaum has taken note of "The Buried Life" in relation to Eliot's early work. See his "New Modes of Characterization in *The Waste Land,*" in A. Walton Litz, ed., *Eliot in His Time* (Princeton: Princeton University Press, 1973), pp. 98-101.

33. There is an unpublished poem in the Berg Notebook that concerns the poet's reaction to a performance of Wagner's *Tristan und Isolde.* He feels a terrible disparity between the passionate self-expression of the music and his own enervated existence, in which so little is expressed. This opera seems to have represented to Eliot the extreme limit of romantic intensity, an intensity that could only destroy itself. Romantic passion ending in self-destruction is also the subject of Arnold's *Tristram and Iseult* (pub. 1852), the structure of which roughly anticipates that of *The Waste Land.*

34. *Facsimile and Transcript,* pp. 12-13. In the final version of this passage, "The hyacinth garden" does not appear.

35. A. Dwight Culler, ed., *Poetry and Criticism of Matthew Arnold* (Boston: Houghton Mifflin, 1961), pp. xii-xiii.

36. Hugh Kenner, *The Invisible Poet: T. S. Eliot* (1959; rpt. New York: Harcourt, Brace, 1969), p. 248.

37. Douglas Bush, *Matthew Arnold: A Survey of his Poetry and Prose* (New York: Macmillan, 1971), p. 69.

38. See Philip Drew, "Matthew Arnold and the Passage of Time," in Isobel Armstrong, ed., *The Major Victorian Poets: Reconsiderations* (Lincoln: University of Nebraska Press, 1969), pp. 199-224.

Chapter 3

1. Cited by Jerome Hamilton Buckley, *The Victorian Temper* (1951; rpt. New York: Vintage, 1964), p. 94. Buckley's chapter, "The Pattern of Conversion," is an excellent account of the Victorian religious sensibility and its expression in the literature of the time.

2. See Thomas Carlyle, *Sartor Resartus* (London: Chapman and Hall, 1896), pp. 125-26.

3. Harold Bloom speaks of the "quest romance" in these terms in "Introduction: First and Last Romantics," *The Ringers in the Tower* (Chicago: University of Chicago Press, 1971), p. 3.

4. John Soldo's 1972 Harvard dissertation, *The Tempering of T. S. Eliot: 1888-1915,* refers to a letter from Eliot's mother to Thomas Lamb Eliot, dated 7 May 1923, now in the Houghton Library's Eliot Collection, in which she talks about the Grail sequel. Perhaps this was only wishful thinking on the part of Mrs. Eliot.

5. Walter E. Houghton and G. Robert Stange, eds., *Victorian Poetry and Poetics,* 2nd ed. (Boston: Houghton Mifflin, 1968), p. 220*n*.

6. T. S. Eliot, *Poems Written in Early Youth* (New York: Farrar, Straus and Giroux, 1967), p. 11.

7. The datings are based on Lyndall Gordon's work; see *Eliot's Early Years* (New York: Oxford University Press, 1977), passim. I am most grateful to Ms. Gordon for her generous help with the Berg Collection material.

8. Stephen Spender, *T. S. Eliot* (1975; rpt. Penguin Books, 1976), p. 35.

9. Grover Smith, *T. S. Eliot's Poetry and Plays,* 2nd ed. (Chicago: Univ. of Chicago Press, 1974), pp. 24-25.

10. Bernard Bergonzi, *T. S. Eliot* (New York: Collier Books, 1972), pp. 20-21.

11. F. O. Matthiessen, *The Achievement of T. S. Eliot,* 3rd ed. (London: Oxford University Press, 1959), p. 134.

12. Bergonzi, p. 21.

13. Ibid.

14. Valerie Eliot estimates that "So through the evening" was written "about 1914 or even earlier" (*FT* 130).

15. "The Death of St. Narcissus" (1914 or 1915), *Poems Written in Early Youth,* p. 29.

16. "Journey of the Magi" (1927), *CPP* 68.

17. Hugh Kenner "The Urban Apocalypse," in A. Walton Litz, ed., *Eliot in his Time* (Princeton: Princeton University Press, 1973), p. 41.

18. Helen Gardner, "*The Waste Land*: Paris, 1922," in Litz, p. 83.

19. Richard Ellmann, "The First *Waste Land,*" in Litz, ed., *Eliot in His Time,* p. 64.

20. Spender, *T. S. Eliot,* p. 95.

21. The translation is Eliot's in "Dante" (1929), *SE* 250. Professor Litz points out that in the "Ithaca" section of Joyce's *Ulysses,* Bloom is described as "Christ or another."

22. *The Dial,* November 1923. Rpt. Frank Kermode, ed., *Selected Prose of T. S. Eliot* (New York: Harcourt Brace Jovanovich, 1975), p. 177.

23. Hugh Kenner, "The Urban Apocalypse," in Litz, p. 41.

24. Sir James George Frazer, *Adonis, Attis, Osiris,* 3rd ed. (1914; rpt. New York: Macmillan, 1935), Vol. I, pp. 179-80.

25. A. T. Murray, trans., *The Odyssey* (London: William Heinemann, 1953), 11. 287-92. Edition of the Loeb Classical Library.

26. See Lyndall Gordon, "Dating *The Waste Land Fragments,*" in *Eliot's Early Years,* p. 145.

27. Headnote for Psalm 107, King James Bible.

28. Charles M. Laymon, ed., *The Interpreter's One-Volume Commentary on the Bible* (Nashville and New York: Abingdon Press, 1971), p. 292.

29. Northrop Frye, *T. S. Eliot* (1963; rpt. New York: Capricorn Books, 1972), p. 58.

30. Martin Svaglic, "Man and Humanist," in David J. DeLaura, ed., *Victorian Prose: A Guide to Research* (New York: Modern Language Assocation of America, 1973), p. 149.

31. John Henry Newman, *The Dream of Gerontius and other Poems* (London: Oxford University Press, 1914), p. 35. All further references to *The Dream of Gerontius* will be cited by line numbers in parentheses.

32. Basil Maine, *Elgar His Life and Works* (London: G. Bell & Sons, 1933), Vol. I, p. 205.

33. Alec Robertson, Notes for the Angel recording (SB-3660) of Elgar's oratorio *The Dream of Gerontius*.

34. G. W. Foster, "The Archetypal Imagery of T. S. Eliot," *PMLA*, 60 (June 1945), p. 577.

35. F. R. Leavis, "T. S. Eliot's Later Poetry," rpt. Hugh Kenner, ed., *T. S. Eliot: A Collection of Critical Essays* (Englewood Cliffs: Prentice-Hall, 1962), p. 111. Leavis's article was originally published in *Scrutiny*, 11 (Summer 1942).

36. Eliot's phrase "the boredom, the horror, and the glory," in "Matthew Arnold" (*UPUC* 106), echoes the final words of the Lord's Prayer. Old Possum is at work, implying that Arnold could not possibly "see" all of these things because he had no real notion of Sin or God.

Chapter 4

1. *CPP* 63. All future references to *Ash-Wednesday* will be cited by section number; e.g., *AW* III denotes *Ash-Wednesday, Part III*.

2. See Ronald Schuchard, "T. S. Eliot as an Extension Lecturer, 1916-1919," *Review of English Studies*, 25 (May 1974), p. 170.

3. V. J. E. Cowley, "A Source for T. S. Eliot's 'Objective Correlative,' " *Review of English Studies*, 26 (August 1975), pp. 320-21.

4. J. H. Newman, *Sermons Chiefly on the Theory of Religious Belief, Preached before the University of Oxford,* 2nd ed. (London: Francis & John Rivington, 1844), pp. 229-30.

5. T. S. Eliot, "Christianity and Communism," *Listener,* 7 (16 March 1932), p. 383.

6. Cardinal Newman, *An Essay in Aid of a Grammar of Assent* (New York: Catholic Publication Society, 1870), p. 478.

7. Frederic Manning, "A French Criticism of Newman," *Criterion,* 4 (January 1926), p. 28.

8. Ramon Fernandez, "The Experience of Newman," *Criterion,* 3 (October 1924), p. 84.

9. Alvan S. Ryan, "Newman and T. S. Eliot on Religion and Literature," in Victor R. Yanitelli, ed., *A Newman Symposium: Report on the Tenth Annual Meeting of the Catholic Renascence Society at the College of the Holy Cross* (New York: 1952), p. 130.

10. I. A. Richards "A Background for Contemporary Poetry," *Criterion,* 3 (July 1925), p. 520*n*.

11. T. S. Eliot, "A Note on Poetry and Belief," *Enemy,* 1 (January 1927), p. 16.

12. T. S. Eliot, "Literature, Science, and Dogma," *Dial,* 82 (March 1927), p. 243.

13. A. Dwight Culler, ed., *Poetry and Criticism of Matthew Arnold* (Boston: Houghton Mifflin, 1961), p. 306. Richards omits the last words of the paragraph, which are as follows: "But for poetry the idea is everything; the rest is a world of illusion, of divine illusion. Poetry attaches its emotion to the idea; the idea *is* the fact. The strongest part of our religion today is its unconscious poetry."

14. T. S. Eliot, "Mr. Middleton Murry's Synthesis," *Criterion,* 6 (October 1927), p. 344.

15. Matthew Arnold, "On Poetry," in R. H. Super, ed., *Complete Prose Works,* Vol. IX, pp. 61-63. This definition of religion was first stated in *Literature and Dogma* (1871). See *Complete Prose Works,* Vol. VI, p. 176.

16. T. S. Eliot, "Poetry and Propaganda," *Bookman,* 70 (February 1930), p. 601.

17. See B. C. Southam, *A Guide to the Selected Poems of T. S. Eliot* (New York: Harcourt, Brace & World, 1968), p. 136. Part II was called "Jausen lo Jorn," Part III "Som de L'Escalina."

18. I Kings xix, 8. See Southam, *Guide,* p. 112.

19. Southam, *Guide,* p. 136.

20. See E. E. Duncan Jones's invaluable essay on "Ash Wednesday" in B. Rajan, ed., *T. S. Eliot: A Study of his Writings by Several Hands* (New York: Funk & Wagnalls, 1949), pp. 37-56. Jones writes that the "repetition of 'because' gives the impression of 'la raison raisonnant'; the intellect is establishing the relations of things" (p. 39).

21. Ezra Pound, trans., *The Sonnets and Ballate of Guido Cavalcanti* (Boston: Small, Maynard, 1912), p. 107. Pound was not quite as reluctant as Eliot to acknowledge a debt to Victorian writers; in the introduction to this volume he writes: "In the matter of these translations and of my knowledge of Tuscan poetry, Rossetti is my father and my mother, but no one man can see everything at once" (pp. xv-xvi).

22. *The Book of Common Prayer . . . According to the Use of the Church of England* (Oxford: University Press, n.d.).

23. Taken from Andrewes' sermon on the opening words of the Epistle for Ash Wednesday; quoted by E. E. Duncan Jones, p. 40.

24. T. S. Eliot, "Poet and Saint . . . ," *Dial,* 82 (May 1927), pp. 428-29.

25. Quoted in Charles Du Bos, *Approximations,* Première Série (1922; rpt. Fayard, 1965), pp. 218-19.

26. T. S. Eliot, "The Silurist," *Dial,* 83 (September 1927), pp. 260-61. This is a review of Edmund Blunden's *On the Poems of Henry Vaughan.*

27. T. S. Eliot, "Baudelaire in Our Time," *FLA* 99.

28. A. C. Swinburne, "Tennyson and Musset," *Fortnightly Review,* February 1881. Rpt. in J. D. Jump, ed., *Tennyson: The Critical Heritage* (London: Routledge & Kegan Paul, 1967), p. 347.

Chapter 5

1. T. S. Eliot, "Introduction: 1928," in *Selected Poems of Ezra Pound* (1928; rpt. London: Faber and Faber, 1948), p. 8.

2. C. K. Stead, *The New Poetic* (1964; rpt. New York: Harper & Row, 1966), pp. 53, 69.

3. T. S. Eliot, ed., *Literary Essays of Ezra Pound* (New Directions, 1954), p. xiii.

4. See C. K. Stead, chapters 3 and 4, pp. 45-95.

5. See J. T. Boulton's introduction, pp. x-xi, in C. F. G. Masterman, *The Condition of England,* ed. J. T. Boulton (London: Methuen, 1960). Future references to this book will be by page number.

6. This passage is referred to (and misquoted) by Vivian de Sola Pinto, *Crisis in English Poetry 1880-1940,* 5th ed. (London: Hutchinson University Library, 1967), p. 100.

7. E. D. H. Johnson, "Alfred, Lord Tennyson," in F. E. Faverty, ed., *The Victorian Poets: A Guide to Research,* 2nd ed. (Cambridge: Harvard University Press, 1968), p. 56.

8. C. F. G. Masterman, *Tennyson as a Religious Teacher,* 2nd ed. (London: Methuen,1910), p. vii. Future references will be cited in the text, by page number.

9. John Killham, "Introduction: Tennyson, A Review of Modern Criticism," in John Killham, ed., *Critical Essays on the Poetry of Tennyson* (London: Routledge & Kegan Paul, 1960), p. 1.

10. J. D. Jump, ed., *Tennyson: The Critical Heritage* (London: Routledge & Kegan Paul, 1967), p. 13. Future references will be by page number.

11. Killham, p. 6.

12. P. F. Baum, "Alfred Lord Tennyson," in *The Victorian Poets: A Guide to Research,* ed. F. E. Faverty (Cambridge: Harvard University Press, 1956), p. 54.

13. Killham, p. 2.

14. W. P. Ker, *Tennyson,* The Leslie Stephen Lecture, Delivered in the Senate House, Cambridge, on 11 November 1909 (Cambridge at the University Press, 1909), pp. 5, 6.

15. *A Short History of Modern English Literature* was first published in 1898 (New York: Appleton). The concluding chapter was called "The Age of Tennyson." In the 1905 Illustrated Edition, this chapter has dates added: 1870-1900.

16. T. Herbert Warren, *The Centenary of Tennyson 1809-1909,* 6 August 1909 (Oxford: Clarendon Press, 1909). Warren's "Tennyson and Dante" is reprinted in his *Essays of Poets and Poetry Ancient and Modern* (New York: E. P. Dutton, 1909).

17. W. P. Ker, pp. 22, 24-25.

18. P. E. More, "Tennyson," in *Shelburne Essays,* Seventh Series (New York: G. P. Putnam's Sons, 1910). Future references to this essay will be by page number.
    In his essay on More in the 5 Feb. 1937 issue of the *Princeton Alumni Weekly,* Eliot wrote:

> When I was an undergraduate at Harvard, More was editor of the *Nation,* and to occupy that position in those days was to be a public figure. I sometimes read the *Nation* and I sometimes read a Shelburne Essay, but I cannot remember that I liked or disliked More's writing: I was interested in other things. . . . It was not until my senior year, as a pupil of Babbitt's, that More's work was forced on my attention. . . . (p. 373)

In "A Note on the American Critic," one of the few pieces Eliot wrote from scratch for *The Sacred Wood,* Eliot discusses P. E. More's work. More was just one in Eliot's gallery of straw men, and he did not escape the dominant tone of condescension:

Mr. Paul More is the author of a number of volumes which he perhaps hopes will break the record of mass established by the complete works of Sainte-Beuve. (*SW* 38-39)

But it becomes clear by the end of Eliot's remarks that he took More quite seriously as a critic; indeed, he goes so far as to let a cat out of the bag, referring to "an interesting essay" (*SW* 42) of More's which turns out to be an unacknowledged source for "Tradition and the Individual Talent." The essay is "Criticism," and it appears in the same volume of essays as "Tennyson."

Years later, reviewing More's *Selected Shelburne Essays* in the January 1936 *Criterion,* Eliot again mentioned the "Criticism" essay, and called More "the finest literary critic of his time" (p. 363).

19. Quoted by Killham, p. 7.

20. Douglas Bush, ed., *Selected Poetry of Tennyson* (New York: Modern Library, 1951), p. xiv.

21. George Saintsbury, *History of English Prosody,* Vol. III (London: Macmillan, 1910), p. 192.

22. Noel Stock, *The Life of Ezra Pound* (1970; rpt. New York: Discus Books, 1974), p. 97.

23. Ernest Rhys, ed., *The Poems of Alfred Tennyson 1830-1863,* Everyman's Library (London: J. M. Dent & Sons, 1906), pp. xiv, vii. Future references by page number.

24. P. E. More, "Tennyson," p. 76.

25. See Richard Le Gallienne, ed., *The Poems of A. H. Hallam, together with his Essay on the Lyrical Poems of Alfred Tennyson* (London: E. Mathews & J. Lane, 1893), pp. xxi-xxii, and W. B. Yeats, "Art and Ideas" (1913), in *Essays and Introductions* (London: Macmillan, 1961), pp. 347, 349.

26. "A. H. Hallam on *Poems, Chiefly Lyrical,*" in J. D. Jump, ed., *Tennyson: The Critical Heritage,* p. 42. Future references will be made by including the page number in the text.

27. H. M. McLuhan, "Tennyson and Picturesque Poetry," in Killham, ed., *Critical Essays,* p. 67.

28. Part of Hallam's review was included in his *Remains,* published in 1863 and in subsequent editions by John Murray. Richard Le Gallienne reprinted it entire in his 1893 edition of Hallam's poems (see above, note 25). And Eliot did own a copy of Rhys's Tennyson edition, which quotes significant excerpts from Hallam's review. He would not have had to dig through stacks of *The Englishman's Magazine,* where the review was originally published in August 1831, in order to find it.

29. Interview with Donald Hall, in *Writers at Work: The Paris Review Interviews,* Second Series (New York: Viking, 1965), p. 93.

30. Hugh Kenner, *The Invisible Poet: T. S. Eliot* (1959; rpt. New York: Harcourt, Brace & World, 1969), p. 14. Kenner's chapter "Laforgue and Others," pp. 13-39, provides an excellent treatment of Eliot's early literary sources, and is one of the few that takes Tennyson into account.

31. Herbert Howarth, *Notes on Some Figures Behind T. S. Eliot* (London: Chatto & Windus, 1965), p. 95.

32. T. S. Eliot, *Poems Written in Early Youth* (New York: Farrar, Straus and Giroux, 1967), p. 11. All future references are to this edition and will be incorporated into the text.

33. Kenner, *The Invisible Poet,* p. 9. The lines come from "Song," *Poems Written in Early Youth,* p. 22.

34. Cf. the following in *Poems Written in Early Youth*: [A Lyric], p. 9; "Song," p. 10; "Song," p. 18; "Before Morning," p. 19; and "Song," p. 22.

35. See Lionel Stevenson, "The 'High-Born Maiden' Symbol in Tennyson," in Killham, ed., *Critical Essays,* pp. 126-36.

36. T. S. Eliot, "Turgenev," *Egoist,* 4 (December 1917), p. 167.

Chapter 6

1. Hugh Kenner, *The Invisible Poet: T. S. Eliot* (1959; rpt. New York: Harcourt, Brace & World, 1969), p. 94.

2. Ronald Schuchard, "T. S. Eliot as an Extension Lecturer, 1916-1919," *Review of English Studies,* 25 (August 1974), p. 303.

3. T. S. Eliot, "Observations," *Egoist,* 5 (May 1918), p. 69.

4. See Eliot, "Professional, or . . . ," *Egoist,* 5 (April 1918), p. 61.

5. "Mr. Leacock Serious," *New Statesman,* 7, No. 173 (29 July 1916), pp. 404-5.

6. "Mr. Doughty's Epic," *Manchester Guardian,* No. 829 (24 July 1916), p. 3.

7. "Mr. Lee Masters," *Manchester Guardian,* No. 906 (9 October 1916), p. 3.

8. "Classics in English," *Poetry,* 9, No. 2 (November 1916), p. 102.

9. "Reflections on Contemporary Poetry I," *Egoist,* 4, No. 8 (September 1917), p. 118.

10. *Literary Essays of Ezra Pound,* ed. T. S. Eliot (New York: New Directions, 1968), pp. 276-77. In his remarks on Tennyson, Pound drew from Walter Bagehot's essay, "Wordsworth, Tennyson, and Browning; or, Pure, Ornate, and Grotesque Art in English Poetry." Pound writes:

> 'Is it credible that his (Tennyson's) whole mind should be made up of fine sentiments,' says Bagehot. Of course it wasn't. It was that lady-like attitude towards the printed page that did it. . . . (p. 276)

Bagehot's essay, largely a review of *Enoch Arden,* first appeared in the *National Review,* November 1864. Pound probably came across it in the Everyman's Library edition of Bagehot's *Literary Studies,* Vol. II, edited by his friend Ernest Rhys and published in 1911 (London: J. M. Dent & Sons). Pound was either drawing incorrectly from memory or deliberately changing the gist of the quotation, for Bagehot was describing the sailor, Enoch Arden, and *not* Tennyson:

> Just so, when he [Enoch Arden] gets home he *may* have had such fine sentiments, though it is odd, and he *may* have spoken of them to his landlady, though that is odder still,—but it is incredible that his whole mind should be made up of fine sentiment.

See Norman St. John-Stevas, ed., *The Collected Works of Walter Bagehot,* Vol. II (Cambridge: Harvard University Press, 1965), p. 349.

11. "The Borderline of Prose," *New Statesman*, 9, No. 215 (19 May 1917), p. 159.

12. "The Letters of J. B. Yeats," *Egoist*, 4, No. 6 (July 1917), pp. 89-90.

13. T. S. Eliot, "Preface," in Maurice Lindsay, ed., *John Davidson; A Selection of his Poems* (London: Hutchinson, 1961), p. [i].

14. *The Princess*, II, 101-8. For Tennyson's note on these lines, see *The Poems of Tennyson*, ed. Christopher Ricks (New York: Norton, 1972), p. 762*n*.

15. W. B. Yeats, *Ideas of Good and Evil* (1903; rpt. New York: Russell & Russell, 1967), p. 254. Quoted by C. K. Stead, *The New Poetic*, p. 12.

16. Harriet Monroe and Alice Corbin Henderson, eds., *The New Poetry* (New York: Macmillan, 1917), p. v. Future references by page number.

17. *Egoist*, 4, No. 10 (November 1917), p. 151. Future references by page number.

18. W. B. Yeats, "Friends of My Youth," in Robert O'Driscoll and Lorna Reynolds, eds., *Yeats and the Theatre* (Macmillan of Canada, 1975), pp. 31-32. My thanks to Herbert J. Levine for pointing this out to me.

19. The essay, originally called "Whether Rostand Had Something about Him," appeared first in the 25 July 1919 *Athenaeum*. There, Eliot had written: "It ['rhetoric'] is one of those words which it is part of the business of criticism to dissolve, finding a variety of particular meanings, each of which is in the end a cluster of particular facts" (p. 665). This was revised for *The Sacred Wood* to read: "It is one of those words which it is the business of criticism to dissect and reassemble." The subject of the revisions Eliot made for his first collection of criticism is worthy of close study. "The Growth of *The Sacred Wood*" would also discuss the strategy behind Eliot's selection of essays out of the many he had written.

20. John Rosenberg, *The Fall of Camelot* (Cambridge: Belknap Press, 1973), p. 1.

21. "A Victorian Sculptor," *New Statesman*, 10, No. 256 (2 March 1918), p. 528.

22. W. B. Yeats, "Friends of My Youth," p. 28.

23. Kenner analyzes the method of the essay in *The Invisible Poet*, pp. 102-5. Here is the complete reference: "Kipling Redivivus," *Athenaeum*, No. 4645 (9 May 1919), pp. 297-98. Future quotations will be noted by page number.

24. Eliot refers to or quotes the following Kipling poems in "Kipling Redivivus": "Danny Deever," "The Ladies," "Mandalay," "McAndrew's Hymn," "Recessional," "Gentlemen-Rankers," "The Sons of Martha," "The Holy War," "A Song in Storm," "The City of Brass," "A Death-Bed," "For All We Have and Are," "The Rowers," and "The Female of the Species." All but the last five are in his 1941 anthology.

25. T. S. Eliot, ed., *A Choice of Kipling's Verse* (London: Faber and Faber, 1941), pp. 11-12. "Whimper" is the "exactly right" concluding word in *The Hollow Men*, too.

26. T. S. Eliot, "The Unfading Genius of Rudyard Kipling," rpt. in Elliot L. Gilbert, ed., *Kipling and the Critics* (New York University Press, 1965), p. 119.

27. Quotations from "Beyond the Pale" are taken from Rudyard Kipling, *Plain Tales from the Hills*, "The Sahib Edition" (New York: Collier, n.d.), and will be noted by page number.

28. "Was There a Scottish Literature?" *Athenaeum,* 4657 (1 August 1919), p. 681. Of course, this also provides a justification in Eliot's own words for studying *his* poetry in relation to the Victorians.

29. *Tennyson: the Growth of a Poet* (Boston: Houghton Mifflin Co., 1965), p. 80. " 'Dora' was written about 1835. Tennyson comments on the 'trouble' its simplicity gave him (*Memoir,* I, 196)" (p. 272).

30. Christopher Ricks, ed., *The Poems of Tennyson* (London: Longmans, 1969), p. 835*n*.

31. " 'The Duchess of Malfi' at the Lyric: and Poetic Drama," *Art & Letters,* III. 1 (Winter [1919/]1920), p. 36.

32. See the entry for Hippolyte Taine in *The Oxford Companion to French Literature,* ed. Harvey and Heseltire (Oxford: Clarendon Press, 1959), p. 694.

33. H. A. Taine, "Poetry—Tennyson," *History of English Literature*; rpt. as "H. A. Taine on Tennyson as the poet of Victorian England," in J. D. Jump, ed., *Tennyson: The Critical Heritage* (London: Routledge & Kegan Paul, 1967), p. 272. Further quotations will be noted by page number.

34. "The Naked Man," *Athenaeum,* 4685 (13 February 1920), p. 209.

35. See Morton Zabel's remarks on F. O. Matthiessen, *The Achievement of T. S. Eliot,* 3rd ed. (New York: Oxford University Press, 1958), pp. 73-74.

36. A. C. Benson, *Edward FitzGerald* (1905; rpt. London: Macmillan, 1925), p. 70.

37. "Notes on Current Letters," *Tyro,* 1 ([Spring 1921]), p. [4]. These "Notes" are divided into two parts: "The Romantic Englishman, the Comic Spirit, and the Function of Criticism," and "The Lesson of Baudelaire." The phrase about Tennyson's Englishman is taken from *The Princess,* Conclusion, line 85:

> And there we saw Sir Walter where he stood, . . .
> No little lily-handed Baronet he,
> A great broad-shouldered genial Englishman. . . .

Eliot was also alluding to Matthew Arnold's quotation of the same line in his chapter on "Barbarians, Philistines, Populace" in *Culture and Anarchy*:

> But in our political system everybody is comforted. Our guides and governors who have to be elected by the influence of the Barbarians, and who depend on their favour, sing the praises of the Barbarians, and say all the smooth things that can be said of them. With Mr. Tennyson, they celebrate "the great broad-shouldered Englishman". . . . (Super, ed., *Prose Works,* V, 150)

38. "Prose and Verse," *Chapbook,* 22 (April 1921), p. 5.

Chapter 7

1. *Poems of Tennyson,* introd. T. S. Eliot (London: Thomas Nelson and Sons, 1936). All further quotations from this introduction will be cited by page number, in roman numerals. The introduction, with revisions, is included in *Selected Essays* (starting with the 1950 American edition), which is far more accessible than the Nelson Classics *Poems of Tennyson.* For those quotations that remain unchanged between the two versions of Eliot's essay, I shall cite the page numbers in *Selected Essays.*

2. T. S. Eliot, *Essays Ancient and Modern* (London: Faber and Faber, 1936), p. 175. Eliot now called the essay "In Memoriam."

3. "Prose and Verse," *Chapbook,* 22 (April 1921), p. 5.

4. "*Prufrock* and *Maud*: From Plot to Symbol," *Yale French Studies,* No. 9 (Spring 1952), p. 92. This issue is devoted to "Symbol and Symbolism." The article is reprinted in Wimsatt's collection of essays, *Hateful Contraries* (1965).

5. For Swinburne's remarks, see *Tennyson: The Critical Heritage,* ed. Jump, p. 345. See also *Poems,* ed. Ricks, pp. 598-99.

6. I am borrowing terms from Swinburne, who spoke of Tennyson's "conscious or unconscious recollection or derivation from a famous passage in the master-work of a mightier predecessor. . . ." See *Tennyson: The Critical Heritage,* ed. Jump, p. 345*n.*

7. *Tennyson: The Critical Heritage,* p. 345.

8. *Petronius,* trans. Michael Heseltine (London: William Heinemann, 1961), p. 87.

9. T. S. Eliot, *Essays on Elizabethan Drama* (New York: Harcourt, Brace & World, 1956), p. 109.

10. Heywood, *A Woman Killed with Kindness,* ed. R. W. Van Fossen (London: Methuen, 1961), p. 74. Scene xiii, 52-64.

11. "London, your people is bound upon the wheel!" See *The Waste Land Facsimile and Transcript,* p. 31.

12. Lyndall Gordon, "*The Waste Land* Manuscript," *American Literature,* 45 (January 1974), p. 557.

13. See the *Facsimile and Transcript,* p. 1.

14. Cited in *Poems,* ed. Ricks, p. 859.

15. See T. S. Eliot, "Reflections on Contemporary Poetry I," *Egoist,* 4, No. 8 (September 1917), pp. 118-19, and "Tradition and the Individual Talent," *SE* 22.

16. Linda Ray Pratt, in her 1971 Emory University dissertation " 'The Neutral Territory Between Two Worlds': A Comparative Study of Alfred Tennyson and T. S. Eliot," does an excellent job of comparing their uses of myth in the chapter on "The Fisher King in Camelot," part of which was published in *Victorian Poetry* as "The Holy Grail: Subversion and Revival of a Tradition in Tennyson and T. S. Eliot" (Vol. 11, Winter 1973). Ms. Pratt's dissertation is perceptive and illuminating, but she pays very little attention to Eliot's own references to Tennyson over the years, and she completely ignores his 1942 broadcast on *In Memoriam.*

17. "*Ulysses,* Order, and Myth," in *Selected Prose of T. S. Eliot,* ed. Frank Kermode (New York: Harcourt Brace Jovanovich, 1975), p. 177. The essay first appeared in *The Dial,* November 1923.

18. Ronald Schuchard, "T. S. Eliot as an Extension Lecturer, 1916-1919," *Review of English Studies,* 25 (May 1974), pp. 169-70.

19. See J. C. C. Mays, *"In Memoriam*: An Aspect of Form," *University of Toronto Quarterly,* 35 (October 1965), p. 44: "There is a great deal in common between the *Four Quartets* and *In Memoriam,* in purpose, theme, form, and images." Mr. Mays does not pursue this statement at all.

20. See Helen Gardner, *The Art of T. S. Eliot* (New York: E. P. Dutton, 1959), p. 47; Harry Blamires, *Word Unheard: A Guide through Eliot's Four Quartets* (London: Methuen, 1969), who does little more than point out the familiar Tennysonian echoes, inventing a few of his own along the way; and the article by J. C. C. Mays, cited in note 26, above.

21. "In Memoriam," *SE* 331. Line 429 of *The Waste Land* alludes to "O Swallow Swallow," another song from *The Princess.*

22. Grover Smith points out this echo in *T. S. Eliot's Poetry and Plays,* 2nd ed. (Chicago: University of Chicago Press, 1974), p. 254.

23. T. S. Eliot, " 'The Voice of his Time,' " *The Listener,* 27 (12 February 1942), p. 212.

24. See P. E. More, "Tennyson," in *Shelburne Essays,* Seventh Series (New York: Putnam's, 1910), passim. I discuss this essay in chapter 5. The opening chapter of G. K. Chesterton's *The Victorian Age in Literature* (1913) is called "The Victorian Compromise and its Enemies."

25. *In Memoriam,* 35. All further quotations from *In Memoriam* will be noted by section heading, in Arabic numerals.

26. Douglas Bush, *Science and English Poetry* (1950; rpt. London: Oxford University Press, 1967), p. 124.

27. E. D. H. Johnson, *"In Memoriam*: The Way of the Poet," rpt. in the Norton Critical Edition of *In Memoriam,* ed. Robert H. Ross (New York: W. W. Norton, 1973), p. 219. This article first appeared in *Victorian Studies,* 2 (1958), pp. 139-48.

28. Mays, p. 28.

29. Information on Eliot's talk was obtained from the British Broadcasting Corporation's Written Archives Centre, Caversham Park, Reading. All quotations from " 'The Voice of his Time': T. S. Eliot on Tennyson's 'In Memoriam,' " published in *The Listener* of 12 February 1942, will be noted by page number.

30. Written Archives Centre files: 910 Eliot, T. S., Talks. File II 1938-1943. Acc. No.: 48111.

31. This is from the little poem beginning "How unpleasant to meet Mr. Eliot!" one of the *Five-Finger Exercises* (*CPP* 93).

32. Ezra Pound, *Personae* (New York: New Directions, 1971), p. 89.

33. *OPP* 32. "The Music of Poetry," the third W. P. Ker Memorial Lecture, was delivered at Glasgow University, 24 February 1942.

34. Derek Traversi, *T. S. Eliot: The Longer Poems* (New York: Harcourt Brace Jovanovich, 1976), p. 190.

35. Stephen Spender, *T. S. Eliot* (Penguin Books, 1976), p. 183.

36. See *OPP* 25.

37. "Rudyard Kipling," *OPP* 267.

38. "You could not say that of Arnold; his charm and his interest are largely due to the painful position that he occupied between faith and disbelief" (*UPUC* 114).

Bibliography

The bibliography is divided into three subjects: T. S. Eliot; Victorian Poets and Poetry; and Other Relevant Works.

T. S. Eliot

Bergonzi, Bernard. *T. S. Eliot.* New York: Collier, 1972.
Bergsten, Staffan. *Time and Eternity: A Study in the Structure and Symbolism of T. S. Eliot's Four Quartets.* Stockholm: Svenska Bokförlaget, 1960.
Blamires, Harry. *Word Unheard: A Guide Through Eliot's Four Quartets.* London: Methuen, 1969.
Eliot, Valerie (ed.). *The Waste Land: A Facsimile and Transcript of the Original Drafts Including the Annotations of Ezra Pound.* New York: Harcourt Brace Jovanovich, 1971.
Foster, Genevieve W. "The Archetypal Imagery of T. S. Eliot." *PMLA,* 60 (June 1945), 567-85.
Frye, Northrop. *T. S. Eliot.* 1963; rpt. New York: Capricorn Books, 1972.
Gallup, Donald. *T. S. Eliot: A Bibliography.* Revised and Expanded Edition. New York: Harcourt, Brace & World, 1969.
Gardner, Helen. *The Art of T. S. Eliot.* 1950; rpt. New York: E. P. Dutton, 1959.
————. "The Landscapes of Eliot's Poetry." *Critical Quarterly,* 10 (Winter 1968), 313-30.
————. "T. S. Eliot." In *Twentieth-century Literature in Retrospect,* ed. Reuben Brower. Harvard English Studies No. 2. Cambridge, Mass.: Harvard University Press, 1971.
————. *T. S. Eliot and the English Poetic Tradition.* Byron Foundation Lecture. Nottingham: The University of Nottingham, 1965.
Gordon, Lyndall. *Eliot's Early Years.* Oxford and and New York: Oxford University Press, 1977.
————. "*The Waste Land* Manuscript." *American Literature,* 45 (January 1974), 557-70.
Gregor, Ian. "Eliot and Matthew Arnold." In *Eliot in Perspective: A Symposium,* ed. Graham Martin. London: Macmillan, 1970.
Howarth, Herbert. *Notes on Some Figures Behind T. S. Eliot.* Boston: Houghton Mifflin, 1964.
Jones, E. E. Duncan. "Ash Wednesday." In *T. S. Eliot: A Study of His Writings by Several Hands,* ed. B. Rajan. New York: Funk & Wagnalls, 1949.
Kenner, Hugh. *The Invisible Poet: T. S. Eliot.* 1959; rpt. New York: Harcourt-Harbinger. 1969.
————(ed.). *T. S. Eliot: A Collection of Critical Essays.* Englewood Cliffs, N. J.: Prentice-Hall, 1962.

Litz, A. Walton (ed.). *Eliot in His Time: Essays on the Occasion of the Fiftieth Anniversary of The Waste Land.* Princeton: Princeton University Press, 1973.

Lobb, Randolph Edward. *T. S. Eliot and the English Critical Tradition.* Princeton University diss., 1974.

Loring, M. L. S. "T. S. Eliot on Matthew Arnold." *Sewanee Review,* 43 (October 1935).

Ludwig, Richard. "T. S. Eliot." In *Sixteen Modern American Authors: A Survey of Research and Criticism.* Ed. Jackson R. Bryer; rev. ed. Durham, N. C.: Duke University Press, 1974.

Margolis, John D. *T. S. Eliot's Intellectual Development, 1922-39.* Chicago: University of Chicago Press, 1972.

Martin, Graham (ed.). *Eliot in Perspective: A Symposium.* London: Macmillan, 1970.

Martin, Mildred. *A Half-Century of Eliot Criticism: An Annotated Bibliography of Books and Articles in English, 1916-1965.* Lewisburg, Pa.: Bucknell University Press, 1972.

Matthews, T. S. *Great Tom: Notes towards the Definition of T. S. Eliot.* New York: Harper & Row, 1974.

Matthiessen, F. O. *The Achievement of T. S. Eliot.* 3rd ed. 1958; rpt. New York: Oxford University Press, 1972.

Moody, A. D. (ed.). *The Waste Land in Different Voices: The Revised Versions of Lectures Given at the University of York in the Fiftieth Year of the Waste Land.* London: E. Arnold, 1974.

Musgrove, S. *T. S. Eliot and Walt Whitman.* Wellington: New Zealand University Press, 1952.

Rajan, Balachandra. *The Overwhelming Question: A Study of the Poetry of T. S. Eliot.* Toronto: University of Toronto Press, 1976.

—————(ed.). *T. S. Eliot: A Study of His Writings by Several Hands.* New York: Funk & Wagnalls, 1949.

Reibetanz, Julia. *A Reading of Four Quartets.* Princeton University diss., 1969.

Scarfe, Francis. "Eliot and Nineteenth-century French Poetry." In *Eliot in Perspective: A Symposium,* ed. Graham Martin. London: Macmillan, 1970.

Schuchard, Ronald. "Eliot and Hulme in 1916: Toward a Revaluation of Eliot's Critical and Spiritual Development." *PMLA,* 88 (October 1973), 1083-94.

—————. " 'First-Rate Blasphemy': Baudelaire and the Revised Christian Idiom of T. S. Eliot's Moral Criticism." *ELH,* 42 (Summer 1975), 276-95.

—————. "T. S. Eliot as an Extension Lecturer, 1916-1919." *Review of English Studies,* 25 (May and August 1974), 163-73 and 292-304.

Smith, Grover. *T. S. Eliot's Poetry and Plays: A Study in Sources and Meaning.* 2nd ed. Chicago: University of Chicago Press, 1974.

Soldo, John. *The Tempering of T. S. Eliot 1888-1915.* Harvard University diss., 1972.

Southam, B. C. *A Guide to the Selected Poems of T. S. Eliot.* New York: Harcourt-Harvest, 1968.

Spender, Stephen. *T. S. Eliot.* 1975; rpt. Penguin, 1976.

Tamplin, Ronald. "*The Tempest* and *The Waste Land.*" *American Literature,* 39 (November 1967), 352-72.

Tate, Allen (ed.). *T. S. Eliot: The Man and His Work.* New York: Delta, 1966.

Traversi, Derek. *T. S. Eliot: The Longer Poems.* New York: Harcourt Brace Jovanovich, 1976.

Unger, Leonard. *T. S. Eliot: Moments and Patterns.* Minneapolis: University of Minnesota Press, 1966.

Writers at Work: The Paris Review Interviews. 2nd ser. New York: Viking Press, 1963.

Victorian Poets and Poetry

Armstrong, Isobel (ed.). *The Major Victorian Poets: Reconsiderations.* Lincoln: University of Nebraska Press, 1969.

Arnold, Matthew. *Complete Prose Works,* ed. R. H. Super. Ann Arbor: University of Michigan Press, 1960—.

————. *The Poems of Matthew Arnold,* ed. Kenneth Allott. London: Longmans, 1965.

————. *Poetry and Criticism of Matthew Arnold,* ed. A. Dwight Culler. Boston: Houghton Mifflin, 1961.

Bradley, A. C. *A Commentary on Tennyson's In Memoriam.* 3rd ed. 1910; rpt. Hamden, Conn.: Archon Books, 1966.

Buckley, J. H. *Tennyson: The Growth of a Poet.* 1960; rpt. Boston: Houghton-Riverside, 1965.

————. *The Triumph of Time: A Study of the Victorian Concepts of Time, History, Progress, and Decadence.* Cambridge, Mass.: Belknap Press, 1966.

————. *The Victorian Temper: A Study in Literary Culture.* 1951; rpt. New York: Vintage, 1964.

Bush, Douglas. *Science and English Poetry: A Historical Sketch, 1590-1950.* 1950; rpt. London: Oxford University Press, 1967.

————. *Matthew Arnold: A Survey of his Poetry and Prose.* New York: Macmillan, 1971.

Carr, Arthur J. "Tennyson as a Modern Poet." Rpt. in *Critical Essays on the Poetry of Tennyson,* ed. J. Killham. London: Routledge & Kegan Paul, 1960.

Chesterton, G. K. *The Victorian Age in Literature.* 1911; rpt. London: Oxford University Press, 1966.

Christ, Carol T. *The Finer Optic: The Aesthetic of Particularity in Victorian Poetry.* New Haven and London: Yale University Press, 1975.

Dahl, Curtis. "The Victorian Wasteland." *College English,* 16 (1955), 341-47.

Davidson, John. *A Selection of his Poems,* ed. Maurice Lindsay. Hutchinson of London, 1961.

Eliot, T. S. "Arnold and Pater" (1930). *SE* 431-43.

————(ed.). *A Choice of Kipling's Verse, with an Essay on Rudyard Kipling.* London: Faber and Faber, 1941.

————. "In Memoriam" (1936). *SE* 328-38.

————. "Kipling Redivivus." *Athenaeum,* No. 4645 (9 May 1919), 297-98.

————. "Matthew Arnold" (1933). *UPUC* 103-19.

————. "Swinburne as Critic" (1919). *SW* 17-24.

————. "Swinburne as Poet" (1920). *SE* 323-27.

————. " 'The Voice of his Time': T. S. Eliot on Tennyson's 'In Memoriam.' " *Listener,* 27 (12 February 1942), 211-12.

————. "Whitman and Tennyson." *The Nation & Athenaeum,* 40 (18 December 1926), 426.

Faverty, F. E. *The Victorian Poets: A Guide to Research.* 2nd ed. Cambridge, Mass.: Harvard University Press, 1968.

Fricker, Robert. "Victorian Poetry in Modern English Criticism." *English Studies,* 24 (October 1942), 129-41.

Gilbert, Elliot L. (ed.). *Kipling and the Critics.* New York University Press, 1965.

Houghton, Walter E. *The Victorian Frame of Mind, 1830-1870.* New Haven and London: Yale University Press, 1957.

————and Stange, G. Robert (eds.). *Victorian Poetry and Poetics.* 2nd ed. Boston: Houghton Mifflin, 1968.

Johnson, E. D. H. *The Alien Vision of Victorian Poetry.* Princeton: Princeton University Press, 1952.

—————. "*In Memoriam*: The Way of the Poet." *Victorian Studies,* 2 (1958), 139-48.

Jump, John D. (ed.). *Tennyson: The Critical Heritage.* London: Routledge & Kegan Paul, 1967.

Ker, W. P. *Tennyson.* The Leslie Stephen Lecture. Cambridge at the University Press, 1909.

Killham, John (ed.). *Critical Essays on the Poetry of Tennyson.* London: Routledge & Kegan Paul, 1960.

Kipling, Rudyard, *The Complete Barrack-Room Ballads of Rudyard Kipling,* ed. Charles Carrington. London: Methuen, 1974.

Masterman, C. F. G. *Tennyson as a Religious Teacher.* 2nd ed. London: Methuen, 1910.

Mays, J. C. C. "*In Memoriam*: An Aspect of Form." *University of Toronto Quarterly,* 35 (October 1965), 22-46.

McLuhan, H. Marshall. "Tennyson and Picturesque Poetry." *Essays in Criticism,* 1 (July 1951), 262-82.

—————. "Tennyson and the Romantic Epic." In *Critical Essays on the Poetry of Tennyson,* ed. John Killham. London: Routledge & Kegan Paul, 1960.

Meynell, Alice. "Some Thoughts of a Reader of Tennyson." In *Hearts of Controversy.* London: Burns & Oates, 1917.

More, Paul Elmer. "Tennyson." In *Shelburne Essays.* 7th ser. New York: G. P. Putnam's Sons, 1910.

Newman, John Henry. *The Dream of Gerontius and Other Poems.* London: Oxford University Press, 1914.

Palmer, D. J. (ed.). *Tennyson.* Writers and their Background ser. Athens: Ohio University Press, 1973.

Quereshi, A. H. "The Waste Land Motif in Tennyson." *Humanities Association Bulletin,* 18 (Fall 1967), 20-30.

Ricks, Christopher. *Tennyson.* Masters of World Literature ser. New York: Collier Books, 1972.

Rosenberg, John. *The Fall of Camelot: A Study of Tennyson's "Idylls of the King."* Cambridge, Mass.: The Belknap Press, 1973.

Sinfield, Alan. "*In Memoriam* and the Language of Modern Poetry." In *The Language of Tennyson's "In Memoriam."* Oxford: Basil Blackwell, 1971.

Squire, J. C. "Tennyson." *The London Mercury,* 2 (August 1920), 443-55.

Swinburne, A. C. *Swinburne: Selected Poetry and Prose,* ed. John Rosenberg. New York: The Modern Library, 1968.

—————. "Tennyson and Musset." In *Miscellanies.* London: Chatto & Windus, 1886.

Taine, H. A. *History of English Literature,* trans. H. Van Laun. Edinburgh: Edmonston and Douglas, 1871.

Tennyson, Alfred. *In Memoriam,* ed. Robert H. Ross. Norton Critical Ed. New York: W. W. Norton, 1973.

—————. *The Poems of Alfred Tennyson 1830-1863,* ed. Ernest Rhys. Everyman's Library. London: J. M. Dent & Sons, 1906.

—————. *Poems of Tennyson,* introd. T. S. Eliot. Nelson Classics ser. London: Thomas Nelson and Sons, 1936.

—————. *The Poems of Tennyson,* ed. Christopher Ricks. London: Longman, 1969.

—————. *Selected Poetry,* ed. Herbert Marshall McLuhan. New York: Holt, Rinehart & Winston, 1956.

—————. *The Selected Poetry of Tennyson,* ed. Douglas Bush. New York: The Modern Library, 1951.

Warren, Alba H. *English Poetic Theory 1825-1865.* 1950; rpt. New York: Octagon Books, 1966.

Wright, Austin (ed.). *Victorian Literature: Modern Essays in Criticism.* New York: Oxford University Press, 1961.

Other Relevant Works

Altick, R. D. *Victorian People and Ideas: A Compendium for the Modern Reader of Victorian Literature.* New York: Norton, 1973.

Bate, W. Jackson. *The Burden of the Past and the English Poet.* 1970; rpt. New York: W. W. Norton & Company, 1972.

Bergonzi, Bernard. "The Advent of Modernism 1900-1920." In *The Turn of a Century: Essays on Victorian and Modern English Literature,* ed. Bernard Bergonzi. New York: Barnes & Noble, 1973.

Bloom, Harold. *The Anxiety of Influence: A Theory of Poetry.* New York: Oxford University Press, 1973.

————. *A Map of Misreading.* New York: Oxford University Press, 1975.

Bush, Douglas. *Mythology and the Romantic Tradition in English Poetry.* 1937; rpt. Cambridge, Mass.: Harvard University Press, 1969.

Hollander, John. Review of *The Anxiety of Influence: A Theory of Poetry,* by Harold Bloom. *The New York Times Book Review,* 4 March 1973, pp. 27 ff.

Holloway, John. "The Literary Scene." In *The Pelican Guide to English Literature: The Modern Age,* ed. Boris Ford. Penguin Books, 1962.

Jones, Peter (ed.). *Imagist Poetry.* Penguin Books, 1972.

Langbaum, Robert. *The Poetry of Experience: The Dramatic Monologue in Modern Literary Tradition.* New York: Norton, 1957.

Masterman, C. F. G. *The Condition of England,* ed. J. T. Boulton. London: Methuen, 1960.

McLuhan, Herbert Marshall. "The Aesthetic Moment in Landscape Poetry." In *The Interior Landscape: The Literary Criticism of Marshall McLuhan,* ed. Eugene McNamara. New York: McGraw-Hill, 1971.

Monroe, Harriet and Corbin, Alice (eds.). *The New Poetry.* New York: Macmillan, 1917.

More, Paul Elmer. "Criticism." In *Shelburne Essays.* 7th ser. New York: G. P. Putnam's Sons, 1910.

Perkins, David. *A History of Modern Poetry: From the 1890s to the High Modernist Mode.* Cambridge, Mass.: The Belknap Press, 1976.

Pratt, Linda Ray. "The Holy Grail: Subversion and Revival of a Tradition in Tennyson and T. S. Eliot," *Victorian Poetry,* 11 (Winter 1973), 307-21.

————. *"The Neutral Territory Between Two Worlds": A Comparative Study of Alfred Tennyson and T. S. Eliot.* Emory University diss., 1971.

Pound, Ezra. *Literary Essays of Ezra Pound,* ed. T. S. Eliot. New York: New Directions, 1968.

————. *The Selected Letters of Ezra Pound 1907-1941,* ed. D. D. Paige. 1950; rpt. New York: New Directions, 1971.

Reardon, Bernard M. G. (ed.). *Religious Thought in the Nineteenth Century.* London: Cambridge University Press, 1966.

Reed, John R. *Victorian Conventions.* Athens: Ohio University Press, 1975.

Ross, Robert H. *The Georgian Revolt, 1910-1922: Rise and Fall of a Poetic Ideal.* Carbondale: Southern Illinois University Press, 1965.

Ryalls, Clyde de L. (ed.). *Nineteenth-Century Literary Perspectives.* Essays in Honor of Lionel Stevenson. Durham: Duke University Press, 1974.

Ryan, Alvan S. "Newman and T. S. Eliot on Religion and Literature." In *A Newman Symposium: Report on the Tenth Annual Meeting of the Catholic Renascence Society at the College of the Holy Cross,* ed. Victor R. Yanitelli. New York: 1952.

Sola Pinto, Vivian de. *Crisis in English Poetry 1880-1940.* 5th ed. London: Hutchinson University Library, 1967.

Stead, C. K. *The New Poetic: Yeats to Eliot.* 1964; rpt. New York: Harper & Row, 1966.

Stock, Noel. *The Life of Ezra Pound.* 1970; rpt. New York: Discus Books, 1974.

Wimsatt, W. I. "*Prufrock* and *Maud*: From Plot to Symbol." *Yale French Studies,* No. 9 (Spring 1952), 84-92.

Index